THE URGENT WEST

By Walter Allen

WRITERS ON WRITING
THE ENGLISH NOVEL
THE MODERN NOVEL
THE URGENT WEST

THE
URGENT WEST

The American Dream and Modern Man

by

WALTER ALLEN

New York: E. P. DUTTON & CO., INC. 1969

Grateful acknowledgment is due the following for permission to reprint copyright
material:

A. Alvarez: *Under Pressure: The Writer in Society: Eastern Europe and the U.S.A.*
Penguin Books, Ltd.

Hart Crane: "The Bridge," from *Complete Poems and Selected Letters and Prose
of Hart Crane,* by Hart Crane. Permission granted by Liveright, Publishers, New
York, copyright 1933, 1958, 1966, by Liveright Publishing Corp.

F. Scott Fitzgerald: *The Great Gatsby,* Charles Scribner's Sons, New York.

Robert Frost: "The Gift Outright," from *Complete Poems of Robert Frost.* Copyright 1942 by Robert Frost. Reprinted by permission of Holt, Rinehart &
Winston, Inc.

Allen Ginsberg: "Howl"— Copyright © 1968 by Allen Ginsberg. Reprinted by
permission of City Lights Books.

Robert Lowell: "For the Union Dead." Reprinted with the permission of Farrar,
Straus & Giroux, Inc., from *For the Union Dead,* by Robert Lowell, copyright
© 1960, by Robert Lowell.

V. S. Pritchett: a review of Wallace Stevens's *Letters,* in *The New Statesman.*

Frederick Jackson Turner: *The Frontier in American History.* Copyright 1920,
1948. Reprinted by permission of Holt, Rinehart & Winston, Inc.

Thomas Wolfe: *Look Homeward, Angel,* Charles Scribner's Sons, New York.

CONTENTS

Whither, O Splendid ship, thy white sails crowding,
Leaning across the bosom of the urgent West?

PART 1

The Making of Americans

[1]

"Ours is the only nation that prides itself upon a dream and gives its name to one, 'the American dream'." In those words the American scholar, Lionel Trilling, has set out what is still the great distinction between the United States and the rest of the world. There are those nations, the Communist countries notably, that live by, or try to live by, a blue print for the future. But a blue print is not a dream. There are those—and they include some of the youngest—that are seeking to restore ancient glories in new forms. And there are the old countries—England and France are obvious examples—that, however much they change, are inevitably shaped even as they change by the consciousness of a great historic past. Continuity and the sense of continuity have made them what they are: the English cannot renounce Chaucer, Shakespeare, Milton, Samuel Johnson, Wordsworth, Dickens and remain English, or the French Montaigne, Pascal, Descartes, Racine, Molière, Stendhal, Flaubert and remain French.

But what is the American dream? Is it anything more than a cliché of political speakers and editorial writers, anything more than a string of pious platitudes generally acceptable because totally innocuous? If all we had to go on were July 4 orations and presidential inaugurations we could dismiss it as almost meaningless, or as a synonym, perhaps, for something called "free enterprise" or "the American way of life". After all, the United States is no longer a young country. It is the oldest independent country of the American continent, as a political entity is older than Italy, Belgium and Germany, and its constitution is the oldest written constitution in the world.

Yet it still remains significantly unlike any other country in the world, and the existence of the American dream cannot be dismissed simply because it is so difficult to define or because definitions at the level of political oratory often seem indis-

tinguishable from claptrap.   The first statement of the dream,
made long before the phrase had been coined, is to be found in
"The unanimous Declaration of the Thirteen United States of
America" drawn up by Thomas Jefferson in 1776: "We hold
these truths to be self-evident, that all men are created equal,
that they are endowed by their creator with certain unalienable
rights, that among these are life, liberty and the pursuit of
happiness."

The Declaration of Independence is very much an eighteenth-
century document.   Its purpose was to justify to the world the
secession of the American colonies from the British crown.
And it contains its built-in contradictions: the man who so
confidently asserted that all men, by virtue of their being men,
were endowed with unalienable rights to life, liberty and the
pursuit of happiness, was, like others who signed the document,
himself an owner of slaves.   Yet his great sentence is still as
revolutionary in its implications as it was almost two hundred
years ago, still as staggering in its assumptions.   It is large,
vague and begs many questions; its power partly resides in this,
which is to say it resides in its magnificent simplicity.   It remains
revolutionary because to this day, in many countries of the world,
liberty is still not admitted as every man's unalienable right;
and, as for the pursuit of happiness as an unalienable right, this
is still, according to most systems of government and religion,
heresy.   The statement is the expression of a dream almost in
the classic Freudian sense, in that it is the fulfilment of wishes
that can probably never be fully realised in actuality.

Six years after the Declaration of Independence was signed,
Hector St-Jean de Crèvecoeur, a Frenchman farming in New
York State, wrote a famous essay, "What is an American?"   It
is again an essay in political propaganda, a   justification of
America. America, Crèvecoeur writes,

is not composed, as in Europe, of great lords who possess everything,
and a herd of people who have nothing.   Here are no aristocratic
families, no courts, no kings, no bishops, no ecclesiastic dominion,
no invisible power giving to a few a very visible one; no great
manufacturers employing thousands, no great refinements of luxury.
The rich and the poor are not so far removed from each other as
they are in Europe.   Some few towns excepted, we are all tillers of
the earth, from Nova Scotia to West Florida.   We are a people of
cultivators, scattered over an immense territory, communicating with

each other by means of good roads and navigable rivers, united by the silken bands of mild government, all respecting the laws, without dreading their power, because they are equitable. We are all animated by the spirit of an industry which is unfettered and unrestrained, because each person works for himself. . . . We have no princes, for whom we toil, starve, and bleed: we are the most perfect society now existing in the world. Here man is free as he ought to be . . .

Who are the people who inhabit this perfect society?

They are a mixture of English, Scotch, Irish, French, Dutch, Germans and Swedes. From this promiscuous breed, that race now called Americans has arisen.

And what of the race now called Americans?

The American is a new man, who acts on new principles; he must therefore entertain new ideas, and form new opinions. From involuntary idleness, servile dependence, penury, and useless labour, he has passed from toils of a very different nature, rewarded by ample subsistence.--This is an American.

Crèvecoeur is describing an ideal society, a Utopia; and it is irrelevant that one knows that the conditions of American life in the last years of the eighteenth century were not nearly so idyllic as he suggests. Like the Declaration of Independence, it is of its time. "Man was born free, and everywhere he is in chains," wrote Rousseau. Crèvecoeur shows us an America in which man has escaped his chains, escaped the domination of kings and priests, and is free. He gives us the American dream in its eighteenth-century form.

But the question, what is an American? is still very much with us; perhaps it has never been more so. On the face of it, this is puzzling. As we have already said, the United States is no longer a young country, and Americans themselves are immediately identifiable, whatever their racial origins, anywhere in the world. Colour apart, an American Negro, for instance, is much more like a white American than an African Negro or even a Negro from the British Caribbean islands. The Americanisation of the rest of the world is one of the features of our time. Yet the problem of American identity, what it means to be an American, remains. It is a problem that obsesses Americans themselves. In a sense, indeed, the problem has been and still is the great theme of American literature. One of the most famous American novels is Theodore Dreiser's *An American Tragedy*. Implicit in the title is the suggestion that the story the novel relates is one that could only have occurred in the United States. Americans, it seems, today as much as at any time, today perhaps more than ever in the past, must always seek to define and evaluate their difference from the other peoples of the world. Are they in fact different, and what has made them so? And, assuming they are different, what have they in common with one another?

This problem of a national identity is obviously not one that bothers people of older countries. An Englishman or a French-man does not have to seek constantly to define his Englishness or his Frenchness, to work out painfully what it means to be English or French. It is only at moments of extreme crisis, as in war, for instance, that he finds it necessary to do so. At other times, his Englishness or Frenchness is something he takes for granted, is as unaware of almost as of breathing. If he were asked what it meant to be English or French, he would probably say, once he had recovered from his initial shock that the question could be asked at all, "Look about you!" He would point to a thousand years of history, to the artistic and architectural monu-ments of a past that has evolved into the present, to centuries of literature.

The inhabitants of Britain or of France are bound together in what has come to seem a natural unity that is the product of a common heritage and common values. There is plenty of disagreement in Britain on religion and politics, but the dis-agreements are fundamental only in a tiny minority of instances; for the overwhelming part they are disagreements within a context of shared assumptions, and this is still true even though citizens of Britain are not invariably white and not invariably Christian in belief. There is no such natural unity in the United States. We find the familiar notion of America as a melting pot even in Crèvecoeur's essay. Crèvecoeur describes Americans as a mixture of English, Scotch, Irish, French, Dutch, Germans and Swedes. But this falls very far short of the mixture today; even to approximate to it, we should have to add to Crèvecoeur's list Negroes, Italians, Greeks, Russians, Poles, Czechs, Slavs of all kinds, Hungarians, Spaniards, Mexicans, Puerto Ricans, Syrians, Armenians, Chinese, Japanese, to say nothing of the original Red Indian stock Crèvecoeur did not mention. There can scarcely be any nationality, race or religion that cannot be found somewhere in the United States.

But it is still a mixture, not a compound. The contents of the melting pot have scarcely begun to fuse in any real sense. This is not to deny that intermarriage between the various national and ethnic stocks takes place, but the fact is, the metaphor of the melting pot is a misleading one. The process of immigration, settlement and assimilation is altogether too complex to be expressed in a single metaphor. In whole states and cities alike, what one has, rather than a melting or merging of peoples one with another, are almost solid blocks of one national stock after another, jigsaw patterns of areas each of which is inhabited by its own national or ethnic groups. The most typical and perhaps the most dramatic instance of this is to be found in the Borough of Manhattan in New York City, where one has the Negro district of Harlem, on the face of it an almost self-contained Negro city, Puerto Ricans on the West Side, the Chinese in Chinatown, again a seemingly self-contained district, and Germans, Hungarians, Czechs in Yorkville on the East River. And, on Jewish holidays, in the midtown area, with stores and offices closed, the streets empty, one has the impression that one is in a Jewish city, as indeed one is.

All are Americans, recognising one another as Americans. Yet a member of one group may well be at a loss to know what he has in common, citizenship apart, with members of others. A white Anglo-Saxon Protestant of an old New England or New York Dutch family, for instance, will inevitably see his country and interpret American experience very differently from a Polish Roman Catholic steel-worker in Cleveland, Ohio, or a Puerto Rican from the West Side or Spanish Harlem; and a man of old Southern stock and a descendant of his family's Negro slaves may feel themselves nearer to each other in significant ways than either is to a New York Jewish intellectual or a Czech farmer from Iowa. The remarkable thing is that they have as much in common one with another as they do, that they are recognised by the outside world impartially as Americans; for their histories in America have been almost as different from one another as the histories of their ancestors in the outside world, and the reasons that brought their forefathers to America were as different too.

Yet all, whatever their origins, colour, religion, occupation, social position, have one thing in common, and it is fundamental. All are descendants of men and women who were, in the strict sense of the phrase, displaced persons. They came to America from somewhere else; not always voluntarily—the Negroes came as slaves; not always willingly—the Irish came to escape starvation, the Jews to escape pogroms, as later they came to escape the persecutions and gas chambers of the Nazis. But all, the Negroes excepted, whatever their background, intelligence or education, once arrived in America had to decide, however inarticulately or obscurely, what being an American was to mean to them.

It is the same story today. The choice and the decision still have to be made. I am an Englishman. But I could fly to New York tomorrow and if at the end of five years I took the oath of allegiance and became an American citizen, I would no longer be an Englishman. I would have opted of my own free will to be American. In a way, I would have decided to become in some sense a new man. It would mean new orientations amounting to a new conception of myself. In a deep part of me, of course, I would remain, whether I wanted to or not, English; but the very act of taking on Americanness, of discovering what Americanness was for me, would include in it a radical modification of my Englishness. To some degree it would be a repudiation of it, for I would have opted for something else I had seen as an alternative.

It was not, of course, quite the same for the early settlers of Virginia and New England, who could legitimately see their new country as an extension of old England, an England beyond the ocean. Nor, probably, was it quite the same, though for different reasons, for millions of the humble, often illiterate immigrants who poured into America from Ireland and central Europe and the Mediterranean lands during the nineteenth century. "The land was ours before we were the land's," begins one of Robert Frost's poems, meaning that the concept of America, of Americanness was not something taken to the New World in the first place but evolved from the experience of living in it. Yet for the first settlers as for the millions who poured into America during the nineteenth century, there was still in the first instance the necessary act of decision, the necessary resolution, however arrived at and for whatever reason, to uproot themselves from home, to go elsewhere, to begin again, to make things new.

[2]

This takes us back to the sentence from Lionel Trilling with which this book begins. It comes from an essay in *The Liberal Imagination* on the American novelist, F. Scott Fitzgerald. Professor Trilling is writing on Fitzgerald's novel, *The Great Gatsby*, published in 1925. "Gatsby," he says, "divided between power and dream, comes inevitably to stand for America itself. . . . We are told that 'the truth was that Jay Gatsby of West Egg, Long Island, sprang from his Platonic conception of himself. . . .' Clearly it is Fitzgerald's intention that our mind should turn to the thought of the nation that has sprung from its 'Platonic conception' of itself."

Gatsby is a mysterious, romantic figure, almost a legend while still alive, whose history we learn through the researches of Nick Carroway, the young man who becomes his neighbour on Long Island and who tells his story. Gatsby gives enormous parties—we are in the early Twenties, the prohibition era—to which all New York flocks. But who is Gatsby? The rumours are many, that he is an "Oggsford man", that he is a cousin of the Hohenzollerns, that he owns a chain of drugstores, that he is a bootlegger, that he has killed a man. In fact he has been an "Oggsford man" in a sense, by circumstance of war, and he is indeed a bootlegger, a criminal. He was born as Jay Gatz in North Dakota, and at the age of seventeen had changed his name to Jay Gatsby. "His parents were shiftless and unsuccessful farm people—his imagination had never really accepted them as his parents at all. The truth was that Jay Gatsby of West Egg, Long Island, sprang from his Platonic conception of himself. He was a son of God—a phrase which, if it means anything, means just that—and he must be about His Father's business, the service of a vast, vulgar, and meretricious beauty. So he invented just the sort of Jay Gatsby that a seventeen-year-old boy would be likely to invent, and to this conception he was faithful to the end."

9

Gatsby, in other words, is a self-made man in a sense that goes beyond the ordinary meaning of the phrase. You might almost say he was a self-created man, which is what Fitzgerald means when he says that Gatsby sprang from his Platonic conception of himself. The victim of what Dr Johnson called "that hunger of the imagination which preys incessantly on life" and unable to satisfy it in the circumstances of his own boyhood, he is living out a dream closer to his heart's desire. It is centred on Daisy, a rich girl whom he met in Louisville during the war while an Army officer, a girl he could never have met had the times not transplanted him, via the Army, into a higher social class than he normally occupied. He had fallen in love with her, and though she had married in his absence he had remained faithful to her. It was because she and her husband lived across the bay that he had taken his house on Long Island; it was in the hope of renewing acquaintance with her that he gave his enormous, notorious parties. He meets her, indeed, through Carroway, who was at Yale with her husband. Carroway says to Gatsby, after Daisy has attended one of his parties.

> "I wouldn't ask too much of her. . . . You can't repeat the past."
> "Can't repeat the past!" he cried incredulously. "Why of course you can!"
> He looked around him wildly, as if the past were lurking here in the shadow of his house, just out of reach of his hand.
> "I'm going to fix everything just the way it was before," he said, nodding determinedly. "She'll see."
> He talked a lot about the past, and I gathered that he wanted to recover something, some idea of himself perhaps, that had gone into loving Daisy. His life had been confused and disordered since then, but if he could once return to a certain starting place and go over it all slowly, he could find out what that thing was . . .

The end is tragic. Gatsby is killed. Both Daisy and her husband are worthless people. Ironically, it is Gatsby, the adventurer from North Dakota, the man who has become rich through breaking the law, who is revealed as the incorruptible. He has remained faithful to a dream and also to the belief, which is part of the dream, that he can conquer circumstances, rearrange them in accordance with his will.

In *The Great Gatsby* Scott Fitzgerald shows us the American dream in its tragic aspect, in other words, as a dream incapable of realisation precisely because it is a dream. But that Fitzgerald equates Gatsby with American man, sees him as a figure symbolic of American experience, is made clear by the final paragraphs of the novel. On his last night on Long Island, Nick Carroway goes over to Gatsby's house, deserted now, and wanders along the foreshore:

> Most of the big shore places were closed now and there were hardly any lights except the shadowy, moving glow of a ferryboat across the Sound. And as the moon rose higher the inessential houses began to melt away until gradually I became aware of the old island here that flowered once for Dutch sailors' eyes—a fresh, green breast of the new world. Its vanished trees, the trees that had made way for Gatsby's house, had once pandered in dreams to the last and greatest of all human dreams; for a transitory enchanted moment man must have held his breath in the presence of this continent, compelled into an aesthetic contemplation he neither understood nor desired, face to face for the last time in history with something commensurate to his capacity for wonder.
>
> And as I sat there brooding on the old, unknown world, I thought of Gatsby's wonder when he first picked out the green light at the end of Daisy's dock. He had come a long way to this blue lawn, and his dream must have seemed so close that he could hardly fail to grasp it. He did not know that it was already behind him, somewhere back in that vast obscurity beyond the city, where the dark fields of the republic rolled on under the night.
>
> Gatsby believed in the green light, the orgastic future that year by year recedes before us. It eluded us then, but that's no matter—tomorrow we will run faster, stretch out our arms farther. . . . And one fine morning—
>
> So we beat on, boats against the current, borne back carelessly into the past.

There, the young man from the Middle West is equated in his innocence with the Dutch seamen who sailed under Hudson in the last years of the sixteenth century. *The Great Gatsby* is a poetic celebration of the American dream, and a comment, pessimistic maybe, upon it. It is tempting to set beside those last paragraphs of Fitzgerald's novel a poem in which the dream is mirrored in its simplest form, a poem written three centuries ago by an English Puritan who never set foot in North America, Andrew Marvell. For us today Bermuda is a West Indian island, but when it was first colonised by the British it was closely linked to Virginia.

Where the remote Bermudas ride,
In the Ocean's bosom unespied,
From a boat, that rowed along,
The listening winds received this song:

"What should we do but sing His praise,
That led us through the watery maze,
Unto an isle so long unknown,
And yet far kinder than our own?
Where He the huge sea-monsters wracks,
That lift the deep upon their backs;
He lands us on a grassy stage,
Safe from the storms, and prelate's rage.
He gave us this eternal spring,
Which here enamels every thing,
And sends the fowls to us in care,
On daily visits through the air;
He hangs in shade the orange bright,
Like golden lamps in a green night,
And does in the pomegranates close
Jewels more rich than Ormus shows;
He makes the figs our mouths to meet,
And throws the melons at our feet;
But apples plants of such a price,
No tree could ever bear them twice;
With cedars chosen by his hand,
From Lebanon, he stores the land,
And makes the hollow seas, that roar,
Proclaim the ambergris on shore;
He cast (of which we rather boast)
The Gospel's pearl upon our coast,
And in these rocks for us did frame
A temple where to sound his name.
Oh! Let our voice His praise exalt,
Till it arrive at Heaven's vault,
Which, thence (perhaps) rebounding, may
Echo beyond the Mexique Bay."

Thus sung they, in the English boat,
An holy and a cheerful note;
And all the way, to guide their chime,
With falling oars they kept the time.

The picture is of a Utopia, though of an earlier pattern than Crèvecoeur's, and again it is irrelevant that the idyllic nature of the life described is wildly at odds with the facts of the early Puritan settlers' experience of America, whether in the Bermudas, which was not a notably successful colony, or in Massachusetts. What is important is the ideal vision. Here, man is free, as he ought to be, "safe from the storms, and prelate's rage".

[3]

There is a sense, however, in which the dream that is fundamental to Marvell, Crèvecoeur and Gatsby alike, existed, admittedly only in the vaguest, most shadowy form, before America itself. From very early times there had been legends in Europe of an ideal land beyond the known limits of the world, beyond the Straits of Gibraltar and the British Isles. There was the submerged island of Atlantis, described by Plato in the *Timaeus* and the *Critias*. The apple-green island of Avalon, the paradise of Celtic mythology, similarly lay westward in the unknown seas. Indeed, the very notion of the west, or of westward, of what lay beyond the sunset, seems always to have had mythical, even mystical connotations. After death, the heroes of Homer went west, and the phrase "to go west" as a synonym for "dying", especially in the case of soldiers, goes back to Middle English and is still current.

And perhaps, even from earliest times, there had been some slight evidence of the existence of a mysterious land beyond the sunset. Indeed, some Europeans, as we now know, had actually been there, the Norsemen in the eleventh century certainly and Madoc, Prince of Wales, conceivably in the twelfth. They left their testimonies behind, testimonies to abundance, of forests, wild animals, grapes, wheat. In any case, beneath both the legends and the fact, meagre and uncertain though the latter is, something else may be guessed at: at once an historic pattern and an historical impulse of western man, which is literally to go west. The great historic migrations that have peopled Europe, those of the Greeks, the Celts, the Slavs, the Goths, the Anglo-Saxons, the Norsemen, have always been from east to west; so that very deep in the European mind there probably lies, almost with the mysterious power of a Jungian archetype, the notion of the West as the site of what Henry James called "the great good place".

We all know that when America was discovered, at the end of the fifteenth century, it was discovered, if not by accident, at any rate by misapprehension: Columbus believed he had reached Cathay. The illusion did not last long; and then America, with all the resources it contained, both real and imaginary, was laid out like a series of blank cheques which the European countries could fill in with their own inordinate demands. These were various and complex, and, as Howard Mumford Jones has shown in *O Strange New World*, were often more the products of European imagination than of American reality. To a large extent, the first European explorers found in America what they hoped to find or at least interpreted what they found in European terms, which were inevitably and fantastically wide of the mark.

For Columbus, Hispaniola (the island of Haiti) was "a land to be desired, and, once seen, never to be left". But, as Mumford Jones points out, Columbus's description of the island "is curiously compounded out of the poetical garden emblematic of the Golden Age and of memories of landscapes in altar pieces and other holy paintings presumably seen by the devout discoverer in Catholic churches". Columbus was much impressed by the fact that the natives "all go naked, men and women, as their mothers bore them"; and as Mumford Jones reminds us, nakedness in Medieval and Renaissance art was a symbol of innocence.

Similarly, the Spanish conquerers of Peru translated the social organisation of the Incas into the pattern of Spanish chivalry. And when, in 1516, Sir Thomas More wrote his *Utopia* it was entirely appropriate that he should locate it in South America, in the New World. For the point is, it *was* a New World, a world in which anything was possible, in which all dreams of perfection might be realised in actuality. Even as late as the last years of the sixteenth century, the Elizabethan poet Michael Drayton could write of Virginia as "Earth's onely Paradise". America was both Utopia and fairyland. Indeed, the very existence of

America was almost proof that fairyland existed; as Spenser wrote in *The Faerie Queen*:

> Right well I wote most mighty Soueraine,
>   That all this famous antique history,
>   Of some th'aboundance of an idle braine
>   Will iudged be, and painted forgery,
>   Rather than matter of iust memory,
>   Sith none, that breatheth liuing aire, does know,
>   Where is that happy land of Faery,
>   Which I so much do vaunt, yet no where show,
> But vouch antiquities, which no body can know.
>
> But let that man with better sence aduize,
>   That of the world least part to vs is red:
>   And dayly how through hardy enterprize,
>   Many great Regions are discouered,
>   Which to late age were never mentioned.
>   Who euer heard of th'Indian Peru?
>   Or who in venturous vessell measured
>   The Amazons huge river now found trew?
> Or fruitfullest Virginia who did euer vew?
>
> Yet all these were, when no man did them know;
>   Yet haue from wisest ages hidden beene:
>   And later times things more unknowne shall show.
>   Why then should witlesse man so much misweene
>   That nothing is, but that which he hath seene?
>   What if within the Moones faire shining spheare?
>   What if in euery other starre vnseene
>   Of other worldes he happily should heare?
> He wonder would much more: yet such to some appeare.

America was the land where everything was possible, the land of infinite riches; and one can probably best appreciate the sense of awe and wonder that its discovery and its promises started in European minds by thinking of Desdemona's response to the tales Othello tells her of his adventures and of Miranda's to Ferdinand, in *The Tempest*: "O brave new world!" Or one may catch the note of triumph, of jubilation at the prospect of illimitable plunder the New World offered, in John Donne's apostrophe to his mistress, "O my America! my new-found-land!" and the lines that follow:

My myne of precious stones, My Emperie,
How blest am I in this discovering thee!

Within scarcely more than twenty years of Columbus's landfall
on Hispaniola the sense of America as a mine of precious stones,
an empery, an inexhaustible treasury of gold, had blotted out
almost everything else. This is not to deny the greatness of the
missionary enterprises among the Indians of Central and South
America of the Jesuits in particular or of the civilisations in
Mexico and Peru the Spanish established in so remarkably small
a time. One remembers that Mexico City was the seat of a
university as early as 1553 and had a printing press even in 1539.
Anglo-Saxon America was not to achieve either until a hundred
years later, and long after that was still shabby and provincial
compared with the splendour of Spanish America, with its great
baroque cathedrals and its vice-regal ceremony and state. But
the splendour and the state, and the civilisation itself, were possible because of the riches the Spanish possessions contained.

[4]

It was the lust for comparable riches that first led the English,
late starters in the colonisation of America, to establish settlements
in North America. No one was more strongly possessed by the
dream of gold, or expressed it more eloquently, than Sir Walter
Raleigh, who sailed up the Orinoco seeking Manoa, El Dorado,
the golden city, in 1594. He did not find it, but he remained
convinced that "whatsoever prince shall possess it, the Prince
shall be Lord of more golde, and· of a more beautiful Empire,
and of more Cities and people, than either the King of Spaine,
or the great Turke". As for Guiana, in which Manao was
supposed to be, Raleigh knew with equal certainty, that it is "the
most eyther riche in golde, or in other merchandises. The
common souldier shall here fight for golde, and pay himselfe in
steede of pence, with plates of half a foote broad, whereas he

breaketh his bones in other warres for provant and penury. Those commanders and chieftaines that shoot at honour and abundance, shall finde there more rich and beautiful cities, more temples adorned with golden images, more sepulchres filled with treasure, than either Cortez found in Mexico or Pizarro in Peru." Guiana, he concluded, "is a countrey that hath yet her maydenhead, never sackt, turned, nor wrought".

It was a kind of madness. Gold was everywhere, and if Raleigh failed to find it for the picking because the Orinoco and the Spanish barred the English entry to South and Central America, there was still all North America waiting to be ransacked. Raleigh's half-brother, Sir Humphrey Gilbert, claimed Newfoundland for Queen Elizabeth in 1583. He was so certain that he would find gold there that he promised to ask no man for a penny towards financing his next expedition; and besides gold, it was believed that silver, copper, lead, tin, turquoise, rubies, pearls, marble, jasper and crystal would also be found there.

In 1584 Raleigh had seized, named and claimed Virginia for the English crown. It was "the most plentifull, sweete, fruitful and wholesome (country) of all the world", and in 1585 the first English settlement in North America was established there, at Roanoke Island, off the coast of what is now North Carolina. It is an ironical story. When the settlers arrived they found the Indians "most gentle, loving, and faithfull, voide of all guile and treason, and such as live after the manner of the golden age". But when the settlers failed to find gold, they "had little or no care for anything but to pamper their bellies", and "lacking fair houses, dainty food, and soft beds, the country to them was miserable". They survived the winter but in the following spring, when Drake's fleet put in to visit them, they returned to England with him. The Indians had not remained friendly for long.

Raleigh tried again. Another company of more than a hundred people, including seventeen women and nine children, were settled on Roanoke. A friendly Indian was baptised into the Church of England and created "Lord of Roanoke". August 1587 saw the birth of Virginia Dare, the first child of English stock to be born in America. Very soon after, the Governor had to return to England for supplies. He was away for three years, and when he got back to Roanoke in August 1500 he found the settlers vanished without trace except for the word CROATAN carved on one tree and the letters CRO on another. Perhaps they had gone to live with and intermarried among the Croatan Indians on a nearby island. It is one of history's unsolved riddles.

Twenty years were to pass before the first permanent English settlement in North America was made, and even so, its survival was touch-and-go for many years. On May 13, 1607, some 140 men and four boys occupied a peninsula, now an island, in the James River in Virginia. They called it Jamestown. Captain John Smith, without whose energetic leadership the settlement might well have disappeared in much the same way as Roanoke, said of Jamestown that "Heaven and earth never agreed better to frame a place for man's habitation", but in fact the site was about as bad as it could have been. It was low and swampy, infested with malaria-carrying mosquitoes, and surrounded by Indians. Within six months about half the colonists had died or been killed by Indians. Smith himself, captured by the Indians, owed his life to the intervention of the chief's daughter, Pocahontas, who later married a settler and returned with him to England. Of the settlers, Smith said there was "no talke, no hope, nor worke, but dig gold, refine gold, load gold". But gold was not found; and though several hundred new settlers arrived in 1608, within a year only about fifty all told survived. During these years, from 1609 to 1611, known as the "starving time", the colonists were reduced to living on horses, dogs, mice, snakes and at least one human body. What remained of the colonists were already on board ship and about to sail for England when, in June 1610, Lord Delaware, with three ships, 150 men and supplies, arrived in the James River and saved the colony.

From then on, things went better, though in 1622 the Indians swept down on Jamestown, killed 350 people, about a quarter of the population, drove off the cattle, burned much of the town and destroyed the ironworks that had recently been built. But at least the basis of Virginia's prosperity had been discovered— tobacco, which sold for as much as five shillings a pound in the London market; and by 1642 the English population of Virginia had risen to 8,000.

By then, there were many European settlements in North America, by no means all of them English. The Dutch had settled New Amsterdam, now New York, on Manhattan Island, in 1624, and had settlements up the Hudson River, and though New York and what is now New York State became English in 1664, memorials of the Dutch occupation still remain in place-names, the Bronx, the Bowery, Broadway, Harlem, Yonkers.

By 1638, there were Swedish settlements on the Delaware, too small to survive except by absorption by the British, though what one thinks of as one of the most characteristic features of American pioneer life, the log cabin, was Swedish in origin. To the north, the St Lawrence River and Quebec were firmly French, and as explorers, missionaries and fur-traders the French were also in the almost 4,000-mile-long valley of the Mississippi and its tributaries. How deeply they penetrated into the interior of what is now the United States may again be seen from place-names—Duluth, Detroit, St Paul, Louisville, St Louis, Des Moines. And the Spanish, of course, held, however sketchily, what are now Florida, Texas, New Mexico, Colorado and California as outlying regions of Mexico itself.

But, in the light of the growth of the United States and of the nature of American experience itself, the most important colonies were undoubtedly those established by the Puritans in New England. The first of these dates from December 21, 1620, when the Pilgrim Fathers, having landed from the *Mayflower* at what is now called Provincetown, settled at Plymouth, the second from June 12, 1630, when six or seven hundred Puritans under John Winthrop founded Salem, Massachusetts.

[5]

Who were the Puritans? The word itself was first used in 1572 and ever since it has been one heavily loaded with emotional connotations. It has been adopted by millions as a badge of pride and defiance; as often, it has been flung about as a term of abuse and contempt. One constant connotation through the centuries is summed up by Shakespeare in the rhetorical question Sir Toby Belch puts to Malvolio, the Puritan steward in *Twelfth Night*: "Dost thou think, because thou art virtuous, there shall be no more cakes and ale?" Here, a Puritan is seen simply as a killjoy, the enemy of pleasure; but this is only a small part of the meaning of the word, even though it has behind it the contrast

popular belief has made for generations between the Cavaliers
and Roundheads of the Civil War.

We associate the Cavaliers, the High Church party, with the
splendours of the Renaissance and tend to see the Puritans as
the enemies of the arts. We remember how they suppressed the
theatre, how Cromwell's soldiers stabled their horses in cathedrals,
how busy the Puritans generally were in rooting up popular
festivals such as May-games and Morris-dancing, interpreting
them, rightly, as survivals from pagan, pre-Christian times. Yet,
while this general interpretation of the Puritans' attitude towards
the arts and pleasure is correct, we still have to bear in mind
that the finest flower of Renaissance humanism in seventeenth-
century England was the greatest Puritan of them all, John
Milton, whose masque, *Comus*—a theatrical performance—was
produced at Ludlow Castle by the children of Lord Fairfax, later
the Puritan general in the Civil War.

Perhaps the first thing to realise about the Puritans who
settled New England, men like William Bradford, John Winthrop,
Myles Standish, is that they were Englishmen of their time,
identified with what may even have been a majority of their
fellow-Englishmen and sundered from the rest by differences very
difficult for us in our century to understand, since we think of
God and society and man's place on earth in terms quite other
than theirs. We may be helped to an understanding if we
remember that throughout the greater part of the seventeenth
century the wars that were fought were religious wars, wars
between states certainly, but states as the champions of differing
interpretations of Christianity. In continental Europe the wars
were between Roman Catholics and Protestants; and in England
the war and the decades of dispute that led up to it were between
rival groups of Protestants, the differences between which may
now seem to us much smaller than what they had in common.

For us, Puritanism and Calvinism are almost synonymous; in
fact, the Church of England as a whole was largely Calvinist.
The important point—and this is the great difference between
that time and ours—is that when the Puritans first settled New
England the western world, Christendom, was still God-
oriented. Everything in it, the forms of the state, men's
behaviour, existed and was governed by reference to God, and
this was as true for Catholics and Anglicans as for Puritans, who,
as Professor Perry Miller has written, "were not unique or
extreme in thinking that religion was the primary and all-

engrossing business of man, or that all human thought and action should tend to the glory of God".

It follows from this that the question of what was man's right relation to God was all-important and the answer to it fundamental in its effects on society. It was in the raising of the question that Puritanism had its origin. It began as an internal quarrel within the Church of England, which, having broken with Rome in the reign of Henry VIII, had become a Protestant church by the reign of Elizabeth. The Puritans were originally that wing of the Church which believed that reformation had not gone far enough, that further purification of Papist and unscriptural forms and ceremonies were called for. For Puritans, the only authority in religion was the Bible; as Milton wrote: "True religion is the true worship and service of God, learned and believed from the word of God only"; and it was upon this that the quarrel between the Puritans and the Church of England hinged, though to put it like that is to be wildly unhistoric, since the Puritans themselves were still part of the Church and often were for many years later. William Bradford and the Plymouth settlers were not, but Winthrop and the company he led to Salem were good Church-of-England men.

For the Puritans their opponents in the Church of England were, like Catholics, in heresy, which Milton defined as "religion taken up and believed from the traditions of men, and additions to the word of God". Anglican theologians like Bishop Hooker and Jeremy Taylor contended, on the other hand, that the Bible was not exhaustive and that to interpret it as such, to see it as the sole vessel of truth, was to rule out the law of reason and the law of nature. God had manifested Himself in many ways, of which the Scriptures, however important, were but one. It was not, it cannot be too strongly emphasised, a quarrel about religion in the narrow sense in which most of us are inclined to conceive of religion today. It went to fundamentals. There is, for example, no scriptural authority for bishops; they belong to "the traditions of men, and additions to the word of God". If the Bible is to be the sole authority in religion, what happens to bishops? James I summed up the consequences of Puritanism in the state in a single terse sentence: "No bishop, no king." He was right: the Puritans of the next generation not only did away with bishops, they cut off his son's head.

The theologians of the Church of England saw the implications of making the Bible the sole authority in religion more clearly than the Puritans did. For if the traditions of man are disregarded and there can be no appeal to the findings of the Church throughout the centuries, then ultimately it is each man for himself. Each man has the right and the duty to interpret the Scriptures as seems best to himself, to make his own religion from it. So that in the end the social and political counterpart of Puritanism is individualism, with all that that implies.

Not, of course, that Puritans like Bradford and Winthrop saw it like that. They may have gone to America in order to worship God as they wished, but it was not a right they granted to others. No more than Catholics and Anglicans of the day did they believe in religious toleration. They were men who had been granted the Truth, there was only one Truth, and like God, it was jealous. Though the Scriptures were their sole authority, not only in religion but also in government and the whole conduct of life, they did not for one moment believe that each man had a right to interpret Scripture as seemed best to him. Interpretation was the work of learned men, of trained divines, and it was because of the necessity of securing a succession of learned men that they so early in New England put such store on education and founded Harvard College in 1636.

For Puritans of different temper, i.e., who interpreted Scripture in a manner other than theirs, there was short shrift. Roger Williams arrived in Massachusetts in 1630, a learned man, a graduate of Pembroke College, Cambridge, and a Puritan minister. He was banished five years later, as a whirlwind whose whirl, to use the words of a Massachusetts Puritan of a generation or so later, was likely to set all America on fire. He went on to found Providence, Rhode Island.

Williams was one of the first men to preach—and practise—religious liberty. Later dissenters from dissent in Massachusetts fared no better than he, no better than if they had stayed at home in England. The Quaker doctrine of the inner light which is accessible to all men and given perfect from God to their inmost spirits, was particularly obnoxious to the Puritans of Massachusetts. The first Quakers came to the colony in 1656: they were banished, and in 1658 the General Court decreed the death sentence for Quakers who returned after banishment. One Quaker, an old man named William Brend, had his head and his heels locked together in irons for sixteen hours and was then given 117 lashes with a tarred rope until he was unconscious. The people of Boston, who protested against this barbarous

treatment of an old man, were assured by the Rev. John Wilson
that the punishment was the will of Jehovah. For extreme
Puritans the only advantage New England had over old England
was that the former offered room for everyone; Massachusetts
Bay could always be left. In old England, the tinker and Baptist
preacher John Bunyan spent almost a dozen years in Bedford Jail;
he might have done little better in Massachusetts, but if he had
been in America he could have gone somewhere else.

[6]

The Puritan settlers as such, then, had no use for religious
tolerance; they had no use, either, for democracy and the notion
of the equality of man and man. They were thoroughly authori-
tarian, and their economic ideas were exactly the same as those
that prevailed in England. They believed in the government
regulation of business and the fixing of just prices. In Boston
tradesmen could be fined by the General Court and rebuked by
the Church for making what were judged to be inordinate profits.
Yet the inner logic of Puritanism ran counter to all this. The
Puritans were God-oriented men, and in this they were like
the Catholics and Anglicans of their time. But they were God-
oriented with a very significant difference. The Catholic's or
Anglican's relation to God was not direct but through the Church,
its traditions, its inherited wisdom and its priests. The Catholic
or Anglican belonged to a community of Christians, a corporate
body of worshippers, through which, as a member of which, he
approached God. But in a very deep sense the Puritan was a
man on his own, alone with God, and this became increasingly
so with the constant proliferation of sects and schisms within
Puritanism that was a consequence of seeing the Bible as the sole
religious authority.

This isolation was rendered all the more intense by the peculiar
nature of the Puritan's relation to God. As a Calvinist, he
believed that if he were one of the Elect, if he were saved, it was

due to no efforts of his own but entirely to the grace of God, which is arbitrary. As the last great Puritan theologian of New England, Jonathan Edwards, wrote in 1741 in his tremendous sermon, "Sinners in the Hands of an Angry God":

> The bow of God's wrath is bent, and the arrow made ready on the string, and justice bends the arrow at your heart, and strains the bow, and it is nothing but the mere pleasure of God, and that of an angry God, without any promise or obligation at all, that keeps the arrow one moment from being made drunk with your blood.
>
> Thus are all you that never passed under a great change of heart by the mighty power of the Spirit of God upon your souls; all that were never born again, and made new creatures, and raised from being dead in sin to a state of new and before altogether unexperienced light and life (however you may have your life in many things, and may have had religious affections, and may keep up a form of religion in your families and closets, and in the house of God, and may be strict in it), you are thus in the hands of an angry God; 'tis nothing but his mere pleasure that keeps you from being this moment swallowed up in everlasting destruction.

The Puritan's conviction that, out of thousands of his fellows, he had been chosen by God to be saved, inevitably separated him, in his own mind at least, from other men. It made him superior to them. He shared his life with God rather than with his fellow-human beings. It could on occasion make for an intolerable arrogance, even at times for an assumption that, since he was chosen by God, he had been lifted above ordinary standards of behaviour, was beyond conventional notions of good and evil. The classic account of this manifestation of Puritanism is to be found in James Hogg's novel, *Confessions of a Justified Sinner*, which is set in Scotland at the end of the eighteenth century and serves to remind us that apart from New England, the other country that saw the complete triumph of Puritanism was Scotland.

Yet for the overwhelming mass of Puritans conviction of Election can never have been absolute. There must always have been a doubt. It expressed itself in constant self-scrutiny, introspection and examination of conscience. Indeed, such a sermon as that of Edwards was in effect an awful minatory blast at the possible complacency of his listeners. The mind of the Puritan has been brilliantly described by V. S. Pritchett in his essay, "A Plymouth Brother", on an English nineteenth-century Puritan, the zoologist Philip Gosse:

Extreme Puritanism gives purpose, drama and intensity to private life. . . . Outwardly the extreme puritan appears narrow, crabbed, fanatical, gloomy and dull; but from the inside—what a series of dramatic climaxes his life is, what a fascinating casuistry beguiles him, how he is bemused by the comedies of duplicity, sharpened by the ingenious puzzles of the conscience, and carried away by the eloquence of hypocrisy. He lives like a soldier, now in the flash of battle, now in the wangling of camp and billet. However much he may bore others, he never suffers from boredom himself.

Yet one pointer to Election there was, both to the individual Puritan himself and in the eyes of his fellows. This was something it is difficult not to call worldly success, prosperity in business, in the man's chosen avocation. Prosperity was taken to be the outward and visible sign of an inward and spiritual grace. It was as though material blessings were assumed to pour down upon the chosen of God. Riches and success became a proof of Election. The connection between Protestantism and the rise of capitalism has long been noted, and it does not seem an accident that capitalism and industrialism first rose in the Protestant countries of northern Europe. In England it was among the merchants, tradesmen and artisans of London and the southern counties, who had most to gain by the break-up of feudalism, that Puritanism first won its way.

It is as though religious individualism went hand in hand with economic individualism; and, if conscience came into it, the Puritan could amass his fortune—and often in eighteenth-century New England it came from what might seem to us very dubious sources, the trade in slaves and rum—in the knowledge that he was doing so to the greater glory of God. Even as late as 1855, Harriet Beecher Stowe, the author of *Uncle Tom's Cabin* and the descendant of a long line of Puritans, could write in a geography book for children: "No people in the world have been more prosperous in every kind of business than those in New England; for God always makes most prosperous those who are most obedient to His laws in the Bible."

With this belief in the relation between salvation and economic success went the belief in its converse: that lack of success in a man was evidence of his rejection by God. The poor were poor because they deserved no better. If poverty was not positively identified with sinfulness it was often presumed to be strong evidence of it. And this goes a long way towards explaining a feature of English and American life that persisted until well into our own time and is still far from obsolete in the United States: what seems to most of us now a heartless attitude towards the poor, the dispossessed, the underprivileged. The notion of the welfare state would have been easily understood in medieval times. Indeed, when the Middle Ages were "rediscovered" in the nineteenth century one of the features in them that were particularly attractive to writers such as Scott and Carlyle and Ruskin, was precisely the balance of obligations and duties of man to man irrespective of rank that seemed to characterise the feudal order. But for the Puritans the idea of a welfare state would have been anathema, blasphemy, an attempt, as wicked as it was foolish, to pervert God's providence. Thus pious men could defend the long hours men, women and children worked in factories by saying that the long hours kept them out of mischief, prevented the occasions for sin. "The Devil still finds mischief for idle hands to do" was very much a Puritan proverb, for idleness was both a sin in itself and the cause of other sins.

In the same way, no people have taken the parable of the talents more to heart than the Puritans. This association between industry and hard work, with their fruits in material prosperity, and virtue survived even in those who had no belief in Puritan theology. Even when the theology disappeared the Puritan ethic remained. The conspicuous example is Benjamin Franklin, both in the ordering of his life as a young man, as he describes it in his *Autobiography*, and in his precepts, such as:

> It would be thought a hard government that would tax its people one-tenth part of their time, to be employed in its service. But idleness taxes many of us much more, if we reckon all that is spent in absolute sloth, or doing of nothing, with that which spent in idle employments or amusements that amount to nothing. Sloth, by bringing on diseases, absolutely shortens life.

Franklin, born in Boston in 1706, was the son of an English immigrant who had left England because of the laws against freedom of worship. He was not a Puritan himself. He was a Deist, and the first American to achieve international fame; he could and did hold his own with English scientists and French *philosophes*. Yet in many respects he remains after two hundred years perhaps *the* representative American. If his father had not migrated, his life obviously would have been very different. It is impossible not to believe the man himself would have been very different.

[7]

The first settlers of New England, then, were Englishmen indistinguishable in belief from hundreds of thousands of Englishmen who stayed at home. All the same, New England—the name was coined not by a Puritan but by Captain John Smith—was very different from old England, most obviously because it was virgin territory. In the most extreme way it represented the chance of a wholly new start of a kind such as probably had never happened in history before.

The parallel the Puritans drew was between themselves and the Children of Israel delivered out of bondage in Egypt into the promised land of Canaan. This is evident from the names they gave their settlements; mingled with those taken from old England, Plymouth, Boston, Worcester, Cambridge and the like, we find such invocations and memorials of the Old Testament story as Salem, Canaan, New Canaan and Providence. In part, this was a product of normal Puritan thinking, for when the Puritans made the Scriptures the sole authority in religion they did not differentiate between the Old and New Testaments and, indeed, sometimes took the former as literally as Orthodox Jews. They were steeped in it. It coloured the way they thought and the way they spoke, so much so that, seeing themselves as the Chosen People, they came very close to identifying themselves with the Children of Israel. One finds this sense of having been chosen by God in Milton's phrase "God's Englishman", which suggests that the Englishman—the Puritan Englishman—exists in a relation to God similar to that of the Jew. The famous phrase for the United States, "God's own country", makes sense in much the same way.

But this process of identification with the Israelites was even stronger in the New England Puritans because they had entered the Promised Land, whereas the English Puritans, except during the interlude of the Commonwealth, could still be seen as in bondage in Egypt. The American critic Edmund Wilson, in his reflections on the Jews and their influence on Puritan America, in *A Piece of My Mind*, recalls that George Santayana makes one of the New England characters of his novel, *The Last Puritan*, say: "We were always a circumcised people, consecrated to great expectations." And the sentence is especially interesting in that it comes from an outsider, for Santayana, though for many years a teacher of philosophy at Harvard, was Spanish by birth and a Roman Catholic in religion.

This conviction that they were the Chosen People accounts for much in the history of the Puritans' settlement of New England, their unrelenting enmity to the Indians, for example. The Indians, it is true, were part of the dangers they had to face, a permanent menace of the frontier. Yet to some degree, as the very different experience of the Quakers in Pennsylvania shows, it was a menace of their own making. For them, the Indians were a lesser breed without the Law, pagans, committed to the Devil, and therefore not much better or more deserving of mercy than wild animals. And perhaps one may trace back to the Puritan attitude the later one, prevalent on the frontier, that the only good Injun was a dead Injun.

This consciousness of their own righteousness, the sense that they had divine approval, must have been a very large factor in the formation of an American characteristic that is never far below the surface of life in the United States and can occasionally emerge in appalling ugliness. This is lack of toleration that manifests itself in a demand for rigid conformity. It often seems like the behaviour of a beleaguered garrison, sometimes indeed like that of a herd of cattle at bay against the alien and unknown intruder, who is feared simply because he is alien and unknown. What is being defended is usually called "Americanism" or "the American way of life", which, it is assumed, is in constant danger of overthrow from the outside world. In our time, the most notorious manifestation of this deep-rooted American characteristic has been McCarthyism.

The heritage of Puritanism cannot be held solely responsible for this ingrained tendency in American life, but some of the seeds of its origin at least lie with it. The Puritans believed very firmly in the Devil, God's eternal enemy, and were constantly seeing the Devil in others. The result was an interpretation of existence in terms of black and white, and even though Puritanism as Bradford and Winthrop knew it has long vanished from the

American scene, this interpretation of the outside world is still with us. It is allied with, is indeed inseparable from, an assumption of moral superiority to the rest of the world that the rest of the world finds baffling and infuriating, partly because it is insulting and partly, and more important, because it stems from a view of life the rest of the world thinks altogether too simple and naïve. When, in the present state of the world, it intrudes into international politics it can obviously be very dangerous. Perhaps the most famous criticism from the outside of this American characteristic is Graham Greene's novel *The Quiet American*.

This assumption of moral superiority is, it must be admitted, one shared, though now to a lesser degree, by the British. In Britain, it reached its peak during the nineteenth century, which witnessed the climax of British power and was also marked by a revival of something like Puritanism, even though the theological bases of it had long been eroded.

[8]

The Puritan settlers of New England were early differentiated from their English brothers not only because they had entered the Promised Land and could live there largely unmolested and uncontaminated by men of different beliefs, but also because of the very nature of the land in which they found themselves. To English eyes, New England remains the most "English" region of the United States. This is partly due to its geography. Though it is a much more rugged country than England—in many ways, with its mountain ranges, its many rivers and narrow valleys, it is more like Scotland—it is at any rate on a scale similar to that of England, unlike the lands to the south and, even more, the prairies beyond the Appalachians. It was a country, in other words, in which Englishmen could feel themselves at home; and, taking their Englishness with them and using as their models for towns and dwelling places those they had left behind, the Puritans made it as English as they could. In Boston, for example, even today the resemblance to eighteenth-century Bristol is still apparent; and New England villages, with the houses clustered round village greens, could only be English in inspiration.

But however much New England in its nooks and corners, both in landscape and townscape, may remind us of old England, the early settlers must have found it, on their first landing and for many years after, intimidatingly different. Though it abounded in forests and game, and its seas and rivers in fish, all of which stood them in good stead—it is not an accident that turkey is the traditional dish at Thanksgiving, which commemorates the first harvest the Plymouth settlers raised—its soil was anything but fertile. By English standards, the climate was extreme, bitterly cold in winter, with blizzards and heavy snows. How the early settlers suffered we know from their records.

Within three months of their settling at Plymouth, half of William Bradford's company were dead, though for this the rigours of the voyage across the Atlantic must be blamed as much as New England. That the rest survived was probably due to the sudden appearance of an Indian named Squanto, who, as William Bradford says in his history of the Plymouth Settlement, "became a special instrument sent of God for their good, beyond their expectation". Squanto had been kidnapped by a sea-captain who intended to sell him as a slave in Spain, but he had escaped to England and knew some English. Squanto showed the settlers how to catch fish, how to plant Indian corn—maize—and how, as was necessary if a harvest was to be obtained, to manure the exhausted soil with fish.

The much larger settlement established ten years later at Salem under Winthrop also suffered bitter loss of life in its first year, again as a result of scurvy, a deficiency disease caused by lack of vitamin C, in other words, of fresh vegetables. But, besides the hazards inevitable in establishing themselves in a new country three thousand miles and many months away from any source of supplies other than those they could produce themselves, the Puritan settlers constantly had other dangers to contend with. Not the least was the presence of other Englishmen whose opinions and ways of life were displeasing, and regarded as hostile, to their own.

This was a situation the Plymouth Colony had to meet early in its history. More than two hundred years later it was to be the raw material of one of Nathaniel Hawthorne's most famous stories. In 1625 an English gentleman named Captain Wollaston arrived in New England with a party of settlers and established an Anglican settlement, called Mount Wollaston, in what is now the town of Quincy, Massachusetts. Wollaston left for Virginia after a few months and control of the settlement fell into the hands of Thomas Morton. The goings-on of Morton and his followers scandalised the Plymouth Colony. As Bradford writes in his history:

They then fell to utter licentiousness, and led a dissolute and profane life. Morton became lord of misrule and maintained, as it were, a school of Atheism. As soon as they had acquired some means of trading with the Indians, they spent it in drinking wine and strong drinks to excess—as some reported, £10 worth in a morning! They set up a Maypole, drinking and dancing about it for several days at a time, inviting the Indian women for their consorts, dancing and frisking together like so many fairies—or furies rather—to say nothing of worse practices. It was as if they had revived the celebrated feasts of the Roman goddess Flora, or the beastly practices of the mad Bacchanalians. Morton, to show his poetry, composed sundry verses and rhymes, some tending to lasciviousness and others to the detraction and scandal of some persons, affixing them to his idle, or idol, Maypole. They changed the name of the place, and instead of calling it Mount Wollaston, they called it Merry Mount, as if this jollity would last forever. But it did not continue long. . . . That worthy gentleman, Mr John Endicott, arrived from England, bringing over a patent under the broad seal, for the government of Massachusetts. Visiting this neighbourhood, he had the Maypole cut down, and reprimanded them to improve their way of living. In consequence, others changed the name of their place again, and called it Mount Dragon!

But that was not the end. Morton discovered the enormous profit the French were making from selling guns, powder and shot to the Indians and thereupon began himself to sell arms to them. "When they saw what execution a gun would do and the advantage of it, they were mad for them and would pay any price for them, thinking their bows and arrows but baubles in comparison." "Oh, the horror of this villainy." Bradford goes on. "How many Dutch and English have lately been killed by Indians, thus furnished; and no remedy is provided—nay, the evil has increased. The blood of their brothers has been sold for profit; and in what danger all these colonies are is too well-known."

The danger, indeed, was obvious, and when the Puritans

discovered that Morton was proposing to import large quantities
of guns from England to trade with the Indians, they sent Myles
Standish and a party of men against Merry Mount. According
to Bradford, the men of Merry Mount were so drunk that they
could not lift their guns; Morton was seized and sent back to
England.

Today, Morton's real crime would seem to have been his trade
in guns and alcohol with the Indians; but the Puritans were just
as outraged by his dancing round the Maypole. It was the
symbol of everything they detested; and they had already had
trouble with what they construed as idleness and dissoluteness
in the Plymouth Colony itself. Admittedly, Bradford describes
it as "rather amusing than serious", but the incident shows how
serious a risk to the ideological bases of New Plymouth Merry
Mount might have been if it had been allowed to flourish. In
1621 a party of new settlers had arrived from England. Bradford
tells us:

> On Christmas Day, the Governor called the people out to work
> as usual; but most of the new company excused themselves, and
> said it went against their consciences to work on that day. So the
> Governor told them, if they made it a matter of conscience, he
> would spare them till they were better informed. So he went with
> the rest, and left them; but on returning from work at noon he
> found them at play in the street, some pitching the bar, some at
> stool-ball, and such sports. So he went to them and took away
> their games, and told them that it was against his conscience that
> they should play and others work. If they made the keeping of the
> day a matter of devotion, let them remain in their houses; but
> there should be no gaming and revelling in the streets. Since then,
> nothing has been attempted in that way, at least openly.

Normally, however, the Puritans' difficulties with their fellow-
Englishmen came from the challenges made to them by other
sectaries, such as the Quakers.

The Indians, until far into the eighteenth century, when they
were often in the pay of or allied to the French, were a constant
menace. Bradford's and Winthrop's histories are full of accounts
of warfare between Indians and settlers, and even as late as 1676,
during what is called King Philip's War, one out of every sixteen
men of military age in New England was killed and sixteeen
towns in Massachusetts were destroyed or abandoned.

What these wars meant for ordinary people may be seen in

such works as Mrs Mary Rowlandson's extremely graphic *The Sovreignty and Goodness of God, Together with the Faithfulness of His Promises Displayed; Being a Narrative of the Captivity and Restoration of Mrs Mary Rowlandson.* Mrs Rowlandson lived in the frontier village of Lancaster, Massachusetts, where she was the wife of the minister. At sunrise on February 10, 1676, while her husband was in Boston, Indians swooped down on the village, burned it and carried off the settlers. Mrs Rowlandson was redeemed from captivity three months later. These raids by the Indians were often interpreted by the Puritans as witnesses of God's displeasure with them: when the Indian chief, King Philip, struck at Massachusetts the General Court decided that it was a visitation from God because the Commonwealth had not persecuted Quakers ardently enough and because her men had taken to periwigs and her women begun to indulge in "cutting, curling and immodest laying out of theire haire".

These wars and skirmishes were as bestial in the atrocities committed on both sides as any in history, and the extent to which the Puritans themselves had become as it were Indianised is shown in a story Thoreau tells in his *A Week on the Concord and Merrimack Rivers*, written in 1839. The anecdote begins:

> On the thirty-first day of March, one hundred and forty-two years before this, probably about this time in the afternoon, there were hurriedly paddling down this part of the river, between the pine woods which then fringed these banks, two white women and a boy, who had left an island at the mouth of the Contoocook before daybreak. They were slightly clad for the season, in the English fashion, and handled their paddles unskilfully, but with nervous energy and determination, and at the bottom of their canoe lay still-bleeding scalps of ten of the aborigines.

The two women had been captured by Indians two weeks before. The younger, Hannah Dustan, "had seen her seven elder children flee with their father, but knew not of their fate. She had seen her infant's brains dashed out against an apple tree, and had left her own and her neighbours' dwellings in ashes." The two women had been forced to march through the snow to an Indian encampment, where they found an English boy, Samuel Lennardson, also held prisoner. Determined to escape, Mrs Dustan had asked the boy how an enemy could be killed most quickly and how scalps were taken. He asked one of the Indians and passed the information on to Mrs Dustan. She rose before dawn on the morning of the thirty-first, took up a tomahawk and killed all the Indians, except a child and a squaw who fled bleeding with him into the woods. "The English boy struck the Indian, who had given him the information, on the temple, as he had been directed." They then seized what provisions they could, together with the Indians' arms, scuttled all the canoes but one, in which they set out down the Merrimack to paddle the sixty miles to Haverhill, Massachusetts. But "after having proceeded a short distance, fearing that her story would not be believed if she should escape to tell it, they returned to the silent wigwam, and taking the scalps of the dead, put them in a bag as proof of what they had done".

[9]

Their isolation in a largely barren land inhabited, except for themselves, only by incomprehensible savages, their religious fanaticism that was unalloyed, or uncompromised, by habitual contact with others of different views, forced the Puritans of New England into attitudes towards the world and assumptions about society significantly different from those of Englishmen at home. What must be especially stressed is their isolation, but their isolation as a community, not as individuals. The New England Puritans were town-dwellers; indeed, it was against the law for settlers to live outside communities. They were not concerned, like later Americans, in pressing westward and opening up new frontiers: they had come to settle and to stay.

They believed no more in democracy or equality than they did in religious toleration; their beliefs made them obdurately opposed to all three. But the plain facts of the nature of their existence in New England forced upon them a measure of democracy and equality that went far beyond anything obtaining in England. They had either to live together or perish, and this meant, in the circumstances in which they found themselves, that they could survive as communities only if the general will of the settlers prevailed. The other European settlements in America, the Spanish, Portuguese, French, Dutch, were planted at the decree of the home governments; they were planned and organised from Europe as instruments of quite conscious imperialism, as we should say today. But when the Puritans went to New England they had no thoughts in their mind of empire; in a way, the Puritan settlements just happened. They were different even from those of the English settlers in Virginia, who had been granted royal authority to make their own local laws. The Puritans had to make their own authority, and the pattern—one cannot say the model—was established right at the beginning in the covenant drawn up on the *Mayflower* even before the Pilgrims landed.

It was imposed upon them by necessity, occasioned, as William Bradford wrote, "partly by the discontented and mutinous speeches that some of the strangers among them had let fall: that when they got ashore they would use their liberty; that none had power to command them. . . ." The Mayflower Compact, as it is called, runs as follows:

> In the name of God, amen. We whose names are underwritten, the loyal subjects of our dread sovereign lord, King James, by the grace of God, of Great Britain, France and Ireland, King, Defender of the Faith, etc., having undertaken for the glory of God, and advancement of the Christian faith, and honour of our king and country, a voyage to plant the first colony in the northern parts of Virginia, do by these presents solemnly and mutually in the presence of God, and of one another, covenant and combine ourselves into a civil body politic, for our better ordering and preservation, and the furtherance of the ends aforesaid; and by virtue hereof to enact, constitute, and frame, such just and equal laws, ordinances, acts, constitutions, and offices, from time to time, as shall be thought most meet and convenient for the general use of the Colony, unto which we promise all due submission and obedience.
>
> In witness whereof we have here underscribed our names at Cape Cod, 11th of November, in the year of the reign of our sovereign lord, King James of England, France and Ireland the eighteenth, and of Scotland the fifty-fourth.

In fact, the Compact was an extension into the realm of civil government of the covenant the men of the *Mayflower* and others of their religious belief, who were later to be called Congregationalists, commonly followed in their church government. The word Congregationalism is almost self-explanatory: every con-gregation, that is every church, is self-governing and democratic. No hierarchy exists; the head of the Church is Christ and the various congregations are fellow-members of the common family of God. During the seventeenth century Congregationalism became virtually the established religion of New England, so it is not difficult to see why something very close to the *Mayflower* Compact was adopted by other small settlements that lay outside established government.

At first, the laws of the Plymouth Colony were made by a mass meeting, called the General Court, of the forty-one men who had signed the Compact. Then, as population increased and more and more colonies were planted as offshoots of Plymouth, it became less easy for all freemen to attend the General Court at Plymouth; and in 1636 the freemen of the three largest settlements outside Plymouth decided to send representatives to the General Court instead of going *en masse*. Three years later, the Pilgrims adopted "The Fundamentals of Plymouth", which among other things legalised the procedure and instituted representative gov-ernment. It also guaranteed trial by jury in the English manner and laid it down that no person should suffer loss of life, liberty or property except by "some express law" of the Colony or of England in matters "wherein we have no particular law of our own". Certain changes followed later. Until 1660, the right to vote was possessed by almost every adult male; but then a small property qualification was imposed. And in 1668 an additional requirement was enacted: voters must be "orthodox in the fundamentals of religions", that is, members of the church.

After its first few years, the Plymouth Colony dwindled in importance by comparison with other colonies, especially with Winthrop's Massachusetts Bay Colony, and in 1691 it was annexed to Massachusetts. Its relative smallness probably made the evolu-tion of democratic procedures, if not of democratic principles, easier than in the large Bay Colony, where for many years there was something like a running battle between the freemen, the original stock-holders of the Massachusetts Bay Company, who had the franchise, and what may be called the ruling class headed by Winthrop.

It was in some ways a class struggle: Winthrop, who was of the English upper classes, in England had been lord of the manor of Groton, in Suffolk, while the Bay Company itself had many Puritan peers and aristocratic gentlemen among its promoters.

Winthrop was quite explicit in his attitude towards democracy. It was, among other things, unscriptural: "If we should change from a mixt aristocratie to a mere democratie, first we should have no warrant in scripture for it: there is no such government in Israel . . . a Democratie is, amongst most civil nations, accounted the meanest and worst of all forms of government . . . and History does record that it hath been always of least continuance and fullest of trouble." These words Winthrop wrote after the case, in 1642, of Goody Sherman, a poor widow, whose stray sow had been impounded and claimed by a rich man named Richard Keaynes, who was well known for his lack of scruples in business. The case was brought before the General Court. A majority of the magistrates favoured Keaynes, a majority of the deputies Goody Sherman. In other words, the magistrates, much smaller in number than the deputies, frustrated the will of the majority.

At this time in the history of Massachusetts Bay, only a small minority of men had a vote. The others would voice their opinions on local affairs at town meetings, though even there they could not vote. The magistrates, who were generally allied with the clergy, were normally opposed to the deputies, who were not precisely representatives of ordinary citizens, since only stock-holders of the Bay Company, members of the church, had the vote, but certainly stood for wider interests than the magistrates and clergy. It was not until more than a century later, at the time of the War of Independence and the break with Britain, that universal male suffrage was found anywhere in North America, but nevertheless democratic processes were inherent in the New England colonies from the beginning, for reasons stated by the French political scientist, Alexis de Tocqueville, in his classic work, *Democracy in America*, published in 1835:

> The religious and political passions which ravaged the British Empire during the whole reign of Charles I drove fresh crowds of sectarians every year to the shores of America. In England, the stronghold of Puritanism continued to be in the middle classes; and is was from the middle classes that most of the emigrants came. The population of New England increased rapidly; and whilst the hierarchy of rank despotically classed the inhabitants of the mother country, the colony approximated more and more the novel spectacle of a community homogenous in all its parts. A democracy, more perfect than antiquity had dared to dream of, started in full size and panoply from the midst of an ancient feudal society.

Tocqueville also notes that

> The political existence of the majority of the nations of Europe commenced in the superior ranks of society, and was gradually and imperfectly communicated to the different members of the social body. In America, on the contrary, it may be said that the township was organised before the county, the county before the state, the state before the Union.

Then, the conditions in which the settlers lived were such as to make considerations of rank and class relatively unimportant and to enforce a rough equality. The very geography of the country prevented the growth of large estates and the rise of great landowners such as characterised Virginia and the Hudson Valley of New York. It produced, instead, men who were fishermen, subsistence farmers, tradesmen and townsmen, men, in other words, working for themselves, living by their own efforts, marked by independence of mind. In the early days of the settlements, especially, when the wilderness had to be cleared and a new country built by hard physical toil and practical sagacity, a strong, healthy, intelligent workman who could turn his hands and his wits to the solving of difficulties as they arose, was infinitely more valuable than a foolish gentleman, however rich.

Money itself was not of great importance in a country where luxuries were almost unobtainable. There is a striking incident right at the beginning of the Bay settlement that shows how preconceptions of rank and society had to go by the board in the face of sheer necessity. Within months of their landing in Massachusetts, Winthrop's party was threatened if not with starvation at any rate with famine. Food was so scarce that one hundred and eighty indentured servants had to be given their liberty, at a cost of something like £400 to their employers. Labour was always scarce, and in a country where free land was readily obtainable there was little incentive for an intelligent, energetic man, however humble his status may have been in England, to work for another. As one settler wrote: "I live a simple life and hath builded a shop, and doth follow the weaving of cloth, but I have bought 450 acres of land in the woods."

How quickly a man might become a master, how rapid social change could be, is indicated by a passage in Winthrop's *Journal* dated April 13, 1645:

The wars in England kept servants from coming to us, so those we had could not be hired, when their times were out, but upon unreasonable terms, and we found it very difficult to pay their wages to their content (for money was very scarce). I may upon this occasion report a passage between one Rowley and his servant. The master, being forced to sell a pair of his oxen to pay his servant his wages, told his servant he could keep him no longer, not knowing how to pay him the next year. The servant answered, he would serve him for more of his cattle. But how shall I do (saith the master) when all my cattle are gone? The servant replied, you shall then serve me, and so you may have your cattle again.

[10]

The scope New England offered to men of initiative and enterprise must have been a powerful lure to immigrants. By 1640 the population had risen to about eighteen thousand. Not that the New England colonies were the only ones. There were about eight thousand Englishmen in Virginia and over thirty-five thousand in the West Indian islands of Barbados, Nevis and St Kitts. In the West Indian islands the brilliant beginnings were not to be maintained; the dawn was false. It was otherwise with Virginia, but its development, its culture, its whole way and temper of life, were to be very different from New England's, in a real sense fundamentally opposed to it, as finally became plain in the tragedy of the Civil War, the war between the States, in the middle of the nineteenth century.

Virginia was colonised in a spirit quite different from that which made New England. Its settlers went there with no Utopian motives; there are no such place-names in Virginia as Salem and Canaan; and it seems significant that whereas the country of the Puritans was called New England Virginia was known as the Old Dominion. It represented a different aspect of England. It was almost entirely Anglican in religion, Anglican in a broad, moderate way, remote from fanaticism and zeal, stressing tradi-

tional institutions rather than doctrine. It came in time almost
to represent an ideal dream of rural England, the rural England
that is summed up in such figures as Addison's Sir Roger de
Coverley and Fielding's Squire Allworthy and Squire Weston.
It looked back, in other words, to an older England.

That it did so was in part a consequence of the nature of the
country, which made it from the beginning a one-crop economy,
the crop being tobacco. At first, the labour consisted of white,
indentured servants who were often convicts shipped from
England. They could earn their freedom, and it was possible
for them to rise in the world. There were no property quali-
fications for the franchise; every free man could vote in the
elections for the House of Burgesses. But by 1699 all this had
changed; only men who owned land were allowed to vote;
tenant farmers were disenfranchised. And the chances of ad-
vancement for the poor man in Virginia became increasingly
smaller after 1680 and the introduction of Negro slaves. Poor
men could not compete with unpaid labour. What might have
developed into a substantial class of yeoman farmers was wiped
out; more and more the economy of the colony depended on
slave labour.

Virginia became a country of large plantations in which there
were few towns. The feudal system, which was disappearing in
England, was re-established in Virginia, with Negro slaves as the
peasants and the country gentlemen who owned them modelling
themselves on the country gentlemen of England. As Daniel
Boorstin has written: "It was as if the landed families of Virginia
had brought with them the text of a drama long played on the
English stage which would now be played on the American."
It was essentially a class society. Boorstin shows us, in *The
Americans: The Colonial Experience*, how horse-racing was made by
law a sport restricted to gentlemen. The gentlemen of Virginia
maintained close relations with England, often sending their
children back to be educated. They were very consciously gentlemen, all-round men, in a modest way patrons of scholarship and
the arts. At the same time they were "working gentlemen", not
absentee landlords. They managed their own estates, which were
often vast, running into thousands of acres and hundreds of
slaves, and managed, too, their own businesses. If they still had
to depend on England for luxuries, in essentials their plantations
were self-supporting and self-contained, like medieval estates.

They produced a style of living, these gentlemen of Virginia, more attractive than anything New England knew, a style of living that, especially when seen from this side of the Civil War, which killed it, invokes in many people a nostalgia which probably falsifies it. We tend, especially if we depend on novels for a view of it, to see it in ideal terms, as Thackeray does in *The Virginians* and recent American novelists like Caroline Gordon and Allen Tate have done in *None Shall Look Back* and *The Fathers*.

Not that these two novels, which stress the feudal sense of obligation of the Southern gentleman, the chivalric code and sense of formal, aristocratic values strikingly like those expressed in the poetry of W. B. Yeats, "where all's accustomed, ceremonious", are necessarily contradicted by what we know of actuality. We may take as representative of the South at its best such a man as Colonel William Byrd of Westover in Virginia, Esq., as he was called, whose *Secret Diary*, first published in our own time, throws valuable light on life in Virginia in the latter years of the seventeenth century and the first four decades of the eighteenth. Byrd was sent to England to school and was a member of the Middle Temple. He also served an apprenticeship to a firm of London merchants. For some years the agent of Virginia in London, he was the friend of writers—gentlemen-wits we may call them—like Congreve and Wycherley, was himself a writer, was interested in the sciences, and elected a Fellow of the Royal Society.

Back home in Virginia, he built the superb Georgian mansion of Westover, "baronial in extent and luxurious in its appointments", on the James River. His library of more than 3,600 books was the largest in Virginia and scarcely rivalled anywhere in British North America. Yet Byrd was anything but a dilettante in the contemporary English manner. He was an astonishingly energetic man of affairs, who personally supervised the working of his plantations, the planting of his orchards and gardens and the planning of his crops. He was busy in schemes of real-estate promotion and, foreseeing its future importance as a port, laid out and developed on his land the city of Richmond.

He maintained a sawmill and gristmill, prospected for coal and iron and copper and wrote an account of his prospecting, bought up tobacco which he shipped and sold in London, traded with the Indians and trafficked in slaves. When members of his family or his slaves were ill, he doctored them himself. He was a member of the Council of State; and to make time for all his many interests, he often rose at three in the morning to read in

Hebrew, Greek or Latin until breakfast. After supper in the evening he read Tillotson's sermons.

Virginia probably came to its finest flowering in the men of the generation that followed Byrd's, in Washington, Jefferson, Madison and Monroe, respectively first, third, fourth and fifth Presidents of the United States, men who did so much to defeat the British in the War of Independence and to launch the new nation on its destiny. They were men used to government. It is true they were oligarchs, but Professor Boorstin argues persuasively when he suggests that it was their aristocratic habit of mind that helped to make them leaders of the American Revolution. They were fiercely independent men, rather as medieval barons had been, and, as Boorstin suggests, their passion for independence, which was the passion to live their lives as they wished to, may well have been the more intense because of its contrast with the slavery all about them.

Certainly it is impossible to conceive the history of the young Republic without them. They were large-minded men, and again one feels it was their special position as great landowners responsible for the lives and the welfare of considerable numbers of retainers that made them so. Today, one can perhaps best realise how they saw themselves from the classical elegance of the houses they left behind them, such as Washington's at Mount Vernon and Jefferson's at Monticello. By eighteenth-century English standards, Mount Vernon is not a large house. Indeed, an Englishman may be struck when first seeing it by its smallness. It is not in any way grand; before anything else, it is a house to be lived in. But in its proportions, the natural taste that breathes through it, its simplicity and lack of ostentation, it seems a perfect expression of the aristocratic spirit. It is one of those manifestations of America at the end of the colonial period and in the early days of the Republic that bring home the force of the parallel Americans themselves made between their country and republican Rome.

Nevertheless, the civilisation of Virginia was a precarious growth. Essentially agrarian, its economy was archaic, and, based as it was on a single crop and a slave system, it was doomed to destruction as soon as the world outside impinged upon it. It depended for its everyday maintenance on a sense of *noblesse oblige*, a chivalric code, among its aristocracy incapable, probably, of being sustained for long. Allen Tate's novel, *The Fathers*, is an elegiac celebration of the code, but the novel also shows how impotent it was in the face of the intrusion of commercial values.

[11]

If from the beginning the Puritan experience of America was poles apart from the Virginian, to use the word as applying to the South generally, that of the Quakers of Pennsylvania was different again. Pennsylvania was founded in 1681 by William Penn, who was granted "the true and absolute Proprietarie" of the colony by Charles II. Penn used his ownership to establish in Pennsylvania what he called a "Holy experiment". Pennsylvania was to be free, self-governing, with complete and religious freedom irrespective of race or belief. Liberty of conscience was at the heart of his ideas of society. As he wrote from London to the settlers already in the colony:

> I hope you will not be troubled at your change and the king's choice, for you are now fixed at the mercy of no governor that comes to make his fortune great; you will be governed by laws of your own making, and live a free, and, if you will, a sober and industrious people. I will not usurp the right of any, or oppress his person. . . . In short, whatever sober and resonable men can reasonably desire for the security and improvement of their own happiness, I shall heartily comply with . . .

The name Penn gave to the city he built—Philadelphia, "brotherly love"—sums up his ideal.

In many respects, the seventeenth-century Quakers strike us as being already natural Americans, meaning by that that they embodied in their lives tenets we now take for granted in democracy, even though we may fall far short of practising them. They believed absolutely in human equality. Their religion was without formal creed or ritual, ceremony was anathema to them, and informality and simplicity was their practice in speech and in dress. Since they believed that religion was an individual, personal, inward matter and that man was essentially good, they were committed fundamentally to religious freedom. They

43

treated the Indians with a fairness, a recognition of their rights, they had never before received from Anglo-Saxons.

Since the Quakers welcomed men of all sects, their colony naturally became a haven for religious dissentients throughout western Europe. Penn encouraged this. Indeed, to use a modern word, he "promoted" Pennsylvania as no colony had ever been promoted before, and his advertising brochures, as we would call them today, were widely circulated not only in England and Wales but also in Ireland, Germany and the Netherlands. In 1682, Welsh Quakers, who had acquired 50,000 acres of land from Penn, began to arrive and establish settlements—Merion, Haverford, Radnor—on the outskirts of Philadelphia. The second large settlement, after Philadelphia, was founded in 1683 and called Germantown, since the majority of its people were German Quakers and Dutch Mennonites, members of a sect closely resembling Quakerism. These settlers, whether German or Dutch in origin, became known generally as Pennsylvania Dutch. They increased rapidly and spread into the interior, where they became extremely able and energetic farmers.

Given scope, the Quakers, like the Puritans, became highly successful business men. For similar reasons. Their religious beliefs cut them off very largely from the ordinary concerns and frivolities of the world, so that their energies easily became channelled in one secular activity their Society approved of, trade. At the same time, their tolerance towards ways of belief not their own gave them an advantage commercially over the Puritans of New England. Philadelphia attracted merchants and artisans not only from England but from the other American colonies. Life there might not be less austere but it was more free; yet it was not so different from that of New England as to prevent New Englanders from feeling at home.

One New Englander who made the transition from Boston to Philadelphia was Benjamin Franklin, whom we think of today as the greatest Philadelphian of them all; and the presence there of men like Franklin, men who were not Quakers, made for a stability the colony might not otherwise have had. For Quaker principles were such as, undiluted, to make the practice of government next to impossible. Quakers, for instance, would take no oaths, which, according to English law, meant, among other things, that they could not be jurymen or take the stand as witnesses in a court trial. It was years before a satisfactory compromise between legal necessity and the demands for conscience was evolved. Similarly, the Quakers were absolute pacifists; they would not kill or take part in any war. And yet the Colony had to be defended, from the French and from the Indians. At such time, it was to men like Franklin that responsibility for the safety and preservation of Pennsylvania passed.

Pennsylvania was the last but one of the British colonies on the Atlantic seaboard to be founded. From the beginning, it was the most successful. Less than fifty years after Penn had been granted his charter, it could be written of the colony that, "From a wilderness, the Lord, by his good hand of providence, hath made it a fruitful field." Before another fifty years were out, Philadelphia was not only the biggest city and port in the colonies but also the second biggest city of the British Empire.

By 1700 the population of the colonies was about 260,000, as compared with about 150,000 Spaniards in South and Central America and a mere 13,000 Frenchmen in the French possessions, which in theory took in the whole of Canada and the Mississipi Valley. There were many differences between English settlement and Spanish and French. Spanish settlement was built upon a large aboriginal population of Indians who were hewers of wood and drawers of water. The French, though they had forts as far west as what are now Michigan, Illinois and Minnesota as well as villages on the banks of the St Lawrence in Quebec, by English standards had scarcely settled at all. Moreover, British colonisation was compact, lying along the length of the continent in the hundred-mile strip between the ocean and the Appalachians, beyond which they had yet to penetrate.

[12]

The more than a quarter million Europeans in British North America at the beginning of the eighteenth century were by no means all British, and each national stock as it arrived threw into the common pot its own specific talents. There were the Dutch in New York. By comparison with the English colonies, the development of what is now New York State was slow and late, for the Dutch were interested in trade with the Indians, mainly in furs, rather than in settlement. This, as it happened, stood the settlers of New England in good stead, for it made New York a buffer territory between them and the French in Canada, who might have reacted strongly against permanent British settlements so near to them. As it was, the Hudson Valley was sparsely inhabited, parcelled out in vast estates which prevented the growth of small farms and intensive farming.

But from its foundation, the city of New York was what it is today, a cosmopolitan city. At the beginning of the eighteenth century it is said that eighteen languages were spoken in it, and this in itself reflects the nature of the original Dutch settlement. During the first half of the seventeenth century the Netherlands were the most prosperous country in Europe, the centre from which new developments in technology, new methods of farming, advances in the standard of living radiated. It was also the most liberal country in Europe, a haven for political and religious refugees from other lands. So there was little inducement for the Dutch themselves to leave Holland, and the settlers who went out to New Netherlands and New Amsterdam under Dutch auspices were extraordinarily diverse in origin, French-speaking Protestants from the Spanish Netherlands, Germans, Danes, Norwegians, Swedes, Finns, Portuguese, Spaniards, Italians, Bohemians, Poles and Jews.

But it was the Dutch influence that was paramount. Dutch was still taught in the schools of New York City until the middle of the eighteenth century and it remained in use as the common tongue in parts of the Hudson Valley until the early years of the nineteenth. And the Dutch set their stamp especially on New York City, giving it a tone that may perhaps still be felt there. It is impossible that they could have been more devoted to trade than the Puritans of Boston or the Quakers of Philadelphia, but they brought with them from Holland a quality which to Puritans and Quakers alike was anathema, a zest for rich, earthy living, a delight in the pleasures of the table and in creature comforts. They made New York something of a materialist's paradise, in contrast with Boston, where plain living and high thinking went hand in hand. New York is still a materialist's paradise, though it is also much more than that; but it was not until the last years of the nineteenth century that it could begin to rival and ultimately, through sheer size of population, take over from Boston as a centre of culture and the arts.

The other European groups of settlers lost their national identities more rapidly than the Dutch because they came to colonies already established by the English, though the Germans in Pennsylvania succeeded in retaining theirs almost until revolutionary days. They did so because they largely shunned the towns. They became highly successful farmers; it is said that the whole of the colonies could have been fed by the German farms of Pennsylvania alone.

A national and religious group that contributed to the growth of the colonies to a degree out of all proportion to its numbers were the Huguenots, who were in great demand throughout the seventeenth century. The first of them came by way of England, Holland and Switzerland, where their fathers had sought asylum after the massacre of St Bartholomew in 1572, but the largest contingent arrived after the revocation of the Edict of Nantes in 1685. They settled particularly in Virginia, South Carolina, Pennsylvania and New York: the town of New Rochelle, in Westchester County, New York, was a Huguenot settlement.

The variety of skills they brought with them is shown in a legal document of South Carolina of 1697, which lists the names and occupations of sixty-three of them; twelve planters, twelve weavers, eleven merchants, four shipwrights, three coopers, three smiths, two goldsmiths, two gunsmiths, two joiners, two leatherworkers, an apothecary, a doctor, a blockmaker, a brazier, a gardener, a saddler, a sailmaker, a watchmaker, a wheelwright, a maker of silk thread. They were often teachers, of the arts, sciences, of polished behaviour. They brought with them, in other words, what one thinks of as especially French virtues of civilisation and elegance. In religion, they were Calvinists, like the Puritans of New England, but they had to a remarkable degree the quality of assimilation. They married into English families and, in the South, often became Anglicans. They provided a civilising leaven in the mass of Anglo-Saxonness in which they found themselves.

Two things must strike one as one contemplates the presence of non-Anglo-Saxon elements in British North America during the first century of its existence. The first is the relative ease with which the English language prevailed, thus setting the pattern for the future, even though today Americans of Anglo-

Saxon origins are a minority of the population. It might have been otherwise; after all, in Canada the French population has remained uncompromisingly French-speaking. It may be that the ease with which English prevailed was helped by the fact that the original English settlers were, irrespective of where they settled on the Atlantic seaboard, relatively homogeneous. Even today, the dialectal differences in British English are much more considerable than they are in American English. Indeed, one can scarcely talk of dialectal differences in American; there are regional differences in pronunciation and speech rhythms, which is not the same thing. In the England of the early seventeenth century dialectal differences were much more extreme than they are today. But the bulk of the early settlers came from the same regions, mostly from London, the south of England, East Anglia and the Midlands, and mostly from the same social classes. In other words, they spoke what was largely a uniform speech which, in the circumstances of the time and place, was a classless speech. From the beginnings, then, a common standard of speech existed as it did not in the home country and even now still does not.

It was certainly not a language non-Anglo-Saxons were unwilling to learn. Yet even though it was the language of what today we should call the Establishment, it was scarcely essential to learn it. The country was sparsely peopled, and communities, often recruited from a dominant national stock, were more or less self-supporting. English prevailed, all the same, and perhaps we can see why from an account of his travels in America in 1748 published by a Swedish botanist, Peter Kalm. He writes, of the Dutch in New York City: "The younger generation scarcely ever spoke anything but English, and there were many who became offended if they were taken for Dutch because they preferred to pass for English. Therefore it also happened that the majority of the young people attended the English church, although their parents remained loyal to the Dutch." The inference is plain. They had succumbed to English influences because the majority culture had more to offer them than their own, even though they were living in a community that was traditionally Dutch.

Which brings us to the second thing that must strike us about the non-Anglo-Saxon settlers in the first century of colonisation. They could not have been so quickly assimilated to Anglo-Saxon ways, and voluntarily assimilated at that, had they not shared a common body of assumptions with the English in North America. If they had been French, Italian and Spanish Roman Catholics it would have been very different. As it was, English and non-English alike were not only of closely related racial stocks, Northern Europeans for the most part, but also in religion overwhelmingly Protestant and refugees from religious persecution at home. They were inner-directed men, to use David Riesman's term; their sanctions for behaviour, their motives for action, they found within themselves. They were men who wished to make their own lives after the fashion it seemed best to them as individuals.

[13]

The first settlers in North America stayed and built their towns very close to where they had landed, and those that followed them did not move far inland. Unlike the French in Canada, who were largely trappers and traders with the Indians for furs, they had come to settle; and they were townsmen primarily. Also, for so long as they had to depend upon England for the bulk of their supplies, the ocean was their lifeline; and they were hemmed into their narrow coastal strip both by the Indians and by the Appalachian Mountains, which run down the eastern side of North America at a distance of never more than a hundred miles from the Atlantic. At first, the mountain barrier was hardly important; while there was plenty of land to be occupied between it and the sea there was little point in pressing on into the interior. The Indians were another matter, for they rightly saw in the Anglo-Saxon settlements, which were plainly to be permanent, a much greater threat to them than the deeper incursions into America of the French who came singly, as traders or trappers, and with no intention of staying; or, if they did stay, intermarried with the Indians and became almost Indians themselves.

But there came a time when the pressure of population upon

the eastern seaboard was so great that, if newcomers wanted land, they must go beyond the mountains to find it. The first people to do so in large numbers were the Scotch-Irish. But first the word itself calls for some explanation. The Scotch-Irish were not Irish. They were Lowland Scots who had settled in Ulster in the seventeenth century when the lands of the chieftains of Northern Ireland were confiscated by the British crown. They went to Ulster in three waves: after 1608, on the foundation of what is called the "Great Plantation", after the Great Rebellion of 1641, and after the defeat of James II at the Battle of the Boyne in 1690. It is said that between 1690 and 1750 50,000 Scottish families migrated to Ulster. Ulster became predominantly Scottish, and the Scotch-Irish, as they were called, retained their Scottish characteristics and their religion. They were Protestants and generally Presbyterians and they did not mingle, much less intermarry, with the native Roman Catholic Irish populations. They were in Ireland very much as conquerers.

Why did they leave Ireland? Simply because of the politics of the English government; one says English government advisedly, because at this time, though they shared a common monarch, England and Scotland were separate countries. It was the English, not the Scots, who controlled Ireland, and in 1699 the English Parliament, in order to protect the English woollen trade, passed the Woollen Act, which made it illegal for the weavers of Ulster, who were Scotch-Irish, to export their cloth abroad. The act meant economic ruin for the Ulster weavers. It was followed by the passing five years later of another act of the English Parliament, the Test Act for Ireland, which made the right to vote or to hold public office conditional on membership of the Church of England.

These two Acts, one of which robbed them of their livelihood and the other of which meant their disenfranchisement if they remained Presbyterians, drove more than 200,000 Scotch-Irish to migrate to America in the space of seventy-five years. They poured in by way of Philadelphia, though Charleston, South Carolina, was also an important port of entry for them. They rarely settled in New England; it was too English for them, and they had no reason to love the English. One must remember that, quite apart from what they had suffered at the hands of the English, this was still a time when Scotsmen saw the English as the hereditary enemy. Indeed, they brought with them a hostility towards the English that certainly played its part in the quarrels that led to Independence. Generally, they made for the free land beyond the mountains, land offered free to settlers in order to prevent it from falling into Indian or French possession. Where land was not free but vacant all the same, they often seized it as squatters, saying "it was against the laws of God and nature that so much land should be idle while so many Christians wanted it to work on and to raise their bread". Together with Germans from the Palatine, the "Pennsylvania Dutch", who composed the other great wave of immigration at this time, they pressed up the Shenandoah River into North and South Carolina and penetrated by Indian trails into the country beyond the mountains.

The Scotch-Irish brought into colonial life qualities that powerfully accelerated the processes that transformed colonial life into something that can be called American life. Followers of John Knox, Calvinists like the Puritans of New England, to whom they yielded nothing in the way of religious bigotry and fanaticism, much of their character is summed up in the prayer attributed to them: "Lord, grant that I may always be right, for Thou knowest I am hard to turn." They were more strongly egalitarian in feeling than the New England Puritans. Wherever they went, from Pennsylvania southwards, they found themselves fighting the vested interests the older settlers had already established, demanding, as against the control of a minority that generally prevailed, equality of representation. At the same time, they brought with them their Scottish passion for education, so much so that in the middle years of the eighteenth century they provided Virginia and Maryland with most of their teachers. In addition to this faith in education firmly based on a knowledge of Latin and Greek, they brought with them, too, a passion for whisky, which, in the absence of barley, they distilled from rye and corn (*Anglice*, maize). Unable to make what we know as Scotch, the Scotch-Irish invented bourbon, named after its alleged place of origin, Bourbon County, Kentucky.

They were not men of special skills, apart from weaving, but they could turn their hands to anything; and this adaptability, combined with their restlessness, aggressiveness and self-confidence, made them ideal frontiersmen. It was the Germans who invented the frontiersman's long rifle, but it was the Scotch-Irish who used it, and they did so against the Indians without hesitation, for to them Indians were heathens whom it was the duty of good Christians to strike down.

[14]

Both as fact and idea, the frontier, which came into existence in its specific American sense in the early years of the eighteenth century, can hardly be made too much of as a factor in the development of America. Indeed, according to Professor F. J. Turner, it was the frontier that made the American. The early history of the United States, according to Professor Turner in his key-book, *The Frontier in American History*, "is the sturdy European germs developing in an American environment". He goes on:

> The frontier is the line of the most rapid and effective Americanisation. The wilderness masters the colonist. It finds him a European in dress, industries, tools, modes of travel and thought. It takes him from the railroad car and puts him in the birch canoe. It strips off the garments of civilisation and arrays him in the hunting shirt and moccasin. It puts him in the log cabin of the Cherokee and Iroquois and runs an Indian palisade around him. Before long he has gone planting Indian corn and ploughing with a sharp stick; he shouts the war cry and takes the scalp in orthodox Indian fashion. In short, at the frontier the environment is at first too strong for the man. He must accept the conditions which it furnishes or perish, and so he fits himself into the Indian clearings and follows the Indian trails. Little by little he transforms the wilderness, but the outcome is not the old Europe.... The fact is, that here is a new product that is American. At first, the frontier was the Atlantic coast. It was the frontier of Europe in a very real sense. Moving westward, the frontier became more and more American.... Thus the advance of the frontier has meant a steady movement away from the influence of Europe, a steady growth of independence on American lines.

It was the frontier, in the sense of a continually receding line, which was the meeting point of "savagery and civilisation", that, according to Professor Turner, made the American. "To the frontier," he says, "the American intellect owes its striking characteristics. That coarseness and strength combined with acuteness and inquisitiveness; that masterful grasp of material things, lacking in the artistic but powerful to effect great ends; that restless, nervous energy; that dominant individualism, working for good and for evil, and withal that buoyancy and exuberance which comes from freedom—these are traits of the frontier, or traits called out elsewhere because of the existence of the frontier."

It was in the frontier states, too, as they entered the Union during the first twenty-five years of its existence, that universal suffrage was pioneered; and it was the influence of these states that made democracy effective in the original thirteen colonies of the eastern seaboard. One can in fact date its triumph precisely: the year 1829, when Andrew Jackson was elected seventh President of the United States. It represented, as Turner says, the triumph of the frontier. The first six presidents—Washington, John Adams, Thomas Jefferson, James Madison, James Monroe, John Quincy Adams—were from Virginia or Massachusetts, representatives of the earliest British America and its values. They were gentlemen by birth, indeed patricians. It would be absurd to suggest that they were in any way less American than Jackson, but they were a different kind of American. Jackson was from Tennessee, which had been admitted into the Union in 1796, was an Indian fighter, a man from the backwoods and their spokesman.

Again, the triumph of the frontier, or the backwoods, may be seen symbolically in the behaviour of the crowds at President Jackson's inauguration. They poured into the White House despite the buckets of punch that were placed on the lawns outside in the hope of distracting them. They stood on the satin chairs and smashed glass and china in their struggle to get to the food and drink. Jackson himself, pressed against a wall by the crowd, narrowly escaped suffocation. Someone who was there said: "It was the people's day, the people's President, and the people would rule."

Of the twenty-nine presidents since Jackson less than half have come from the original thirteen states of the Union, and almost half have come from the Middle Western states that were the receding frontier of the first fifty years of the nineteenth century. In a way, the greatest of all the presidents, Lincoln, sums up in himself the westward movement of those years. Born in 1809 in a log cabin in Kentucky, he drifted with his parents, who were "illiterate and shiftless", first to the woods of Indiana and then to Illinois, so that by the time he was twenty-one he had lived in three frontier states.

The frontier not only shaped itself, it also continued to shape anew the long-settled lands behind it. But one can distinguish stages in the development of the frontier. In his essay, "The Significance of the Frontier", Turner quotes an extremely illuminating passage from John Mason Peck's *New Guide to the West*, published in Boston in 1837. Peck was a Baptist minister of New York who founded missions and schools in Illinois, Indiana and Missouri; he had, in other words, seen the frontier and its settlement for himself. He writes, as Turner quotes him:

Generally, in all the western settlements, three classes, like the waves of the ocean, have rolled one after the other. First comes the pioneer, who depends for the sustenance of his family chiefly upon the natural growth of vegetation, called the "range", and the proceeds of hunting. His implements of agriculture are rude, chiefly of his own make, and his efforts directed mainly to a crop of corn and a "truck patch". The last is a rude garden for growing cabbage, beans, corn for roasting ears, cucumbers and potatoes. A log cabin, and, occasionally, a stable and corn-crib, and a field of a dozen acres, the timber girdled or "deadened", and fenced, are enough for his occupancy. It is quite immaterial whether he ever becomes the owner of the soil. He is the occupant for the time being, pays no rent, and feels as independent as the "lord of the manor." With a horse, cow, and one or two breeders of swine, he strikes into the woods with his family, and becomes the founder of a new county, or perhaps state. He builds his cabin, gathers around him a few other families of similar tastes and habits, and occupies till the range is somewhat subdued, and hunting a little precarious, or, which is more frequently the case, till the neighbours crowd around, roads, bridges, and fields annoy him, and he lacks elbow room. The pre-emption law enables him to dispose of his cabin and cornfield to the next class of emigrants; and, to employ his own figures, he "breaks for the high timber", "clears out for the New Purchase", or migrates to Arkansas or Texas, to work the same process over.

The next class of emigrants purchase the lands, add field to field, clear out the roads, throw rough bridges across the streams, put up hewn log houses with glass windows and brick or stone chimneys, occasionally plant orchards, build mills, school-houses, courthouses, etc., and exhibit the picture and forms of plain, frugal, civilised life.

Another wave rolls on. The men of capital and enterprise come. The settler is ready to sell out and take the advantage of the rise in property, push further into the interior and become, himself, a man of capital and enterprise in turn. The small village rises to a spacious town or city; substantial edifices of brick, extensive fields, orchards, gardens, colleges, and churches are seen. Broadcloths, silks, leghorns, crapes, and all the refinements, luxuries, elegancies, frivolities, and fashions are in vogue. Thus wave after wave is rolling westward; the real Eldorado is still farther on.

A portion of the first two classes remain stationary amidst the general movement, improve their habits and condition, and rise in the scale of society.

The writer has travelled much amongst the first class, the real pioneers. He has lived many years in connection with the second grade; and now the third wave is sweeping over large districts of Indiana, Illinois and Missouri. Migration has become almost a habit in the West. Hundreds of men can be found, not over fifty years of age, who have settled for the fourth, fifth, or sixth time on a new spot. To sell out and remove only a few hundred miles makes up a portion of the variety of backwoods life and manners.

Lincoln's father was a man of this kind; and it must be plain that the frontier, and the freedom it offered, attracted not only many of the best men but also many of the worst, fugitives from justice and those unable to cope with the responsibilities of life in society, criminals and social misfits. For in one sense the lure of the frontier represented the flight from civilisation and the restraints civilisation imposes on men.

If, as Turner suggested, it is to the frontier that the American intellect owes it most striking characteristics, it is to the frontier, too, that the American character owes other qualities, both good and bad. Its most important effects, according to Turner, were the promotion of democracy and individualism. On the frontier, community, as Boorstin puts it, existed before government. Men got together and made common cause to provide themselves and their families with the essentials of social life, schools, roads, water supply, drainage, etc. There was no existing authority they could turn to for those things. If they wanted them, they had to provide them for themselves. Government came into being as a result.

But individualism has two sides. As Turner says:

> Complex society is precipitated by the wilderness into a kind of
> organisation based on the family. The tendency is anti-social.
> It produces antipathy to control, and particularly to any direct
> control. The tax-gatherer is viewed as a representative of
> oppression.

Since the frontier was beyond the law it bred lawlessness and
violence. What justice it had was essentially rough justice, im-
promptu and summary, as one sees it reflected in such a story as
Bret Harte's "The Outcasts of Poker Flat". Its law was lynch
law, which is capital punishment carried out by self-appointed
groups of private persons, the term being derived from the
name of Charles Lynch, a Virginia planter and Revolutionary
officer who suppressed a Loyalist conspiracy by taking, as we
say, the law into his own hands. There is a superb dramatisation
of lynch law at work on the frontier in Walter Van Tilburg
Clark's fine novel of Nevada in the eighteen-eighties, *The Ox-Bow
Incident*.

And though the frontier as a geographical entity has long been
closed—the usually accepted date for its disappearance is 1880—
it remains psychologically a conditioning factor of the greatest
importance in the minds of Americans wherever they live. This
can be seen in any number of ways, some of which may appear
to contradict one another. There is the famous and very real
tradition of American hospitality, the open-handed welcome for
the stranger in their midst, which overwhelms most visiting
Europeans. There is also the disregard for law, which manifests
itself in the great cities in the violence that, it sometimes seems
to Europeans, Americans tend to take for granted as a necessary
evil of life, whether it takes the form of quarrels between car-
drivers involved in accidents or the trigger-happiness of hoodlums
and the tendency of policemen to shoot first and ask questions
afterwards.

The influence of the frontier is apparent too in the nomadism
of Americans, their mobility, their willingness still to "break for
the high timber" at a moment's notice. There was never time
for local loyalties to crystallise. This has its all-too-visible
consequences in American life. It accounts, for example, for
what impresses the European visitor again as the apparently
temporary nature of the centres of towns now quite old, which
often have an air of shabbiness and dereliction, as though they

had been run up in a hurry as purely provisional quarters meant
to be abandoned almost as soon as built.

Another aspect of this is the squalor that often surrounds
American towns, the acres upon acres of abandoned cars and
junk-yard litter. Again, one has the sense of habitation seen as
necessarily temporary: why clean up the mess when you are not
staying more than a few months or years and there's all the open
world lying ahead and waiting to be seized? In these days, this
civic dinginess of so many American towns, this expression of
social irresponsibility which is the consequence of no one's being
responsible, exists in the sharpest possible contrast with the
obvious community spirit, the care for formal order, the pride
in home, gardens and possessions, that characterise the suburbs
that so frequently comprise the outer circle round the central
municipal squalor.

The face of the United States still has an air of restless im-
provisation, almost as though impermanence was a necessary
part of its being. This is true even of great cities like New York
and Chicago, which seem always to be in process of being torn
down and rebuilt. Robert Lowell catches this aspect of the
American scene admirably in his fine poem, "For the Union
Dead", the setting of which is Boston:

> The old South Boston Aquarium stands
> in a Sahara of snow. Its broken windows are boarded.
> The bronze weathervane cod has lost half its scales.
> The airy tanks are dry . . . .
>
> One morning last March,
> I pressed against the new barbed and galvanised
> fence on the Boston Common. Behind their cage,
> yellow dinosaur steamshovels were grunting
> as they cropped up tons of mush and grass
> to gouge their underground garage.
>
> Parking spaces luxuriate like civic
> sandpiles in the heart of Boston.
> A girdle of orange, Puritan-pumpkin coloured girders
> braces the tingling Statehouse,
> shaking over the excavations, as it faces Colonel Shaw
> and his bell-cheeked Negro infantry
> On St Gaudens' shaking Civil War relief,
> propped by a plank splint against the garage's earthquake . . .

"For the Union Dead" is a nostalgic poem, a poem of regret for contemporary America's impiety towards its past. Yet this obsessive urge to tear down and rebuild has its attractiveness as compared with what sometimes seems the equally obsessive European—or English—urge to preserve relics of the past at all costs simply because they are of the past. It points to a dissatisfaction with what has been and is and a confidence in the future; it stresses becoming rather than being; and there is obviously a sense in which the future may be said to be the frontier in time just as the furthest forward line of settlement was the frontier in space.

The frontier, the movement westward, remains the great image of the American sense of possibility. As such, it is one of the main components of the American dream, one might say of America as dream. It is summed up in a peculiarly American book, a seminal book, Mark Twain's *The Adventures of Huckleberry Finn*, especially in its last sentences: "I reckon I got to light out for the territory ahead of the rest, because Aunt Sally she's going to adopt me and sivilize me, and I can't stand it. I been there before." The dream of the frontier, then, from one point of view, is the dream of the escape from Aunt Sally, from respectability, the constraints of civilisation and society, indeed from civilisation and society itself into the life of uninhibited freedom. Twain was not the first to state it in American fiction: it is embodied in the figure of Natty Bumppo, 'Deerslayer', 'Pathfinder', 'Leather-Stocking', in Fenimore Cooper's sequence, *The Pioneers, The Last of the Mohicans, The Prairie, The Pathfinder* and *The Deerslayer*. Published between 1826 and 1841, they reflect among other things, through the idyllic, chivalrous character of Bumppo, their patriotic author's disenchantment with what seemed to him the materialism and narrowness of American society.

The dream of the frontier as expressed by Twain and Cooper, is no doubt a romantic dream, even an adolescent or neurotic dream. For many years it has been contradicted by the facts of the real situation. The Okies of John Steinbeck's novel, *The Grapes of Wrath*, when dispossessed of their farms in Oklahoma by soil-erosion or by the banks that own the land, pile their belongings into their battered, all but broken-down cars and drive the thousand miles across the desert to the promised land of California, flowing with milk and honey. But California is already owned and occupied; there is no welcome for them there. There is in fact no place for them to go.

The Grapes of Wrath, written out of Steinbeck's passionate indignation against the miseries caused by the economic depression of the Thirties, was published in 1939. Twelve years later, another equally famous novel was published, on the face of it very different from Steinbeck's: J. D. Salinger's *The Catcher in the Rye*. But it too is concerned with flight. *The Grapes of Wrath* describes flight motivated by economic misery towards more prosperous lands. *The Catcher in the Rye* describes a more hopeless flight, the flight from what seems to the boy-hero the crippling evasions and hypocrisies, the absence of generosity, of adult American life. Like the Okies, but unlike Huck, who is in many respects his exemplar, he finds nowhere to fly to, no place to go. There is no escape for young Holden Caulfield except the psychoanalyst's couch, after which, one must assume, follows conformity with the society rebelled against.

These two novels in their different ways are seemingly criticisms of the American dream in that they show its inadequacy in the face of the brute facts of American life. It could also be said that the dreamers themselves are inadequate: Steinbeck's Okies are illiterates, some of them indeed almost morons, and Salinger's Holden is a boy in early adolescence; neither he nor the Okies are in a position to know the reality of their situations. Yet there can be no question at all where the authors' sympathies lie: they are with the dream, against the brute facts of reality, and their criticism works both ways. And this criticism of the nature of American life, made as it were from the standpoint of the dream itself is, as we shall see, a constant element in American literature.

The movement westward of the Okies of *The Grapes of Wrath* is towards a frontier that no longer exists. Yet the movement westward itself duplicates one made by the ancestors of all Americans, whether of old families or of recent origin. All, whether they came in hope or were driven by persecution or by the threat of starvation at home, crossed a frontier, the frontier of the Atlantic. They made a leap into a country where it seemed to them a better life was possible. The leap is what differentiates them from the men who remained at home, is what makes them American. And even though the frontier is no more, the possibilities it represents are still there as powerful elements in the American mind.

[15]

The frontier was settled and pushed back by successive waves of migration throughout the eighteenth and nineteenth centuries. Not of course that all the immigrants poured into the open spaces at the frontier or, for that matter, that the only settlers at the frontier were immigrants. Far from it. During the nineteenth century the development of the frontier went on at the same time as the development of industrialism in the states to the east. Indeed, industrialism, first in the form of the Erie Canal from Albany to Buffalo, which was opened in 1825 and linked the eastern seaboard and New York with what was then the west, and then in the shape of railroads, was itself a major factor in the opening up of the frontier; and rapidly expanding industries called for labour no less than the frontier. Whole national groups of immigrants were drawn into them. Roman Catholic Irish, for instance, who flocked into the United States after the great famine of the eighteen-forties by the hundred thousand until the Irish population in America exceeded that of Ireland herself, stayed mainly on the east coast, in Boston and New York. They came as labourers: in 1961 they gave the United States its first Roman Catholic president in the person of John F. Kennedy. The Poles and Hungarians went largely to the coal and steel towns of New York, Pennsylvania and Ohio. The Jews fleeing the pogroms of imperial Russia in the last years of the nineteenth century and up to 1914 also remained largely on the Atlantic coast and made New York the largest Jewish city in the world.

At the same time, during the second half of the nineteenth century, the states of what is now the Middle West, Ohio, Michigan, Indiana, Illinois, Minnesota, Iowa, Wisconsin, Kansas, the Dakotas and Nebraska, were settled by immigrants from Germany, Bohemia, Sweden and Norway, who had come to farm and therefore to stay, so much so that whole towns were given over to distinct national stocks; Milwaukee, Wisconsin, was and remains a largely German city, as, on a smaller scale, Cedar Rapids, Iowa, is Czech.

Yet to state it thus is to put the facts of European immigration in the nineteenth century and the opening up of America all too simply. Just as the waves of immigration came from many countries, so they came from more than one class within those countries. For example, after the suppression of the German Revolution in 1848 there was a wholesale influx into America of refugees, middle-class, liberal in outlook, educated, scholarly. They made the towns they settled in centres of German culture, music and philosophy—during the second half of the nineteenth century St Louis, Missouri, was a conspicuous instance—and their liberalism reinforced native liberal sentiments. It is from Germans of this kind that General Eisenhower is descended.

A somewhat similar immigration, and perhaps of even great importance, was that in the late nineteen-thirties and early war years of the refugees, mainly Jewish and often of great intellectual attainments, from Nazi oppression. Of these refugees Einstein's is the greatest name, but Einstein was merely the most famous of thousands of men of distinction who chose at that time to become American. One could pick out, from the world of music alone, Bloch, Schoenberg and Stravinsky.

The effect of this last great wave of immigration on the science and culture of the United States has been incalculable. Yet it is doubtful whether it exceeds the contribution made by the Jews whose parents came to America a generation earlier as refugees from Tzarist Russia. They came as poor men from the ghettoes, quite outside any Anglo-Saxon or western European tradition. Many remained poor; but what they contributed to America may be seen in the names of their children and grandchildren, Saul Bellow, Bernard Malamud, Norman Mailer, Lionel and Diana Trilling, Henry Roth, who are among writers of Jewish origin who have transformed American writing during the last two decades. These two waves of Jewish immigration have made American science and the arts more international; they have not made them less American.

[16]

Nevertheless, when one looks at the development of the United States, including the forward march of the frontier, it is still to the colonists of the first century and their descendants that one comes back. Large numbers of them, of course, took their place among those who opened up the frontier. "After the War of 1812," Turner writes, "New England, its supremacy in the carrying trade of the world having vanished, became a hive from which swarms of settlers went out to western New York and the remoter regions." But the significance of the part played by the east, and particularly New England, in the development of the American interior goes far beyond this.

From the earliest days of westward expansion there was tension between the east and the new states and territories of the west, wherever the west might be located at any particular time. We have seen how it was the example of the states that entered the Union in the generation after the War of Independence, Ohio, Kentucky, Indiana, Illinois, which forced political democracy upon the old states of the Atlantic seaboard. This tension still remains. Indeed, the New Englander often reacts towards the phenomenon of, for example, contemporary California in much the same way as an Englishman or European will, as one sees from Alison Lurie's entertaining novel, *The Nowhere City*, which describes the bewilderment experienced by a young couple from an academic New England background when they go to the altogether "freer" world of Los Angeles. In the years after independence the East feared the West, feared that the new states might themselves become independent and the new Republic undergo a process of Balkanisation. This did not happen, but after the first forty years or so of national history the centres of political power that arose in the West were to challenge and counter-balance those of the East.

There was another fear. It was expressed in 1835 by the famous

Presbyterian minister, Lyman Beecher, whom Turner quotes as saying in a speech: "A nation is being born 'in a day'. . . . But what will become of the West if her prosperity rushes up to such a majesty of power, while those great institutions linger which are necessary to form the mind and the conscience and the heart of that vast world?" Linger, that is to say, behind in the East. The fear was the loss of the West to the religion of the East, Turner quotes a writer in a religious magazine as saying in 1850, on reports that settlements had been established as far west as Wisconsin, "we cannot forget that with all these dispersions into remote and still remoter corners of the land the supply of the means of grace is becoming relatively less and less".

Today, the fear looks as though it was unreal. After all, the traffic between West and East was always a two-way one. If the West democratised the East, it was from the Eastern states that the new states took the model for their laws and legal systems, which in the first place were largely English. Yet in the first half of the nineteenth century the fear was genuine enough. It was disguised by what can only be called missionary endeavour. Lyman Beecher himself is an example of this. Born in Connecticut, and a graduate of Yale, he became a Presbyterian minister and had pastorates on Long Island, at Litchfield, Connecticut, and in Boston before going to Cincinnati in 1832 to become the first president of Presbyterian theological seminary in Cincinnati, Ohio, which was then the West.

Another and perhaps more telling example for us today, because of his fame as a poet and critic, is to be found in the family history of T. S. Eliot. In many respects Eliot is quintessentially New England; but he was born in St Louis, Missouri, whither his grandfather had gone as a Unitarian minister from Harvard in the days when St Louis was the West. And Eliot's grandfather was not only a minister, he was also the founder of what is now Washington University, St Louis.

Religion and education have always gone together in the New England mind. Indeed, education had been seen as the handmaiden of religion; in the mid-eighteenth century the President of Yale had even defined colleges as "Societies of Ministers for training up persons for the work of the Ministry". It was the important function of New England to provide such colleges in the Middle West in the nineteenth century. Yale, a Congregational foundation, and Princeton, Presbyterian, were especially active in the fathering of Western colleges. There was, for example, the "Yale Band", a group of seven young men from that university who declared their "readiness to go to the state of Illinois for the purpose of establishing a seminary of learning such as shall be best adapted to the exigencies of that country— a part of us to engage as instructors in the seminary—others to occupy—as preachers—important stations in the surrounding country." A similar group was the "Iowa Band", eleven young graduates from Andover, Massachusetts, whose aim was "each to found a church and all a college" in the new state of Iowa.

Even when the impetus to found a college was local the money was often raised in the East, sometimes even in England. For example, Kenyon College, at Gambier, Ohio, one of the most famous of American liberal arts colleges, was founded in 1824 as a seminary for the training of Episcopal clergymen by Bishop Philander Chase, who toured England to raise funds for its foundation. He found his chief source in the Lord Kenyon of the day, after whom the College is named. There is a rhyme about Bishop Chase:

> The King, the Queen, the lords, the earls,
> They gave their crowns, they gave their pearls
> Until Philander had enough
> And hurried homeward with the stuff.
>
> He built the college, built the dam.
> He milked the cow, he smoked the ham,
> He taught the classes, rang the bell,
> And spanked the naughty freshmen well.

Those last lines show how much education in the West depended upon the single-minded effort of individual men, handicapped by lack of money, buildings and adequately trained staffs. They had no choice but to be all-round men. Educational standards could hardly help being low, though not necessarily lower than at some long-established Eastern institutions—in the middle of the nineteenth century at Columbia University, New York, founded as early as 1754, mental and moral philosophy, history, political economy, logic and English literature were all taught by one professor. What mattered was that the colleges existed. Not all of those founded by men like Chase and the "Yale Band" survive. But many do, and some have developed into great universities like the University of Indiana, at Bloomington, and Western Reserve at Cleveland, Ohio. Others have remained small liberal arts colleges of high reputation like Kenyon, Grinnell, Iowa, and Wabash, Indiana. They preceded the state universities—Wisconsin was the first, at the end of the Civil War—and for many years were their pace-makers. Even today they probably hold some advantages over the state universities at the undergraduate level. As for the state universities, they too, according to F. J. Turner, were "for the most part the result of the agitation and proposals of men of New England origin".

They became, Turner goes on to say, "characteristic products of Middle Western society". He was writing in 1918; but they remain, such universities as Illinois, Wisconsin, Kansas, Indiana, Minnesota, the State University of Iowa, in some special sense characteristic of their region, partly because their functions were always rather different from those of elsewhere, whether in the East or in Europe. They had to be not only the training grounds of scholars, lawyers, doctors, but also the forcing houses of the science and culture of their states, forcing houses of the fine arts, music, painting, sculpture, drama and literature, as well as of the applied sciences, especially agricultural science, so vital to the development of new regions. They were and continue to be centres from which civilisation radiates.

The debt of the Middle West—and of the West generally, for what happened in the Middle West was repeated as the frontier was pushed still further west—to the men of New England who came to the new states in the nineteenth century. whether as ministers, teachers or business men, can scarcely be exaggerated. They educated it, they kept it in the main stream of American thought and culture, for they did not lose their links with New England, then the intellectual heart of the United States, the fountainhead of its ideas. Again one goes back to T. S. Eliot, a third-generation Missouran who was sent back east as a boy to be educated at Milton Academy, Massachusetts, and Harvard University. And even today the ties are often close. One finds, for instance, wealthy Iowans of New England stock, descendants of the founding fathers of the state, who still, almost automatically, send their children east to school, to Dartmouth or Harvard or Smith.

New England is no longer the unrivalled intellectual centre of the United States. In the arts, literature and publishing it long ago yielded to New York. Even so, the concentration of great universities and research institutions it contains give it an intellectual influence out of all proportion to its size.

The men of New England, as preachers and teachers, fertilised the Middle West intellectually, so much so that they made it almost a province, for all it was so enormously bigger, of New England. Because of the religious beliefs of the majority of the settlers, the Middle West became and to a considerable extent remains the second great Puritan settlement. The symbol of this New England fertilisation of the Middle West is the New England-type chapel one sees so often on Middle West campuses, the replica of the simple white timber-and-brick village church of Massachusetts and Connecticut. Yet this intellectual fertilisation is merely an aspect of something else. The Middle West and later the further West were the utmost frontier for New Englanders as they were for European immigrants. They attracted some of the best and some of the worst of men from the East. For some it was the Promised Land; for others it fulfilled the same function as the "Colonies" did for Victorian England, as a place into which failures and ne'er-do-wells could conveniently disappear. Dickens's Mr Micawber, a bankrupt in London, could become a magistrate at Botany Bay: the American novelist Harold Frederic, as late as 1896, could send the hero of *The Damnation of Theron Ware*, a failed Methodist minister, to what was then Washington Territory, in the far North West, to redeem himself. "Who knows?" Ware remarks on leaving New York, "I may turn up in Washington a full-blown senator before I'm forty. Stranger things than that have happened, out West!" For he is bound for "a formless sort of place which was Seattle", a place where anything was possible.

[17]

The influence of the states of the eastern seaboard on the hinterland has been decisive not only in cultural spheres: it has also established the traditional ideological pattern of American life and society. Or rather, the influence of New England, together with New York and Pennsylvania, has been decisive, for the South is the great exception to all generalisations about America. But to the world outside America it has always been the North and its values that have represented the United States, and it was by way of the Northern ports that, throughout the nineteenth century, immigrants from Europe flocked into the United States. It was in the North that the differences between Americans and the rest of the world were asserted; and when immigrants came to the United States they came to a nation already conscious of its differences from the rest of the world, differences, in the form of principles and customs, that they had to accept, that were in fact inescapable since, even when they went west into the hinterland, men of the Northern states had gone there before them.

It would scarcely be an exaggeration to say that the immigrant, regardless of national origin or religion, became a Yankee. The Yankee was the type to which all the pressures of American life impelled him to approximate. "Yankee" is a word the rest of the world applies indiscriminately to all Americans, however inaccurate historically this may be. The derivation of the word is uncertain, but it was first used, specifically for New Englanders, in the eighteenth century. During the Revolutionary War it was applied derisively by the British troops to the "rebel" Americans and adopted by them as a term of defiance. During the War between the States it was used by Southerners for soldiers in the Army of the Union generally. It came, in other words, to stand for Northern values, and since its application was so often pejorative the qualities it stood for were rarely flattering. Cleverness, cunning and cold calculation are among the connotations listed in the Oxford Dictionary.

But translated into non-pejorative terms, these are qualities that may equally well be called ingenuity, adaptability, enterprise and versatility. In many ways, the seas that beat upon their rocky coast were more valuable to the New Englanders than the land. Great fishermen and then great smugglers and privateers, they became an essentially mercantile people, their ships trading all over the world. It was New Englanders who opened up the China trade. The port of Salem, for instance, became the world's centre for trade in peppercorns, which in the days before refrigeration were needed everywhere for the preservation of meat. Into Salem, according to Boorstin, New England ships brought almost the entire peppercorn crop of Northwest Sumatra, seven and a half million pounds of it, and from Salem it was re-exported throughout the world. Similarly, the ports of New Bedford and Nantucket came near to monopolising the whaling industry.

New Englanders even succeeded in turning what seemed the disadvantages of their country to profit. New England, it was said, produced nothing but granite and ice. Boorstin has some entertaining pages in which he describes how New Englanders made fortunes precisely out of granite and ice in the early days of the nineteenth century. Ice in particular, if only it could be preserved, was a valuable, almost a precious commodity in the days before refrigeration. New Englanders mastered the art of preserving it, and by the middle of the century Boston was shipping more than one hundred thousand tons of ice a year to the rest of the world, especially to India and the Far East. Ice had become a major American export.

But Yankee versatility, ingenuity and adaptability are seen at their most striking in the development of industrial and manufacturing processes. Again, what seemed national inadequacies and deficiencies were turned into sources of strength. There had always been a shortage of labour, skilled or otherwise, in America, and there was no tradition of craftsmanship such as existed in Europe. From the earliest colonial days, the American had been a jack-of-all-trades. On the face of it, the United States was particularly ill-equipped to meet the challenge of the Industrial Revolution that was already under way in Britain. Yet it was in the United States that what we now think of as the characteristically modern means of production were first developed, and developed years before anything resembling them occurred in Europe.

Here the great representative name is that of Eli Whitney. He was born in 1765 and died in 1825. A graduate of Yale, he had already, in 1793, while tutor to the children of a planter in Georgia, invented the cotton gin that revolutionised the harvesting of cotton and was to bring unprecedented prosperity to the South. It was three years later that he hit upon the manufacturing system that was to change the whole nature of industry. In 1798 the United States was threatened with war by France. The country was virtually unarmed, there was no armaments industry, and the muskets of its soldiers were those that had been used in the Revolutionary War fifteen years earlier.

Whitney offered the Government the resources of his factory and labour force for the manufacture of muskets and signed a contract for the delivery of ten thousand. Now Whitney was not a gunsmith, which in Europe was a highly skilled craft. In one way, his very ignorance of gun-making was an important

factor in his success.   Had he been a gunsmith, he might well
have been blinded by reverence for his craft; as it was, he had no
such inhibitions.   He broke down into its component parts the
French musket he had to reproduce and devised the moulds and
machines with which to make them.   He had invented what he
called the Uniformity System, the system of production of a
complex article by the assembling of standardised, interchangeable
parts that could be made by relatively unskilled labour.

The purpose of the Uniformity System was defined by Whitney
as "to substitute correct and effective operations of machinery
for that skill of the artist which is acquired only by long practice
and experience; a species of skill which is not possessed in this
country to any considerable extent".   He is here placing the
emphasis not on manual skill but on the power of machines to
do the work men had formerly done, the power of machines
designed for special purposes and operable by the relatively unskilled.   He is looking forward to mass production as it was first
applied to the motor car by Henry Ford at Detroit at the end of
the nineteenth century.

In *The Americans: The National Experience*, Boorstin calls the
changes Whitney innovated in methods of production the "Know-
how Revolution", and it seems a fact of some significance, throw-
ing light on the American nature, that the expression "know-
how" was coined as long ago as 1857.   It did not reach Britain
until the second world war.   Know-how is not easy to define,
but it implies a special cast of mind, free-ranging, empirical,
which sees how to apply fundamental knowledge to immediate,
practical ends.   It thinks in terms of techniques and technology,
of ways of doing things and making them work.   An early master
of know-how—and in this as in so many other ways he appears
the representative American—was Benjamin Franklin, who applied
a restless, questing, organising mind to projects ranging from the
establishment of a city police force and the paving, cleaning and
lighting of the streets of Philadelphia to the invention of the
Franklin stove and the lightning conductor.

The great nineteenth-century master of know-how was
Thomas Alva Edison.   By the time of his death at the age of
eighty-four in 1931 he had more than 1,200 patents to his name.
Now Edison was not a scientist and he had, indeed, little formal
education, no more than three months' regular schooling, before
he started work on the railway at the age of twelve.   He made no
contribution to fundamental knowledge; his genius lay in his

ability to harness fundamental knowledge to immediate needs and to perfect existing inventions. For example, Joseph Swan, an Englishman, had already devised the electric lamp with a carbon filament, but the light that resulted was not bright enough for it to be practically useful. Nearly twenty years later, working with Swan, Edison produced a much improved lamp which was the forerunner of the light bulb we know today. Similarly, with Alexander Bell, he turned the telephone from a commercial possibility into a commercial success. Among his other inventions were the gramophone and one whose wide-scale application still seems to lie in the future, the electric automobile.

Master of know-how though he was, Edison was still in this respect a representative American of his time. As Perry Miller has shown in *The Life of the Mind in America*, the American temper in the nineteenth century found its expression not in pure science, the discovery of fundamental knowledge, but in the application of science to utility. Perhaps this was in part dictated by the facts of the geography of the country and of contemporary history. Miller quotes from a speech on the steam locomotive delivered by an orator in 1841:

> Here we shall be taught to behold him, a Titanic colossus of iron and of brass, instinct with elemental life and power, with a glowing furnace for his lungs, and streams of fire and smoke for the breath of his nostrils. With one hand he collects the furs of the arctic circle; with the other he smites the forests of Western Pennsylvania. He plants his right foot at the source of the Missouri—his left on the shores of the Gulf of Mexico; and gathers into his bosom the overflowing abundance of the fairest and richest valley on which the circling sun looks down.

Miller comments: "Here was surely a creature to roam the land of the mythologised Davy Crockett, who released the sun from an ice pack and returned to earth with a piece of daylight in his pocket." If the United States were to endure as a nation, if it were not to lapse into separate states, distances on a scale utterly remote from the experience of European countries had to be overcome. Edison's work on the telephone is significant here. But the great symbol of the American conquest of distance is, the locomotive. Unlike the steamship, the locomotive was not an American but a British invention. For all that, railway systems were extremely rapidly developed in the United States.

The difference between British and American railway construction and engine design, however, were great, and they grew out of differences between the geography and history of the two countries. One fundamental difference was noted by a Scotsman, James Stirling, who visited the United States in 1856–57. Boorstin quotes him as follows:

> There seems a natural, preordained fitness between railway and the prairie; for the prairie is as eminently suited to the formation of railways, as railways are essential to the development of prairies. For hundreds of miles you have only to raise the turf, and lay your sleepers; for hundreds of miles you need neither grading nor bridging; no engineering; hardly any surveying. In one long, unwavering line your iron road passes over the level plain. And that plain, remember, costs nothing; or at most a dollar and a quarter an acre. The artificial hindrances are still fewer than the natural ones. There are no cities to be circumvented, or bridged over, at enormous cost; no gentlemen's seats whose "amenity" is to be preserved. . . . But again: the prairies absolutely make their own railways without cost to anyone. The development of the country by means of a railway is such, that what was yesterday waste land is today a valuable district. There is thus action and reaction: the railway improves the land; the improvement pays for the railway . . . there is nothing in history to compare with this seven-league progress of civilization.

In some essential respects, the functions of the railway differed in the two countries. In Britain, railways were built to bring closer together ports, cities, towns, villages that had been settled for centuries; and the railways themselves largely followed the system of roads and canals that had been developed over the centuries. They were imposed, as it were, on what was already a densely populated and relatively small country. There was nothing comparable in the United States. Beyond the Appalachians, settlements were few and small, the fewer and smaller the further west one went, until, beyond the frontier, they disappeared altogether. The railways, in fact, preceded population. They did not follow known roads; and it was in their vicinity, along their tracks, that towns sprang up. In a real sense, they made the country and dictated the localities of settlements. And the distances the railways had to cover were immense. These, together with the need for speed in building the railways, stimulated what Boorstin has called a technology of haste.

In England and Europe generally, the emphasis in railway construction was on safety, and locomotives were built to last. The English point of view was put by Edward Watkin, a railway engineer who visited the United States at the middle of the century. Boorstin quotes him as saying: "We have deemed the invention of railways a final improvement in the means of locomotion, and we have, therefore, constructed our works to last 'for ever' of bricks and mortar. We have made our rails strong enough for any possible weight of engine; our drainage capacious enough to remove any conceivable flood . . . our bridges firm enough for many times the weight that can ever come upon them." Boorstin's comment is that British railway builders "became prisoners of their rigid expectations", but this is really to imply comparisons between the two countries that at the time scarcely held. By contrast, American railway construction was dictated by the need to build as quickly as possible. To this, almost everything else was sacrificed—the safety and comfort of passengers, permanence of track, durability of engines. One could almost say that American railway building was characterised by a calculated flimsiness of construction. The hazards of American railway travel and its sheer discomfort horrified English travellers from Fanny Kemble to Dickens. Accidents were so common as to be taken almost for granted.

The important thing is, American railroads worked. They opened up the continent. And there is something else, related to the very flimsiness and impermanence that marked their construction. They were not meant to last, because something new and better would take their place. The present, as it were, was provisional; the future would be bigger, and different. As Boorstin puts it, "belief in obsolescence became an article of American faith". We have become used to the expression "built-in obsolescence", to the notion that a motor car, for example, will be so built as to last only a limited number of years; and the practice, indeed, is now an essential part of the American economic system and, in the end, perhaps of all systems of mass production and mass consumption. But historically, in the United States, built-in obsolescence was a fact long before a theory was invented to justify it or an economic structure built upon it. It was dictated by the need for speed in construction, by the shortage of workers skilled in traditional crafts, and by the application of science to satisfy the demands of an increasingly high standard of living.

This characteristic American industrial development is closely allied to, is part of, other aspects of American life that seem just as characteristic of it. It is allied to the American philosophical system called Pragmatism. The word was first used in its present philosophical sense by William James in 1898 and its meaning developed at length in his lectures delivered at the Lowell Institute, Boston, and at Columbia University in 1906–7, under the title *Pragmatism: A New Name for Some Old Ways of Thinking.* "A pragmatist," James said, "turns away from abstraction and insufficiency, from verbal solutions, from bad *a priori* reasons, from fixed principles, closed systems, and pretended absolutes and origins. He turns towards concreteness and adequacy, towards facts, towards action and towards power." Basic to pragmatism is the belief that the truth of a proposition is to be judged by its results, that is, by experience; and the emphasis throughout is on the empirical. The decisive question in any context is Will it work? When the famous radical journalist, Lincoln Steffens, visited the Soviet Union in the early nineteen-twenties and returned to say, "I have seen the future, and it works," he was, whether he knew it or not, speaking like a good pragmatist, though the remark itself could have been equally justly applied to the United States at almost any moment of its history.

The way of thinking that receives philosophical definition in William James seems inherently of the American grain; it is characterised by an impatience with the accepted or traditional, a delight in solving technical problems, a belief that the only criterion of success is functional, and a general sense that what exists in the present is provisional because it is of the present and the future will be better. The stress is on results. And with this goes what seems to be another consistent element in American life and experience, an attitude to work and to business, which perhaps can be brought together under the single heading of making money, that is quite different still from what exists in Britain.

This can be seen in any number of ways. Perhaps as good a first instance as any can be taken from the history of industrialism in Britain during the nineteenth century. In many respects, the prevailing tone of middle-class feeling in Victorian England was similar to that in the United States then and now. It was an expression of the Puritan tradition both countries shared. In nineteenth-century England there was much talk about the dignity of labour; Carlyle preached the gospel of work—and when we read Emerson after Carlyle we realise how much indebted the Yankee was to the Scot. At the popular level, the chief spokesman of the gospel of work was Samuel Smiles, whose *Self-Help* was published in 1859. The title is the clue to the contents: the book preaches the virtue of individual endeavour, personal application to what lies to hand, and points out the material success that will follow. *Self-Help* was followed by *Character, Thrift* and *Duty*, titles that are again self-explanatory, and, more important, by *The Lives of the Engineers* and *Industrial Biography*, which trace the success-stories of engineers and industrialists from humble origins, success-stories brought about by study, application, ambition and an eye that saw where technical development was needed and how it could be achieved. The archetype of the Smilesian hero was George Stephenson, the railway engineer and the subject of Smiles's first book. The virtues of industry, diligence and self-reliance that Smiles celebrated were very similar to those preached by Benjamin Franklin a century earlier, but if one is looking for a contemporary American counterpart to Smiles it is to Horatio Alger one must go. From 1866 onwards, he wrote nearly 130 popular books for boys, showing that the struggle against poverty and temptation leads to wealth and fame, and biographies of self-made statesmen, of which the best known is probably *From Log Cabin to White House*, the life of President James A. Garfield.

Great industrial organisations were built up and great fortunes made in Britain during the second half of the eighteenth century and throughout the nineteenth by self-made men of humble origins. It was in Britain, after all, that the Industrial Revolution began. But if one compares what happened to the children of these self-made men with what happened to those of their American equivalents a significant difference is immediately apparent. In Britain there was an exceedingly powerful influence at work on them that simply did not exist in America. This was the pull of aristocracy and, more particularly, of aristocratic values, which were quite other than and opposed to commercial and industrial values.

One sign of this was the development of the public school system, which, as we now know it, was almost wholly nineteenth century in origin. There had, of course, for centuries been a handful of great schools, pre-eminent among them Eton, Winchester, and, in London, Westminster and St Paul's. But the notion of the public schools as the preserve of a special privileged class, in other words, as the reverse of public, was something new. It dates from 1828, when Thomas Arnold was appointed headmaster of Rugby School. Arnold broadened the curriculum, adding modern history, mathematics and modern languages to the traditional subjects of Greek and Latin. But what was much more important was his determination that his boys should be trained as Christian gentlemen, leaders of men, whose lives should be devoted in one form or another to public service. Rugby became the model for scores of other schools, some entirely new foundations, others old grammar schools that had become almost moribund in the eighteenth century and now, under the influence of evangelical religion, turned themselves into boarding schools staffed by enthusiastic Arnoldians. They had a new class to educate, the sons of the new-rich industrialists, whom they were to make into gentlemen. They succeeded admirably, with the result that newly inherited wealth tended to take over the values associated with aristocracy. It was men from the public schools who administered India and the developing empire. They went into the rapidly expanding civil service. They went into Parliament; the greatest of all nineteenth-century prime ministers, Mr Gladstone, was the son of a Liverpool merchant. His name is synonymous with nineteenth-century Liberalism, but he began his career in politics as "the rising hope of those stern and unbending Tories", identifying himself with the old landed gentry.

In other words, in nineteenth-century England the acquisition of wealth through business or industry was not regarded as an end in itself but as a means to an end. With the acquisition of wealth, the aristocratic principle of *noblesse oblige* tended to assert itself. Successful industrialists like Joseph Chamberlain, a Birmingham screw-manufacturer, went into politics, and indeed his son, Sir Austen, became, with his eyeglass and orchid, almost the walking embodiment of the English aristocrat as he exists in the popular imagination.

Nothing like this happened in the United States, at least not for many years. The great foundations based on enormous personal fortunes such as the Guggenheim and the Ford belong to this century. The tycoons of the nineteenth century appear by comparison with their British equivalents as robber barons driven by lust for money and the power money bestows. There was no aristocratic tradition to condition them, and the genteel tradition of cultivated New England was impotent to influence them. From one point of view, the consequences were bad. Politics, government, became the adjunct of financial power, dirty, corrupt, often criminal, so that gentlemen would take no part in them. The attitude of the American gentleman, one might say the American aristocrat, towards government is plainly shown in Henry Adams's novel, *Democracy*, published in 1880. It was not until the present century, with the election to the Presidency first of Theodore Roosevelt and then of Woodrow Wilson, a professor of history and one-time President of Princeton University, that the American gentleman, meaning by that a man who combines wealth with a disinterested sense of the public good, returned to politics. Even so, the business man, and perhaps especially the man who goes out to get the business, the "drummer", the salesman, the commercial traveller, remains much more representative of American values than his English counterpart does of British. It was, after all, an American president, Calvin Coolidge, who said that the business of America is business. A British prime minister might conceivably think much the same of the British Government but he would hardly dare say it. And it was President Eisenhower's Secretary of Defence, Charles Wilson, a business man in the government service, who said, "What is good for General Motors is good for the United States."

Mr Wilson's remark aroused, it is true, derision in many quarters of the United States, and he never lived it down. But it was merely the extreme statement of the fact that, beyond any other in the world, American civilisation is a commercial civilisation; which is why commercial values, especially when elevated into the dogma of free enterprise, which is as much philosophical as economic, are accorded veneration of a kind usually reserved for those things that are considered of divine origin. And in the American context this is not so far wrong, since these values are not only inculcated by the facts of early American existence but also sanctioned by all the authority of Puritan religion.

One result of this is evident in American attitudes towards work, which are significantly unlike English attitudes. An example of this is the function of the British trade unions as contrasted with the American. In Britain trade unions have traditionally existed to protect and extend workers' rights and privileges. Employers have been thought of as the enemy. The British Labour Party, whose aim, in theory at any rate, is to change the economic system and replace private ownership of industry by public ownership, was brought into existence largely by the trade unions in order to fight and defeat the owning, i.e., the ruling class in the political sphere. Now the history of industrial disputes, of strikes and lockouts, in the United States has been marked by considerably more violence than has that of Britain; but the American trade unions have never founded their own political party or become socialist. Indeed, over the years they have become increasingly committed to the American industrial system, and their leaders have aimed increasingly not only at protecting and extending their members' rights but also at obtaining greater production.

This difference in attitudes towards work may be shown in another way. Almost any American professional man—clergyman, university professor, lawyer, doctor—will have had more first-hand experience of work, which here means manual labour, than his English counterpart, who may very well have had none at all, though this will probably be much more rare in the future. The American during his student days will almost certainly have worked with his hands, as waiter, petrol pump attendant, truck driver, welder. He may have worked his way through college; but whether or not manual labour has been forced upon him by necessity, it may be taken for granted that at some time or other he has performed it, if only in order to pay for a trip abroad or to buy himself a car.

From his schooldays onwards, the American expects to earn money, and all the traditions of the society he is born into encourage him to do so. He is expected to be self-reliant and to act on his own initiative, and this gives him a sense of initiative and independent action, a sense of his being in control of his environment and his destinies, beyond anything that is common to the young in Britain and in Europe. And this almost universal experience of physical work has other effects. It blurs the distinctions between the classes; it is one of the factors—the relative absence of class differentiations through accent is another —that make for the social homogeneity of America, the general feeling of equality between man and man irrespective of occupation. And if it is a product of American flexibility, of the belief that, if necessary, any man can turn a hand to anything, it also promotes it.

From this American phenomenon of expansion, boost and boom, which was unparalleled in history, the South was cut off; so much so that in retrospect the War between the States, the Civil War, seems the inevitable consequences of irreconcilable differences between it and the rest of America. Within the United States itself the South existed almost as a foreign country, as it still often appears to be today, not only to Europeans but also to many Northerners. What set it apart from the rest of the country was the presence of the Negro slave, the "indelible immigrant", as Boorstin has called him, whose very colour seemed to make his assimilation into American life impossible.

Not that Negro slavery was unique to the South, at any rate in the early years of the settlement of America. There were Negro slaves in New England; there were even Negro slaves in England itself, something like 12,000 of them in 1772. In fact, when the Negro was first introduced into America in the seventeenth century his position in law seems to have been no different from that of the indentured servant or transported convict from Britain. Neither was "free", but freedom was achieved at the end of his term of service; he was free then to go on to become a landowner and the master of other unfree men. Indeed, in the seventeenth century the indenture system was one of the main means by which immigrants were attracted to America; it was not unlike the contract by which an apprentice was bound to a master for so many years. And as the demand for labour in America increased, so the term of indenture became less stringent and the years of service to be worked shorter. At the end of his time, the European indentured man merely became an American increasingly indistinguishable from other Americans.

But the Negro, simply by being a Negro, was in a quite different situation. He was not in America by any voluntary act of his own; and when free it seemed impossible that he could be assimilated, that he could ever become an American more or less indistinguishable from other Americans. It might even be said that, cast as he was in a society utterly and bewilderingly different from the Africa he had been born into, there was no advantage to him in being free so long as he was in America. And since he was owed nothing, had signed no contract with his master, there was no obligation, either, to set him free. So we find Maryland passing a law declaring that all Negroes should "serve" for the term of their lives; and in 1670 Virginia passed a similar law, adding for good measure that conversion to Christianity would not set a slave free. In a very real sense, the institution of Negro slavery in America, like Topsy, the Negro girl slave in *Uncle Tom's Cabin*, "just growed".

Unfortunately for the Negro, it grew outside the law. As Boorstin shows in *The Americans: The National Experience*, the very concept of slavery did not exist in English law; which is why, when Lord Mansfield made his historic judgement in the Court of the King's Bench in 1772, in which he said that "the state of slavery was so odious, that nothing can be suffered to support it but positive law" and that there was no law in England to support it, the several thousand Negro slaves in England found themselves free men—and, interestingly enough, were lost without trace in the population of England within a few generations.

In countries like Spain, where slavery was legal, slaves were protected; they had rights and their masters obligations, which could be legally enforced. In America, the Negro, existing in a society that had no body of laws regulating slavery, became a chattel, a thing, with fewer rights than an animal has today.

In the Northern states, where slaves had never played any significant part in the economy, slavery was abolished between 1777 and 1804. In 1794 it became illegal for American citizens to engage in the slave trade, and in 1808 the importation of African slaves into the United States was prohibited. At this time it might have been possible for slavery to be abolished in the South, though there would still have been the problem of what to do with the slaves; in 1790 there were 200,000 of them in Virginia alone; and the only solution seemed to be to send them back to Africa. It was widely believed in the South that slavery had to continue in order to prevent the dangers of race conflict that would arise from emancipation, a belief reinforced by the fear generated by slave risings, especially that led by Nat Turner in Virginia in 1831, in which fifty-four white people were killed.

It seemed significant that Turner was a free Negro who as a slave had been well treated by his owner and, indeed, taught to read by his owner's son.

In fact, by the time of Turner's rising, or the Southampton Insurrection as it is sometimes called, slavery was once again firmly established in the South. Southern prosperity depended upon it. The South had become the Cotton Kingdom. By the last years of the eighteenth century the South had fallen on lean days; the old crops of tobacco, rice and indigo were no longer as profitable as they had been. Economically, the South was saved when in 1793, Eli Whitney, invented the cotton gin. The world demand for cotton was increasing and would continue to increase at an enormous rate; for years it exceeded the supply. In 1791, out of a world production of 490,000,000 pounds, the United States produced only 138,000 pounds. Ten years later, as a result of Whitney's invention, it was producing 35,000,000 pounds. Within a decade, it was producing ten times as much, most of which went to feed the mills of Lancashire.

The cultivation of cotton became the South's way to riches, and cotton-growing depended on slave labour at a time, ironically, when the slave trade was no longer legal, even though the laws against it were constantly evaded; it has been estimated that as many as two million slaves were smuggled into the country after the trade was prohibited. Slaves became increasingly valuable possessions, beyond the reach of ordinary men. When the Civil War broke out the slave population of the South was owned by less than five per cent of the white population. All the same, it was slavery that made life in the South what it was, gave it its especial quality and differentiated it from life in the rest of America. It was the great isolating factor, and as such it operated in many ways.

To many people in the North, in New England particularly, it was a moral outrage, and not necessarily to Abolitionists alone. It set up a tension between the free states and the slave states that dominated and bedevilled national politics for half a century. The Union was maintained only by a series of compromises, the first of which, the Missouri Compromise of 1820, largely set the pattern for the rest. To maintain equal representation of free and slave states in the Senate it was agreed that Maine, a free state, and Missouri, a slave state, should be admitted to the Union simultaneously. But one result of such compromises was to implicate the North itself in the perpetuation of slavery. The

Fugitive Slave Act of 1850 gave the Government the right to
pursue runaway slaves into free states and return them to the
South.   In effect, it meant that the slave could no longer free
himself by escaping to the North.   One consequence of the Act
was that Harriet Beecher Stowe wrote *Uncle Tom's Cabin*, one of
the most dynamic propaganda works ever written and a much
finer novel than it is often given credit for, a novel, moreover,
that squarely faces up to the North's financial involvement in the
institution of slavery.

Many attempts were made to lessen the tension; always they
aggravated it.   There was, for instance, the Kansas–Nebraska Bill
of 1854, which allowed the citizens of Kansas and Nebraska
Territories to decide for themselves, before state governments
were set up, whether they should be free or slave.   This led
Kansas, immediately to the west of the slave state of Missouri,
to be flooded with "settlers" who had come not to settle but to
vote against slavery, and to be invaded by "border ruffians" from
Missouri who voted for slavery.   One of the Abolitionists who
"settled" in Kansas was John Brown, who murdered five of his
neighbours, Southern sympathisers, in cold blood.   The state of
civil war that prevailed gave the Territory the name of "Bleeding
Kansas".

In the end, as each side became more and more intransigent
in its attitude towards slavery, the tension was such that it could
be resolved only by war.   The Civil War, the War between the
States, the first shot of which was fired by the volunteer forces
of South Carolina on April 12, 1861, was not fought on the issue
of slavery but on the issue of the South's right to secede from
the Union; but it was in defence of slavery and the way of life
based upon it that the South seceded and declared itself the
Confederate States of America.

As for the conditions of Negroes under slavery, it is impossible
to generalise.   In 1853 Thackeray visited a plantation near
Savannah, Georgia, and inspected the slaves' quarters.   He wrote
home: "They're not uncomfortable, they have half a pound of
bacon a day, plenty of flour, nice treacle and a little tobacco—
they're kindly treated that's the truth—no planter but is anxious
you shall see his people at any hour and unknown to him if you
like.   Of course there are bad and savage masters too, but the
general condition is far from unhappy."   Perhaps this was so.
Certainly it seems that the extremely severe laws on the statute-
books, which among other things made it illegal to teach slaves

to read and write, were rarely enforced. Southern apologists for slavery made much of the affection that they maintained often existed between slaves and masters. Boorstin quotes one as saying that the "first" law of slavery "is that of kindness from the master to the slave. . . . Slavery becomes a family relation, next in its attachments to that of parent and child." It seems natural to assume that there were very often strong bonds between white children and the "black mammies" who had largely brought them up.

One observer who found nothing good to say of slavery and saw no extenuating factors in the system was Fanny Kemble, one of the most brilliant members of the famous English family of actors and actresses. She came to America in 1832 after a successful career on the English stage, enjoyed for two years a triumphant reception wherever she appeared—"Fanny Kemble", one historian of the American theatre has written, "was to New York something of a divine manifestation"—and then in 1834 married Pierce Mease Butler, a wealthy Philadelphian whose fortunes were based on the family plantations in Georgia. Well-educated, sensitive, a product of the Romantic movement and a liberal, Fanny went with her husband to stay on his plantations in 1838. Before she went she wrote to her sister: "I am going prejudiced against slavery, for I am an Englishwoman, in whom the absence of such a prejudice would be disgraceful." What she saw she recorded in her remarkable *Journal of a Residence on a Georgian Plantation in 1838-39*. The detail and the tone in which she records it are such as to make one accept the journal as an accurate account of what she saw. Admittedly, her husband was an absentee landlord; his slaves were controlled by managers. In the circumstances, it would probably be too much to expect to find in Fanny Kemble's pages any family attachments between slaves and Butler's white employees. Certainly Fanny Kemble found none; she found instead, not cruelty in any gratuitous or sadistic sense, but a disregard for the ordinary dictates of humanity. The Negroes were work-animals.

Yet the Butler slaves considered themselves well off in comparison with those on some of the neighbouring estates. One of these she visited; and perhaps the passage sums up as well as any other criticism the effect of slavery on the life of the South:

> On driving through my neighbour's grounds, I was disgusted more than I can express with the miserable Negro huts of her people;

they were not fit to shelter cattle—they were not fit to shelter
anything, for they were literally in holes, and, as we used to say of
our stockings at school, too bad to darn.   To be sure, I will say, in
excuse for their old mistress, her own habitation was but a very
few degrees less ruinous and disgusting.   What would one of your
Yankee farmers say to such abodes?   When I think of the white
houses, the green blinds, and the flower plots of the villages of New
England, and look at these dwellings of lazy filth and inert degradation, it does seem amazing to think that physical and moral conditions
so widely opposite should be found among people occupying a
similar place in the social scale in the same country.   The Northern
farmer, however, thinks it no shame to work, the Southern planter
does; and there begins and ends the difference.   Industry, man's
crown of honour elsewhere, is here his badge of utter degradation;
and so comes all by which I am here surrounded—pride, profligacy,
idleness, cruelty, cowardice, ignorance, squalor, dirt, and ineffable
abasement.

But to see the whole range of possible conditions under which
slaves might live, *Uncle Tom's Cabin* is still the book to go to, as it
is also, despite Mrs Stowe's uncompromising opposition to
slavery, probably the best anthology of Southern justifications
for slavery.   One of these was that, though slavery was evil, it
was not more evil than the exploitation of the working classes
that was found in advanced industrial systems such as those of
England and the Northern states.   It is Augustine St Clare, the
Southern slave-owner who sees slavery as a curse laid on his
country and as a tragic doom that must be endured, who tells
his Abolitionist cousin:

> "Alfred . . . says, and I think quite sensibly, that the American
> planter is 'only doing, in another form what the English aristocracy
> and capitalists are doing by the lower classes'; that is, I take it,
> *appropriating* them, body and bone, soul and spirit, to their use and
> convenience."

When his cousin retorts that the "English labourer is not sold,
traded, parted from his family, whipped", he replies:

> "He is as much at the will of his employer as if he were sold to him.
> The slave-owner can whip his refractory slave to death—the capitalist
> can starve him to death.   As to family security, it is hard to say
> which is the worst—to have one's children sold, or to see them
> starve to death at home. . . . I've travelled in England some, and

I've looked over a good many documents as to the state of their lower classes; and I really think there is no denying Alfred, when he says that his slaves are better off than a large class of the population of England."

All one can say is that Fanny Kemble, who was the friend of George Stephenson, the engineer from the working class who designed the *Rocket* locomotive, would not have been persuaded by St Clare's almost Marxist view of slaves and wage-slaves; nor would the factory-hands of the north of England, of the mills of Lancashire, have been pleased by the bracketing of them with Negro slaves. This indeed is shown by the fact that, during the Civil War, it was the politically radical industrial working classes of the north of England that supported the Northern States, even though their livelihoods largely depended on Southern cotton, while it was the conservative aristocracy that supported the Confederacy.

Slavery was also justified on the ground that it was the essential basis of a high civilisation; Alfred St Clare maintained "that there can be no high civilisation without enslavement of the masses, nominal or real". But the claims of the nineteenth-century South to be a high civilisation are pretty dubious. If one gauge of a civilisation is the number of excellent writers it produces, then in this respect the South was obviously far inferior to New England; and the same is true if it is universities that are thought of. Life in the pre-war South has been so romanticised in the fiction of the past thirty years that it is now difficult to penetrate through the magnolia blossoms to the truth. It seems clear, however, that the quality of upper-class life had greatly degenerated since the days of William Byrd, Washington and Jefferson. One reason for the degeneration is suggested by Boorstin. Unlike New England, where from the earliest days the centre of life had been the town, the South had always been rural. The population of Williamsburg, the eighteenth-century capital of Virginia itself, had never exceeded 1,500, and though by the beginning of the nineteenth century there were cities in the South, one of them, Baltimore, the third largest in the States, they were recent in origin and, as it were, superimposed on the South. They were commercial centres; the real life of the region went on outside them, in the country.

But the fact that the South was rural did not mean that its ruling class in the eighteenth century was provincial—anything but. The Southern planter was probably much less so than his corresponding figure in New England. He had his agent, his factor, in London, who sold his crop there on commission and generally acted as his man of business and at times as more than this. He sent the planter the latest books, the latest news of political and intellectual events, bought wine for him and apprised his wife of the latest fashions. He found English schools for the planter's children. He was, in other words, the planter's direct line to the centre of things.

This ended with the Revolutionary War. The place of the factor in London was taken by the factor in Baltimore or Richmond, in one of the new or greatly enlarged Southern ports. Boorstin sums up the change in the words: "While commerce went to town, leadership stayed in the country." The local factor took over more and more of the business that the planter had had to do himself in the days when he was dealing directly with London. Commerce was divorced from leadership, one might almost say from aristocracy. And the factor's power rose with the rise in importance of cotton. He normally took over a planter's whole crop and it was he who decided how and at what price it was to be sold. Economically he became the planter's dictator.

The effect of the change was two-fold. By cutting off the planter from London it forced on him a provincialism, a narrowness, that his ancestor in America had never known; and it also deprived him of the need to be versatile, and versatility had been the Southern gentleman's outstanding characteristic. As important, it made commerce seem no longer the business of a gentleman, just as to the poorer white man work carried with it the stigma of the Negro slaves who did most of it.

It undercut the very foundations on which Southern civilisation in the full sense rested. This is beautifully brought out by Allen Tate in *The Fathers*, the most moving celebration of Southern civilisation in fiction. The action covers the period 1860–61, the months immediately before and after the outbreak of the Civil War. At the centre of the novel is Major Buchan—Buchan of Pleasant Hill. He is in his way a feudal landowner; he refers to his neighbours by the names of their plantations, Carter of Ravensworth, Carey of Vaucluse. His is a house where, in Yeats's words, "all's accustomed, ceremonious". His life is ruled by custom and ceremony; manners have made the man and, one could add, the civilisation he represents. His son, Lacy, who tells the story from a point in time long after that of the events described, says: "Our lives were eternally balanced upon a pedestal below which was an abyss that I could not name. Within that invisible tension my father knew the moves of an intricate game that he expected everybody else to play." Lacy recalls "the only time I had ever seen my father blush; someone had tried to tell him his private affairs, beginning, 'If you would allow me to be personal,' and father had blushed because he would never allow anybody to be personal."

Yet, governed by forms though he is, Major Buchan is not a merely formal man. As his behaviour shows, he is a great gentleman. At his wife's funeral, it is her old Negro maid, Lucy, whom he takes by the hand to lead the funeral procession. His closest friend is his old Negro valet, Coriolanus, who shares his study. His values are completely uncommercial, feudal; his life governed by obligations in which money has no part. He is in fact deeply in debt, but he would never dream of selling his slaves: they are part of his family. He believes, indeed, that he has made the necessary arrangements to give them their freedom on his death; but when he dies they are immediately sold. An anti-secessionist, he disinherits his elder son for joining the Confederate Army; but when the Federal troops arrive at Pleasant Hill and a Union officer gives him half an hour in which to leave his house before it is burnt, he retorts, "There is *nothing* that you can give me, Sir,"—and goes off and hangs himself.

Major Buchan's foil in the novel is his son-in-law, George Posey. Posey does not know the moves of the intricate game Major Buchan expects everybody else to play. He does not, in the Major's sense, know how to behave. His attitude towards the Buchans' values is shown in his behaviour at Mrs Buchan's funeral, when he mounts his horse and rides away, saying, "I can't even remember their names. I meet them but I don't know who they are. And by God they'll starve to death, that's what they'll do. They do nothing but die and marry and think about the honour of Virginia." He too is a Southerner, but an uprooted one. Significantly, he no longer lives in the country, in Maryland, where the Poseys were once landowners, but in a town, in Georgetown, now a suburb of Washington, D.C. He lacks any kind of code to mediate between him and life; he "receives the shock of the world at the end of his nerves"; the boy Lacy always sees him as "a horseman riding over a precipice". Tate obviously means him to represent traditionless modern man. He has no piety in the fundamental sense, no awareness of the obligations owed to others and to the universe. This comes out plainly when he sells a Negro for fifteen hundred dollars to buy a bay mare, saying to the slave, "You're liquid capital; I've got to have the money." "He rode away on the back of a bay Negro," is the comment of one of the Buchans, whose horror is not due simply to the fact that he has sold one of his slaves but that the slave is his half-brother.

Tate's theme in *The Fathers* is the break-up of a civilisation. The character of Major Buchan is a remarkable rendering of a man of honour, and honour was the Southerner's concern to the point of obsession. Yet, admirable as Major Buchan is as a man, it is difficult not to think that the culture he represents must have been extremely precarious if his simplicity in the worldly, commercial sense was also representative. Tate is obviously describing an ideal Southern gentleman, ideal in that his very simplicity may be seen as the tragic flaw in him. In fact, Southern honour as it manifested itself in practice could look very different to outside observers from its ideal manifestation in Major Buchan. It looked very different to Fanny Kemble. During her months in Georgia she had seen it at first hand in the form of particularly bloody vendettas and duels; and when *Uncle Tom's Cabin* was attacked in leading articles in the London *Times* she wrote a long letter to the editor in support of the novel. She has this to say of the Southern gentleman:

> The gentry of the Southern states are pre-eminent in their own country for that species of manner which, in contrast with the breeding of the Northerners, would be emphatically pronounced "good" by Englishmen. Born to inherit landed property, they are not inevitably made clerks and countinghouse men of, but inherit with their estates some of the invariable characteristics of an aristocracy. The shop is not their element; and the eager spirit of speculation and the sordid spirit of gain do not infect their whole existence, even to their very demeanour and appearance, as they too manifestly do those of a large proportion of the inhabitants of the Northern states. Good manners have an undue value for an Englishman, generally speaking; and whatever departs from their peculiar standard of breeding is apt to prejudice them, as whatever approaches it prepossesses them, far more than is reasonable. The Southerners are infinitely better bred men, according to English notions, than the men of the Northern states. The habit of command

gives them a certain self-possession, and the enjoyment of leisure a certain ease. Their temperament is impulsive and enthusiastic, and their manners have the grace and spirit which seldom belong to the deportment of a Northern people. But, upon more familiar acquaintance, the vices of the social system to which they belong will be found to have infected them with their own peculiar taint; and haughty, overbearing irritability, effeminate indolence, reckless extravagance, and a union of profligacy and cruelty, which is the immediate result of their irresponsible power over their dependents, are some of the less pleasing traits which acquaintance develops in a Southern character.

Elsewhere in her letter, Miss Kemble points out that the parts of the South most commonly visited by Englishmen were Maryland, Virginia and Kentucky, where "the outward aspect of slavery has ceased to wear its most deplorable features," where, indeed, slavery was in decline. In fact, most of the romantic notions of the South seem to be based on memories of eighteenth-century Virginia, the "Old Dominion", but life in other parts of the South, in the Deep South especially, could be very different, at best a gimcrack *parvenu* parody of what had been a genuinely aristocratic society. For it is too often forgotten that the South is not in any geographical, climatic or cultural sense an entity. Its homogeneity is rooted solely in the fact of the *"Peculiar Institution"*, slavery, that prevailed there. For the inner truth about the institution and its effect on the South, we cannot do better than turn to another novel of our times, William Faulkner's *Absalom! Absalom!*

What Faulkner does in the novel is to tell, in terms of a violent telescoping of time, which still apparently chimes with historical fact, the essential history of the South from the first introduction of the Negro. The scene is Mississippi, which did not enter the Union until 1817 and is therefore one of the later Southern states. The central character is Thomas Sutpen, whose history we learn at second-hand through the neurotic memories of his aged sister-in-law, the reminiscences of Jason Compson III, whose father had been Sutpen's friend, and the sleuthing and surmising, the imaginative reconstructions, of young Quentin Compson and Shreve McCannon, his Canadian room-mate at Harvard. Sutpen's story, as it emerges from Faulkner's tortuously complex method of narration, is this.

Born in West Virginia in 1807, the son of a poor-white

mountaineer, Sutpen as a boy was shocked at being treated as an inferior by a Negro butler at a great plantation house. He thereupon conceived his "great design", to found a Southern dynasty. As a young man working as a plantation manager on a Caribbean island, he saved the lives of his employer and family and married the planter's daughter, only to divorce her when he found she had Negro blood. In June, 1833, he arrived in Yoknapatawpha County, Mississippi, as it were out of nowhere at the head of a band of Negroes of a wildness and ferocity unknown in the state before, and bought a hundred square miles of virgin territory from the Indians, on which he established his plantation, Sutpen's Hundred. A year later, he married Ellen Coldfield, by whom he had two children, Henry and Judith.

As a student at the University of Mississippi, Henry became the friend of an older student, Charles Le Bon, of New Orleans. He was Sutpen's unacknowledged son by his first wife. To all appearances he was white. In the vacation he accompanied Henry to Sutpen's Hundred, his relation to Sutpen being known by them both. Sutpen refused to recognise him and refused to consent to his betrothal to Judith. As a result of this seemingly groundless refusal, Henry repudiated his birthright and went with Charles to New Orleans. When the Civil War broke out Sutpen raised his own troop to fight against the Yankees. Henry and Le Bon also went to the war. Near its end, the two young men rode back to Sutpen's Hundred, where Le Bon was shot by Henry to prevent his marrying Judith, shot not in order to prevent incest, for he already knew Le Bon was his half-brother, but because he had learned that he had Negro blood.

Sutpen returned from the wars to find his plantation in ruins and Henry disappeared. A doomed titan, as Rosa Coldfield sees him, he set out to re-establish his estate and fortune and beget more sons to inherit it. His wife dead, he proposed to Rosa but alienated her by suggesting that they should see before marriage whether she was capable of bearing a son. Rebuffed by her, he turned to the daughter of Wash Jones, his poor-white employee. The girl bore him a daughter. He repudiated the mother and child with such brutality that Jones murdered him.

Judith continued to live at Sutpen's Hundred with her Negro half-sister, Clytie, whom she sent to New Orleans to bring back the boy Charles Etienne Saint-Valery Bon, Charles's son by an octoroon. The boy, white to all appearances, was brought by Judith and Clytie to think himself as black. In consequence, he rejected his white blood and married a Negress of extreme blackness and extreme ugliness who bore him an idiot son called Jim Bond. Both Judith and Etienne died of yellow fever, so that Clytie and Jim Bond were left in possession of Sutpen's Hundred. In 1909, Rosa Coldfield discovered that someone else was also living in the plantation house; visiting the house with Quentin Compson, she found it was Henry Sutpen, ill and in hiding. Some months later, Miss Compson went out to Sutpen's Hundred with an ambulance to take Henry to hospital. Clytie, assuming that Henry was being arrested for the murder of Charles Le Bon more than fifteen years earlier, set fire to the house over her and Henry's heads. All that remained of the Sutpen dynasty was the Negro idiot Jim Bond, howling and gibbering in the overgrown plantation.

Thus the fall of the House of Sutpen. All that Charles Le Bon asks of Sutpen is recognition, as a son, as a human being. It is refused him; and herein lies Faulkner's diagnosis and criticism of the South. Sutpen is a symbolic figure; that he has built his great house and established himself in so short a space of time is merely the dramatic telescoping of a process that in Virginia and North Carolina had taken generations, even though it seems historically true for Mississippi, which did not become a state until 1817. Sutpen symbolises the profound impiety on which the South was based, the impiety which sees human beings not as ends in themselves but as means, as things, as property. This impiety degraded slaves and slave-owners alike. It is as though the institution was bearable, even to the owners, only when the slaves were not men like themselves but black men. They had to be seen as men different in kind from their masters; yet since white owners never scrupled to sleep with slave women and beget more slaves, the institution perpetuated a perversion of human relations. In terms of human beings, the South was based on rape. It seems clear that this set up in the minds of the whites feelings of guilt towards the Negro which expressed themselves in fear of him and contempt for him. It set up, too, an obsessive concern with the purity of the race, so long as the race thought of was white. The Negro became the enemy, the ever-present menace, the indelible immigrant who could not and must not be assimilated.

To the white man who did not possess slaves, the rural poor-white, the Negro was another kind of enemy in addition—his economic enemy. Poor-whites were often scarcely better off materially or culturally than slaves; Fanny Kemble has some vivid impressions of them in her *Journal*. In the labour market they could always be undercut by slaves; and even when they were skilled artisans they had to face competition from slave-artisans hired out to other white men by their owners. The only advantage over the slave they possessed was their whiteness; and this became all-important.

The fact of slavery cut the South off from the rest of the nation and made it a static, indeed a stagnant society. It was unaffected, for instance, except for the presence of some Germans in Texas, by the never-ending flood of immigrants from Europe during the nineteenth century with all the labour and special skills they had to offer America. They by-passed the South; as Boorstin has said: "Refugees from serfdom did not want to compete with slaves."

And when the South fell in defeat in the War it did so with the terrifying thoroughness that characterised the fall of the House of Sutpen in Faulkner's novel. The War was followed by the Reconstruction, which in important psychological respects was worse than the War itself. If Lincoln had not been assassinated, things might have been different, for Lincoln was for leniency and the reinstatement as quickly as possible of the power of the seceded state governments. But Lincoln was murdered and lesser men took over, men who believed that by secession the South had forfeited all rights, who declared that the South must be treated as "conquered provinces", to be settled with new men. "No civilised victor", James Truslow Adams has written of the North, "was ever more ungenerous." For more than a decade the South was ruled by "carpetbaggers", members of the victorious Republican Party who went South seeking office or spoils, and "scalawags", Southerners who cashed in on the Reconstruction. In Adams's vivid description, "Crowds of Northern muckers, and blacks who had been slaves a short time since, swaggered about, smoking and drinking at the States' expense, ruling the South".

The Reconstruction and the evils it brought with it were among the consequences of the corruption that had set in in the North as a result of the War. The years immediately after the War are often called the "Gilded Age", the phrase coming from the title of Mark Twain's novel published in 1873. The War had led to an enormous expansion of industry in the North; it was a time of unscrupulous individualism in which the

aggressive and self-seeking could become rich very quickly, a time
when financial greed seemed to dominate the nation and private
interests were put before public good. How government at the
centre, in Washington, struck one observer of the day, Henty
Adams, the grandson of one President of the United States and
the great-grandson of another, may be seen in his novel,
Democracy. Fifty years later, Theodore Dreiser was to portray
the ruthless and amoral acquisitiveness of the Gilded Age in the
character of Cowperwood in his novels *The Financier* and *The
Titan*.

The Reconstruction, which lasted until 1876, completed the
economic and social ruin of the South. Moreover, its effect was
to harden white Southerners in their pre-war attitudes towards
the Negroes, who had been hastily enfranchised by the victorious
North in order to counterbalance the Southern whites. The
immediate result of this was the appearance of secret societies
such as the Ku Klux Klan whose aim was to keep the freed
Negroes down by policies of calculated terrorism, which ranged
from midnight parades of masked and white-robed men who
lighted fiery crosses to whippings, tarring-and-feathering, even
lynching. In fact, when Republican power, which meant the
power of the North, was finally broken in the South and
Southerners themselves resumed control of their affairs, all but
a small minority of Negroes were speedily disenfranchised
through inability to fulfil the property or literacy requirements.

The Reconstruction and its aftermath widened the gulf between
the South and the rest of the United States. This may be put in
another way. The South is the only part of the United States
that has been defeated in war, that has experienced tragedy. And
it is in this that its peculiar importance for America as a whole
lies. This comes out with remarkable clarity in the twentieth-
century imaginative writing the South has produced. It has been
a writing characterised, in Allen Tate's words, by "the image of
the past in the present: the pervasive Southern subject of our
time". This indeed defines the nature of modern Southern
writing as compared with most American writing. It is rooted
in its tragic history and scrutinises the present in the perspective
of that history. It is fiercely self-critical, as is shown equally in
the fiction of Faulkner, Allen Tate, Robert Penn Warren and
Carson McCullers and in the poetry of Tate, Warren and John
Crowe Ransom. It is not an optimistic literature; there is no
Emersonian optimism in it—and Emersonian optimism or its

derivatives, which are a constant element in the American mind, can run very shallow indeed.   At the same time, it opposes to the commercial values, the industrial materialism of the North, other values, disinterestedness and obligation.   They are Faulkner's constant themes, as they are Tate's and Ransom's in poetry. We are back, perhaps, with the Southern conception of honour. But what is important now is that, as re-interpreted by this century's Southern writers, it has become the criterion by which American habits of mind and ways of behaviour can be judged, particularly the all-too-easy, self-delusive optimism, based on a naïve faith in total efficacy of techniques, of know-how, which has always been America's besetting sin.

PART 2

American Spokesmen

[19]

Reviewing the memoirs of General Grant in 1887, Matthew Arnold poured scorn on the very idea that there could be such a thing as American literature. "To be always seeking to institute comparisons," he says, "and comparisons to the advantage of their country, is with so many Americans a *tic*, a mania, which sometimes drives their friends half to despair. . . . If there is not superiority, there must be at least balance. Therefore in literature we have 'the American Walter Scott', the 'American Wordsworth';" and he goes on:

> Nay, I see advertised *The Primer of American Literature.* Imagine the face of Philip or Alexander at hearing of a primer of Macedonian Literature! Are we to have a Primer of Canadian Literature too, and a Primer of Australian? We are all contributaries to one great literature—English literature. The contribution of Scotland to this literature is far more serious and important than that of America has yet had time to be; yet a 'Primer of Scotch Literature' would be an absurdity.

Arnold is seeing the claim that there is such a thing as American literature as an instance of American boosting, which is a way of making the wish father to the fact; Webster defines it as shoving upwards, lifting from below, hence aiding by speaking well of. But the passage is interesting beyond this. We do today habitually talk of American literature, Canadian literature, Australian literature, and it would seem unnatural not to do so. And we are not using these expressions simply as a form of shorthand, for English literature written by Americans, Canadians and the rest. We see a distinction between them and English literature which transcends the similar languages in which they are written, which for Arnold was the all-important element, and the distinction is one to do with differences in national experience, differences which do not primarily have anything to do with language.

This Arnold himself might have realised, for even by the time he was writing some of the greatest works of American literature had already been published: the essays of Emerson and Thoreau, the fiction of Hawthorne and Melville, the poetry of Whitman, the early work of Mark Twain, including *Huckleberry Finn*, the early work of Henry James, including *The Portrait of a Lady*. All these seem to us today in their various ways specifically and characteristically American, and some of them, those of Whitman and Twain in particular, were enthusiastically welcomed in England because they were so obviously American. They fascinated because they illuminated a civilisation significantly different from English or European civilisation.

Indeed, what must immediately strike anyone looking back over the history of American literature is how American it was from the very beginning. It was consciously so because American writers saw themselves as the spokesmen of the New Man in a new society, the New Man—and this is the point—who was significantly different from the Englishman or the European. Central to the difference was the "complex fate" entailed in being an American. The phrase is Henry James's. The complex fate is made up of many elements, but the most fundamental is still probably the one James picked out: "It's a complex fate, being an American, and one of the responsibilities it entails is fighting against a superstitious valuation of Europe."

On this James could speak with the authority that came from his being an American who spent the last forty years of his life in England. He became a British citizen in the last months of his life as a gesture demonstrating his solidarity with Britain in the early days of the first world war, but he was none the less an American for that. Though he had made his home in England, it was always as an outsider that he saw her. When he warned his young compatriot against a "superstitious valuation" of Europe he meant, one can only suppose, a valuation based not on reason and objective observation but dictated by emotional considerations, whether guilt, resentment, envy or feelings of superiority or even abasement. This complex fate, as James goes on to show, is a defining factor in Americans. "The burden is necessarily greater for an American—for he *must* deal, more or less, even if only by implication, with Europe, whereas no European is obliged to deal in the least with America."

This aspect of the complex fate needs to be looked at in some detail, for it is at the heart not only of a great part of American

literature but also of much in American life and attitudes outside
literature.

In 1796, when Thomas Jefferson was Secretary of State, the
French Minister in Washington wrote to his government in Paris:
"Jefferson, I say, is American, and by that name, he cannot be
sincerely our friend. An American is the born enemy of all
European peoples." In 1796 the generalisation was probably
true. It is obviously not today, yet even today the American's
relations with and attitudes towards Europe are likely to be
anything but simple and straightforward. Whatever the reasons
that caused the individual American's ancestors to flee it, Europe
is the place that has been fled. For millions of Americans Europe,
and England in particular, because of its special historical relation
to the United States, has been for generations a symbol of injustice, oppression, of all that is the negation of freedom and equality.
As late as the nineteen-twenties, "Big Bill" Thompson, Mayor
of Chicago, could win votes by boasting that he had kept "King
George's snoot out of Chicago". Voters who could be so
influenced were probably not people who made any distinction
between King George III and King George V; but we have to
remember that the first enemies the American child meets in his
school history book are the British. After all, the United States
was born of war with England and within less than half a century
after that war had fought a second war with England, during
which British soldiers burnt down the White House.

No doubt this simple notion of England as the hereditary
enemy is soon discarded; but it is reasonable to assume it still
lingers with varying degrees of potency below the surface of the
American mind, no matter how sophisticated it may be. This
suspicion is partly the result of ancestral fear. It is partly the
result, too, of an inferiority feeling towards England, as the
representative of a greater measure of culture, sophistication,
worldly wisdom, that is paralleled now by similar feelings of
inferiority that Texans, for example, often show towards the
older areas of the United States, New York and New England
in particular. It need have no basis in objective reality at all;
but it expresses itself, as inferiority feelings commonly do, in
aggressive attitudes, boastings of superiority such as those that
drove Matthew Arnold "half to despair", and a touchiness in the
presence of what is construed as British criticism or condescension.
Englishmen in the United States quickly learn how, all unwittingly,
they can give offence; and the touchiness is aggravated by the

patronising attitude that some Europeans, Englishmen in particular, do in fact often adopt towards Americans and American institutions, either unconsciously or out of sheer ignorance.

The truth is, in the Anglo-American relationship feelings of superiority are as much built into the English as feelings of inferiority into Americans, and for similar reasons. Englishmen in America, even those who know and love the country, constantly surprise themselves by criticising features of American life in a way in which they would never dream of criticising, say, French, Swedish or German. They do so because, unconsciously, they are outraged by what seem to them departures from English norms. This is obviously not a standard by which they would think of judging life in continental European countries. Unconsciously, they think American life should be an extension, as it were, of English life, and if they are not on their guard, they are tempted to interpret differences as inferior versions of aspects of English life. They find it extraordinarily difficult to accept the foreignness of America. At the same time, Americans, intellectuals and academics especially, often show a deference to things English that seems to many Englishmen absurd and certainly not warranted by fact.

There is another strand in this tangle of American attitudes towards Europe: guilt—again, needless to say, at the unconscious level. The abandonment of Europe meant the abandonment of an ancient heritage, of a birthright, the rejection indeed of the parents. It was a kind of parricide or matricide, and these are acts that, even when merely metaphorical, are not undertaken without interior psychological conflict and perhaps psychological injury. At the least, there will be the sense that, though much may have been gained by the rejection of Europe much also has been lost; and perhaps this will be even more strongly felt by the immigrant's descendants than by the immigrant himself. For it must not be forgotten that immigration often meant diminishment of personality and sometimes even mutilation of it. As Lewis Mumford writes in *The Golden Day*: "If the nineteenth century found us more raw and rude, it was because our minds were not buoyed up by all those memorials of a great past that floated over the surface of Europe. The American was thus a stripped European; and the colonisation of America can, with justice, be called the dispersion of Europe—a movement carried on by people incapable of sharing or continuing its past."

The loss suffered by the immigrant, which was in the widest

sense a cultural loss, not an economic or political one, is strikingly
brought home in many American novels. Take Willa Cather's
My Antonia, published in 1918. Here Willa Cather draws upon
her own childhood experiences and memories. Born in 1873 in
Virginia, where her ancestors had settled in the late eighteenth
century, she was taken at the age of ten by her parents, who had
bought a farm there, to Nebraska, then a frontier state still un-
fenced and only recently abandoned by the Indian and the buffalo.
The novel purports to be the recollections written in middle age
by Jim Burden, a successful New York lawyer, of his childhood
in Nebraska. Like his creator, he had been taken there at ten,
arriving at the same time as the Shimerdas, an immigrant Czech
family, whose daughter, Antonia, slightly older than himself, he
had taught English and who had become his friend, constant
companion and protector. Antonia is at the centre of his
memories; but nothing in this beautiful, elegaic novel is more
moving than the rendering of the suicide of Antonia's father, who
kills himself, as Burden realises even as a boy, out of despairing
homesickness for a culture older and richer than that which he
has come to.

This cultural loss, which could result in the immigrant's
conscious diminishment or mutilation as a man, is brilliantly
dramatised also in Henry Roth's *Call It Sleep*, published in 1934.
The setting and the kind of immigrants described are very
different from Willa Cather's Nebraska and its Czech farmers:
the scene is the slums of New York, the characters Russian Jews
who poured into them in the years immediately before the first
world war. The rawness and crudity of big-city slum-life, as
experienced by a terrified child, are rendered with uncompromising intensity. Among other ways, they come out in the speech
of the characters, in the barbarous mutilations of the English
language as spoken by the children of these Jewish immigrants.
Roth catches them with a horrible fidelity: "My ticher called id
Xmas, but de kids call id Chrizmas. Id's a goyish holiday any-
ways. Wunst I hanged op a stockin' in Brooklyn. Bod mine
fodder pud in a eggshell wid terlit paper an' a piece f'om a ol'
kendle. So he leffed w'en he seen me. Id ain't no Sendy Klaws,
didja know?"

From the evidence of their speech, any number of conclusions
about the cultural background of these children could be made;
and they would be wrong. For the fact is, at home their parents
speak Yiddish; and when his characters are speaking Yiddish,

Roth puts into their mouths a singularly pure English. It is as though a kaleidoscope has suddenly been shaken: we see the characters in a quite new light. The contrast makes us aware in the sharpest possible way of the degradation, the reduction in human dignity, that was often the immigrant's lot when he transplanted himself from an environment with a traditional culture to one with almost none at all or, at any rate, with none accessible to him.

In Roth's novel the situation is seen at its most poignant in the representation of the Hebrew teacher, Reb Yidel Pankower. At first sight, a dirty, irascible, petty sadist, a Dickensian character conducting an almost Dickensian parody of religious education, it is he who realises the promise of Roth's hero, the boy David, and he who makes what seems the final comment on the Promised Land to which David's parents have brought him:

> A curse on them: He glared about him at the children and half-grown boys and girls who crowded the stoops and overflowed in the sidewalks and gutter. The devil take them: What was going to become of Yiddish youth? What could become of this new breed? These Americans? This sidewalk-and-gutter generation?

It is not, of course, the final comment. Reb Yidel Pankower could not know that some of them, like Roth himself, were to become masters of the English language and to succeed in fusing their traditional Jewish culture with American Anglo-Saxon culture. Nevertheless, Reb Yidel Pankower's cry of anguish was the recognition of something real, of a loss resulting from a descent into something like cultural barbarism.

A third example, from another and quite different group of immigrants, may be found in the novels of James T. Farrell, in particular his trilogy, *Studs Lonigan* (1932–35), and *The Face of Time* (1954), which exist in illuminating contrast with one another. *Studs Lonigan* must be one of the most depressing novels ever written. It is a coldly savage criticism of the quality of American big-city life, the criticism being implied in the character and fate of Studs Lonigan, a lower middle-class Irish Catholic boy living on Chicago South Side, a youth with nothing in his environment worthy of the response of his imagination, so that his mind becomes sodden with dreams of the seedy violence of films, the pulp magazines and the crime reports of the press. He lives in a cultural wasteland which the Catholic Church, to which Studs nominally belongs, does nothing to redeem.

To this novel Farrell prefixes a quotation from Plato's *Republic* which exactly sums up the point of view from which he is criticising Studs's environment: "Except in the case of some rarely gifted nature there never will be a good man who has not from his childhood been used to play amid things of beauty and make of them a joy and a study." Studs has been brought up in a vast urban jungle from which the things of beauty that should surround a child are brutally absent.

Studs is the son of Irish immigrants. In *The Face of Time* Farrell deals with immigrants themselves. The novel describes the life of the O'Flaherty family in working-class Chicago during the early years of the century. The O'Flahertys are much poorer than the Lonigans, and the scene of the novel is no more promising or agreeable than that of the earlier book. Materially, the O'Flahertys, man and wife, now old, are defeated. Yet *The Face of Time* produces an effect of beauty; it has a pastoral quality. Why this is so becomes clear when we look at it in the light of the passage from the *Republic* quoted above. Compared to the native-born American, Studs, the O'Flahertys are, as it were, so much nearer grace. They are immigrants, and for them reality is still largely the Ireland of their childhood. America is a place they do not understand, and it consists, for all its material prosperity, of broken promises. But they have as children played among things of beauty; they have kept their innocence and survive, in spite of poverty, adversity and disappointment, as examples of simple human dignity.

These novels of Willa Cather, Henry Roth and James T. Farrell serve to show, among other things, the extraordinary complexity of the American relationship with Europe. This was a main subject of the fiction of Henry James. It falls into two parts. The first is what James himself called the "international subject", which means in effect the relationship between America and Americans on the one hand and Europe and Europeans on the other. The second is that of the innocent, who are corrupted or more often despoiled by the sophisticated in whom the good things sought by the innocent appear to reside. The innocent tend to be American, their exploiters Europeans or, in some instances, Americans corrupted by Europe. As we see it illustrated in the two great novels, *The Portrait of a Lady* and *The Wings of the Dove*, innocence, aspiring, idealistic, can scarcely not be equated with America; cynicism, corrupt and luxurious, with Europe. In her English and Italian contexts, Isabel Archer, the heroine of *The Portrait of a Lady*, strikes one as particularly American: "She spent half her time thinking of beauty and bravery and magnanimity; she had a fixed determination to regard the world as a place of brightness, of free expansion, of irresistible action. . . . She had an infinite hope that she would never do anything wrong." She recognises no limits to possibility; and in the end, of course, she is defeated.

This equation of America with idealistic innocence and of Europe with cynical corruption, which is worked out by James with infinite subtlety, was a common American attitude in the nineteenth century and, one suspects, lurks not far below the surface today. But it is anything but a simple thing. If at one extreme it can be represented by the novelist Thomas Wolfe's blanket phrase of condemnation, "European and fancy", at the other it can be represented by James himself. James, after all, preferred to live in England rather than in the United States and spent more than half his life in Europe; and though it is of immigration into America one thinks of first of all, it must not be forgotten that from Crèvecoeur, who went back to France, onwards, to T. S. Eliot and beyond, emigration from America, the return to Europe, has been a constant factor in American history. For the American, Europe is the great other place, the great opposite place, as America tends to be for the European. It may be the Great Bad Place; it may also be the Great Good Place. It has at times the attraction of the forbidden, of that which is renounced and therefore often envied. Generally, it is seen probably as somehow wicked, and the more insidiously attractive because of that. But it may also represent an ideal of freedom, as it seems to in John Horne Burns's novel of wartime Italy, *The Gallery* (1947). For Burns, though not for all the characters in his book, Italy comes to mean liberty, a freer, more civilised attitude, in sexual matters especially, than is found in the United States. In *The Gallery* it is the Americans, their fundamental assumptions and their behaviour, that are found wanting. There is, in other words, a discovery of loss.

[20]

The immigrants in *My Antonia, Call It Sleep, Studs Lonigan* and *The Face of Time* are debarred by race, religion, language or national tradition from participation in American life except at the lowest levels. They are "stripped Europeans" in the fullest sense. Yet the awareness of deprivation in some sort, of being "stripped" almost as a condition of American life, was strongly felt by native Americans, WASPS (White Anglo-Saxon Protestant Americans), as they are often called, in the early days of American literature. It was recognised precisely as a differentiating factor between American literature and English. So in 1828, Fenimore Cooper, the first significant American novelist and the first to win a world audience writes in his book *Notions of the Americans*:

> There is scarcely any one which contributes to the wealth of the author, that is found, here, in veins as rich as in Europe. There are no annals for the historian; no follies (beyond the most vulgar and commonplace) for the satirist; no manners for the dramatist; no obscure fictions for the writer of romance; no gross and hardy offences against decorum for the moralist; nor any of the rich artificial auxiliaries of poetry.

American institutions, he goes on, are not "favourable to novelties and variety", and all Americans, he observes—and it is an observation that is echoed and re-echoed down the years— tend to behave like one another.

Thirty years after Cooper, we find Nathaniel Hawthorne writing:

> No author can conceive of the difficulty of writing a romance about a country where there is no shadow, no antiquity, no mystery, no picturesque and gloomy wrong, nor anything but a commonplace prosperity, as is happily the case with my dear native land.

The very words Hawthorne uses betray the tension in his mind.

However unwillingly, he seems to be asserting a paradox: material prosperity generally diffused, the absence of injustice, appear as inimical to the making of literature. He is almost, one feels, on the point of wondering whether the price is worth paying. As we know, he need not have worried: within a matter of years, the Civil War and the Reconstruction that followed were to provide at least one part of his dear native land with all the shadow, mystery, and picturesque and gloomy wrong that even the most demanding writer of romance could wish for.

Thirty years later, in his critical biography of Hawthorne, Henry James paraphrases Hawthorne's lament in terms of consciously humorous exaggeration:

> One might enumerate the items of high civilisation, as it exists in other countries, which are absent from the nature of American life, until it should be a wonder to know what is left. No State, in the European sense of the word, and indeed barely a specific national name. No sovereign, no court, no personal loyalty, no aristocracy, no church, no clergy, no army, no diplomatic service, no country gentlemen, no palaces, no castles, nor manors, nor old country houses, no parsonages, nor thatched cottages, no ivied ruins; no great universities, nor public schools—no Oxford, nor Eton, nor Harrow; no literature, no novels, no museums, no pictures, no political society, no sporting-class—no Epsom nor Ascot: Some such list of that might be drawn up of the absent things in American life of forty years ago, the effect of which, upon an English or French imagination, would probably as a general thing be appalling. The natural remark, in the light of such an indictment, would be as if these things are left out, everything is left out.

It is difficult to read this passage from James now without recalling Crèvecoeur's "What Is an American?". What was a source of pride in Crèvecoeur has become one of humorous dismay in James. The point is, James's list of the things absent from American society represents all those elements in English and European society many immigrants came to America in order to escape.

In fact, there was an immediate comeback to James's indictment from his friend, the American novelist William Dean Howells. Everything left out? Not at all, exclaimed Howells: there remains "simply the whole of human life". There is a sense in which this may be true, but so far as the novel is concerned, Howells was wrong and James was right; as European fiction shows. One has only to think of the crowded canvases of Fielding, Jane Austen, Scott, Dickens, Thackeray, Trollope, George Eliot, Bennett, Joyce and Lawrence; of Balzac, Flaubert, Zola and Proust; of Turgenev, Tolstoy, Dostoevsky, even the stories of Chekhov. These are fictions in which society is present in all its aspects, the supreme conditioning factor on the characters in them. Society is the element in which they live, and without it they could not live; and this is true even when, as with Dostoevsky and Lawrence, the depiction of society is not the novelist's primary concern. Hawthorne has an interesting comment in this connection on the novels of Trollope; "They precisely suit my taste; solid, substantial, written on strength of beef and through the inspiration of ale, and just as real as if some giant had hewn a great lump out of the earth and put it under a glass case, with all its inhabitants going about their daily business, and not suspecting that they were made a show of."

It was the kind of fiction Hawthorne would have liked to write himself; but he could not, nor could any other American of his time and for years to come, not through lack of talent but because of the conditions of life in America. Society of the density and proliferation which gave birth to the English novel and shaped its progress not only did not exist in the United States, it was also what the forebears of men like Hawthorne had left England to escape. How, then, with a large part of the traditional and normal material of literature simply not available to them, could Americans make a literature?

Well, as we have seen, it was a problem the early American writers were highly conscious of. But they were also—and perhaps this is more important—highly conscious of themselves as Americans. They knew that the American experience was a unique experience and therefore demanded unique expression. They knew that what they had to do was something different from the traditional ends proposed for themselves by English writers. So we find Hawthorne asking for his fiction to be judged not as novels but as romances. He writes in the preface to *The House of the Seven Gables*:

When a writer calls his work a Romance, it need hardly be observed that he wishes to claim a certain latitude, both as to its fashion and material, which he would not have felt himself entitled to assume had he professed to be writing a Novel. The latter form of composition is presumed to aim at a very minute fidelity, not merely to the possible, but to the probable and ordinary course of man's experience. The former—while, as a work of art, it must rigidly subject itself to laws, and while it sins unpardonably so far as it may swerve aside from the truth of the human heart—has fairly a right to present that truth under circumstances, to a great extent, of the author's own choosing or creation. If he thinks fit, also, he may so manage his atmospheric medium as to bring out or mellow the lights and deepen and enrich the shadows of the picture. He will be wise, no doubt, to make a very moderate use of the privileges here stated, and especially, to mingle the Marvellous rather as a slight, delicate, and evanescent flavour than as any portion of the actual substance of the dish offered to the public.

Hawthorne, then, considered *The House of the Seven Gables*, which was based on the legend of a curse pronounced on the novelist's family when his great-grandfather was a judge in the Salem witch-trials of 1692, in the light of this:

> The point of view in which the tale comes under the Romantic definition lies in the attempt to connect a bygone time with the very present that is flitting away from us. It is a legend prolonging itself, from an epoch now gray in the distance, down into our own broad daylight, and bringing along with it some of its legendary mist, which the reader, according to his pleasure, may either disregard, or allow it to float almost imperceptibly about the characters and events for the sake of a picturesque effect . . .

In fact, the distinction between the romance and the novel had already been made, much more crudely and even chauvinistically, sixteen years earlier by a much lesser writer, William Gilmore Simms, in his preface to *The Yemassee*, a story of Indian warfare in South Carolina in colonial days. In a sense, the value of Simms's exposition lies in its crudity:

> You will note that I call *The Yemassee* a romance, and not a novel. You will permit me to insist on the distinction. . . . What are the standards of the modern Romance? What is the modern Romance itself? The modern Romance is the substitute which the people of present day offer for the ancient epic. The form is changed; the matter is very much the same; at all events, it differs much more seriously from the English novel than it does from the epic and the drama, because the difference is one of material, even more than of fabrication. The reader who, reading *Ivanhoe*, keeps Richardson and Fielding beside him, will be at fault in every step of his progress.

The domestic novel of those writers, confined to the felicitous relation of common and daily occurring events, is altogether a different sort of composition; and if, in a strange doggedness or simplicity of spirit, such a reader happens to pin his faith to such writers alone, circumscribing the boundless horizons of art to the domestic circle, the Romances of Maturin, Scott, Bulwer and others of the present day, will be little better than rhapsodical and intolerable nonsense.

When I say that our Romance is the substitute of modern times for the epic or the drama, I do not mean to say that they are exactly the same things, and yet, examined thoroughly . . . the differences between them are very slight. These differences depend upon the material employed, rather than upon the particular mode in which it is used. The Romance is of a loftier origin than the Novel. It approximates the poem. It may be described as an amalgam of the two. It is only with those who are apt to insist upon poetry as verse, and to confound rhyme with poetry, that the resemblance is unapparent. The standards of Romance . . . are very much those of the epic. It invests individuals with an absorbing interest— it hurries them rapidly through crowded and exciting events, in a narrow space of time—it requires the same unities of plan, of purpose, and harmony of parts, and it seeks for its adventures among the wild and wonderful. It does not confine itself to what is known, or even to what is probable. It grasps at the possible; and, placing a human agent in hitherto untried situations, it exercises its ingenuity in extricating him from them, while describing his feelings and his fortunes in the process.

The key to the passage is the recognition of Scott as the model for the writer of romance. Scott was concerned with history and he made his readers conscious of history and his Scottish readers in particular conscious of their national heritage. It is here that the international importance, which can scarcely be exaggerated, of Scott as a novelist lies. Scott, the novelist who created the consciousness of a national heritage, became a pattern for novelists throughout the world. He was followed by Balzac in France, by Manzoni in Italy, by Turgenev in Russia, by Cooper and Simms in the United States. And here Scott's achievement *was* close to epic, the historic function of which has been to express the formative experience of a race or a people, to sum up in symbolic terms its idea of itself. As Richard Chase has noted, commenting on the passage from Simms in his book, *The*

American Novel and Its Tradition: "There are many American fictions besides *The Yemassee* which remind us of epics, large and small: Cooper's *Prairie*, *Moby-Dick*, *The Adventures of Huckleberry Finn*, Faulkner's *As I Lay Dying*, for example."

The list could be vastly extended; it would include Fitzgerald's *The Great Gatsby*; and of the central characters of these novels the thing to be noted is that, for all the individualisation that has gone to their making, they are, in a way different from that we find in the heroes of English novels, representative figures, men seen, it is difficult not to think, specifically as American. They tend also to be—and here the contrast with English heroes is striking—men alone, solitary figures, and the relative isolation in which they have their being makes them often somewhat larger than life. They are, as Simms says, human agents in hitherto untried situations; they are subjected to a test. And though of course they are near enough in kinship to the characters of realistic fiction to be convincing as representations of human beings who might conceivably have existed, they are also akin, as the characters of English fiction not necessarily are, to the characters of poetic drama. They are attended to some degree by mystery; they are poetic conceptions.

[21]

The first of these heroes is Fenimore Cooper's Natty Bumppo, the hero of the "Leatherstocking Tales", *The Pioneers* (1823), *The Last of the Mohicans* (1826), *The Prairie* (1827), *The Pathfinder* (1840) and *The Deerslayer* (1841). Cooper was born in New Jersey in 1789 and taken as a child to what is now Cooperstown, near Lake Otsego in New York state. The settlement, then on the frontier, had been founded by Cooper's father, who at one time owned 750,000 acres of land there and built himself the manorial hall of wood which is described in *The Pioneers*. Cooper was by birth, then, a member of the American landowning gentry and he was highly conscious of his position as an American gentleman. Before he was fifteen he had been expelled from Yale, and he thereupon went to sea, serving in the United States Navy as a midshipman. He left the sea in 1811 in order to marry and for the next few years lived the life of a gentleman farmer in New York state. He lost the greater part of his fortune in the economic depression of 1817–19 and turned to writing as a livelihood. His second novel, *The Spy*, a romance of the Revolutionary War, was an immediate success both in the United States and in Europe. *The Pioneers, The Last of the Mohicans* and *The Prairie* were even more successful. The first American writer to win world fame, he was hailed as the American Walter Scott—to his vast irritation: he knew that no one would ever have dreamt of calling Scott the Scottish Fenimore Cooper. Yet the compliment was not necessarily condescending. It contained within it the recognition that he was doing something similar to what Scott had done, as we see him interpreted by William Gilmore Simms; and in fact within a matter of years the tales of Natty Bumppo became part of the mythology of Europe. It is sometimes said that Scott "invented" Scotland; in a similar way Cooper "invented" the American West. That children throughout the world play Cowboys and Indians is traceable back to Cooper, even though Natty is a trapper, not a cowboy, for Natty, simple, chivalrous, solitary, the Indian-fighter, is the ancestor of the cowboy hero, simple, chivalrous, solitary, of the traditional Western story and film.

In 1826 Cooper, having been appointed to the sinecure-office of United States Consul at Lyons, took his family to Europe, and remained there for six years. In Europe he became the champion of things American, arguing for the republican idea against the monarchical and rebutting English criticisms of American society and government in his still extremely readable *Notions of the Americans*. But he returned to America to find himself repelled by many things he saw there, by what seemed to him a falling away from the old republic ideals of public and private virtue and by the excesses and vulgarity of Jacksonian democracy; and, a highly irascible man, he spent the rest of his life, apart from writing, in quarrelling with his fellow-countrymen. He was, in fact, the representative of an older America, of the patrician class of landowners and gentlemen who had made the Republic. He was a deeply conservative man, and from one point of view the Leatherstocking Tales may be seen as the celebration of a heroic age that had ended, of an idyllic past that enshrined the American virtues and by comparison with which the American present was found wanting.

This comes out especially in the first of the Leatherstocking Tales he wrote, *The Pioneers*. In this novel Natty Bumppo is conceived as a minor character, "the kind of peripheral character", it has been said, "who in a play by Shakespeare would have talked in prose". The setting is the New York frontier town of Templeton, which is based on the author's childhood memories of Cooperstown; the time is 1793. Natty is a surly, quarrelsome, pathetic old man, almost an outcast, who lives in a squalid shack on the outskirts of the town, a derelict who poaches deer out of season, is in constant trouble with the authorities, and is unable to cope with the encroachments of the civilisation that has destroyed his way of life. He is a displaced person, and his counterpart and companion is a similarly displaced person, a drunken old Indian called Indian Joe. He is in fact the old Mohican chief, Chingachgook.

The next novel in the sequence as Cooper published it is *The Last of the Mohicans*. We are back in the year 1757, in the tangled frontier wars between the English and the French in which the various Indian tribes fought on one side or the other. Natty appears as the Scout, Hawkeye, and with his friend Chingachgook, the Mohican aristocrat, is instrumental in rescuing a group of Englishmen and girls from the Hurons and bringing them back to civilisation. Hawkeye returns to the frontier.

The third novel, *The Prairie,* jumps forward to 1804. In this Natty has redeemed himself from the degradation and bewilderment in which we found him in *The Pioneers*. Almost ninety, he has gone back to the frontier, which is now the Western plains. Natty is again a scout and again he leads a party of white settlers to safety through the hazards of capture by hostile Indians, of prairie fires and buffalo stampedes, in the end to surrender to his years and die peacefully, surrounded by his Indian and white friends. He does so, one feels, just in the nick of time, for already the real enemies of his way of life have appeared on the prairie in the form of settlers, the squatters, represented by the Bush family, who, for all their picturesqueness, are shown as being wholly materialistic, without reverence for man or nature. They are the civilisation, if that is the word, which Natty in his extreme old age has gone west to escape. But the implication is plain: there can be no escape.

In *The Pathfinder* and *The Deerslayer*—the titles are soubriquets

for Natty—we go back to his early life and his years of comradeship with Chingachgook. The time of the action of *The Pathfinder*
is 1756, that of *The Deerslayer* even earlier: it recounts Natty's
initiation into manhood.

The "Leatherstocking Tales" grew rather than were planned.
They are not in any normal sense great or even good novels, and
the case against them as novels was put with all his comic skill
by Mark Twain, who suggested that the name Chingachgook
should be pronounced "Chicago". More seriously, he wrote, of
The Deerslayer specifically:

> It has no invention; it has no order, system, sequence, or result;
> it has no lifelikeness, no thrill, no stir, no seeming of reality; its
> characters are confusedly drawn and by their acts and words they
> prove that they are not the sort of people the author claims that
> they are; its humour is pathetic; its pathos is funny; its conversa-
> tions are—oh! indescribable; its love-scenes odious; its English
> a crime against the language.

All of which is true and yet beside the real point, which is Cooper's
creation of the mythic figure of Natty. In his preface to the
collected edition of the "Leatherstocking Tales" Cooper wrote:

> The author has often been asked if he had any original in mind,
> for the character of Leatherstocking. In a physical sense, different
> individuals known to the writer in early life, certainly presented
> themselves as models, through his recollections; but in a moral
> sense this man of the forest is purely a creation. The idea of
> delineating a character that possessed little of civilisation but the
> highest principles as they are exhibited in the uneducated, and all
> the savage life that is not incompatible with these great rules of
> conduct, is perhaps natural to the situation in which Natty was
> placed. He is too proud of his origin to sink into the condition of
> wild Indian, and too much a man of the woods not to imbibe as
> much as was at all desirable, from his friends and companions.
> In a moral point of view it was the intention to illustrate the effect
> of seed scattered by the way side. To use his own language, his
> "gifts" were "white gifts", and he was not disposed to bring them
> discredit. On the other hand, removed from nearly all the tempta-
> tions of civilised life, placed in the best associations of that which
> is deemed savage, and favourably disposed by nature to improve
> such advantages, it appeared to the writer that his hero was a fit
> subject to represent the better qualities of both conditions, without
> pushing either to extremes.

Natty has been called the "peculiarly American Adam". His Garden of Eden is the wilderness. He cannot be said to eat of the Tree of Knowledge and he suffers no Fall; simply he shrivels and all but dies when in contact with settled communities, as in *The Pioneers*. It is as though Cooper is saying that innocence, the simple fundamental virtues, cannot survive in society. The element of parable in the "Leatherstocking Tales" is obvious here. In his *Studies in Classic American Literature*, a book of the foremost importance on the subject and the one from which a host of later interpretations of American literature descends, D. H. Lawrence writes: "True myth concerns itself centrally with the onward adventure of the integral soul. And this, for America, is Deerslayer. A man who turns his back on white society. A man who keeps his moral integrity hard and intact. An isolate, almost selfless, stoic, enduring man, who lives by death, by killing, but who is pure white." In these respects Natty Bumppo is an archetypal figure in American literature. He is the ancestor not only of the Gary Cooper hero of Western films but also of the Hemingway hero from the short stories of *In Our Time* onwards; indeed it is in Hemingway that we find the completest modern equivalents of Natty. But he may be linked, as Richard Chase shows, with Melville, Thoreau and Faulkner, with the interior, psychological drama of Poe and Hawthorne, and even with certain American characters in Henry James, for all their sophisticated European backgrounds. And he has his affinities too with Huck Finn, with his eternal necessity to light out for the Territory; and Huck, it may be said, even has his Chingachgook in the Negro Jim.

Yet, as Chase also says, "Cooper's hero succeeds in being profound only by being narrow." The American Adam has no Eve. Natty's virtue and power depend on his being celibate, sexless. Instead of Eve, he has Chingachgook; comradeship, blood-brotherhood with a man of another race instead of love. There are, of course, women in the "Leatherstocking Tales", but they are so wooden and lifeless as scarcely to exist as characters. More, probably, than that of any other fiction ever written, Natty Bumppo's world is an entirely masculine one. Which means that, for all its epic qualities, it is severely limited and, as reflection of any real world, severely distorted.

Perhaps this is no more than to say that essentially Cooper's is a boy's world or a world before the Fall. It stands in the sharpest possible contrast with Nathaniel Hawthorne's. And there is, of course, a fundamental difference between the two men in that Cooper, who was not a New Englander, had been spared the heritage of Calvinisn—for him Puritans were largely figures of fun—whereas for Hawthorne the Calvinist inheritance of sin, guilt and evil was the inescapable element of his life, for he was the quintessential New Englander.

[22]

Hawthorne was born in 1804 in Salem, Massachusetts, where his family had lived ever since his first American ancestor had arrived in America with John Winthrop in 1630. As a magistrate, this first ancestor had ordered the whipping of a Quakeress in Salem. His son, Hawthorne's great-great-grandfather, was one of the three judges who presided over the Salem witch trials in 1692 in which nineteen people were hanged, one pressed to death, fifty-five frightened or tortured into confessions of guilt, one hundred and fifty imprisoned, and more than two hundred named as deserving arrest. Among this Hawthorne's actions was the committal of a four-year-old child to prison, where she was fettered in irons; and he was publicly cursed by a man who had been forced to watch his wife being tortured.

In a sense, Hawthorne took his ancestors' guilt upon himself. As he writes in "The Custom House", the essay prefixed to *The Scarlet Letter*:

I know not whether these ancestors of mine bethought themselves to repent, and ask pardon of heaven for their cruelties; or whether they are now groaning under the heavy consequences of them, in another state of being. At all events, I, the present writer, as their representative, hereby take shame upon myself for their sakes, and pray that any curse incurred by them—as I have heard, and as the dreary and unprosperous condition of the race, for many a long year back, would argue to exist—may be now and henceforth removed.

But, if he identified himself with his ancestors, he also identified himself with their victims; and it has been suggested that he felt himself doubly accursed, both as the inheritor of his ancestors' guilt and as the kind of man they would have condemned. He was an artist, and the Puritans had no use for artists, had indeed sternly put them down; and Hawthorne goes on in "The Custom House" to say:

> Doubtless, however, either of these stern and black-browed Puritans would have thought it quite a sufficient retribution for his sins, that, after so long a lapse of years, the old trunk of the family tree, with so much venerable moss upon it, should have borne, as its topmost bough, an idler like myself. No aim that I have ever cherished would they recognise as laudable; no success of mine—if my life, beyond its domestic scope, had ever been brightened by success—would they deem otherwise than worthless, if not positively disgraceful. "What is he?" murmurs one gray shadow of my forefathers to the other. "A writer of storybooks! What kind of a business in life—what mode of glorifying God, or being serviceable to mankind in his day and generation—may that be? Why, the degenerate fellow might as well have been a fiddler!"

Out of this division within himself, this deep disquiet about his forebears and himself, Hawthorne made his complex, ambiguous, many-faceted art. As we have seen, he chose to call his fictions romances rather than novels, partly because of the thinness of American life as compared with European. This was something he was always conscious of, and it is one of the subjects of his fiction. But there were other reasons why he was more at home with the romance than with the novel. It allowed him, as the novel could scarcely have done, to take up a neutral position between the past and the present, to present both simultaneously or to see the one in terms of the other; it enabled him also to inhabit impartially the real world and the world of the supernatural and to blur or shift the boundaries between them; it permitted him to exploit his capacities for allegory and symbol and multiple interpretation. The world of his fiction is a shadowy, twilight world in which much is suggested but little stated with absolute certainty. It confers on him—and the reader—something of the freedom, or at least the emancipation from the severely rational, that we experience in dreams.

Perhaps the best way into Hawthorne's interpretation of the American experience is through his short stories. Two, "The Maypole of Merry Mount" and "Young Goodman Brown", are

particularly helpful here. The former is Hawthorne's version of
the incident in the early history of the Plymouth Colony narrated
in William Bradford's history and discussed on page 31. While
remaining faithful to the facts of history, Hawthorne very
considerably changes the emphases. Those who dance round
the maypole in Hawthorne's tale are not the mere drunken
revellers we find in Bradford's history. Hawthorne obviously
approached them with Milton's *Comus* in mind and he trans-
figures them, presents them as figures from a pagan, even pre-
Christian past:

> But what was that wild throng that stood hand in hand about the
> Maypole? It could not be that the fauns and nymphs, when driven
> from their classic groves and homes of ancient fable, had sought
> refuge, as all the persecuted did, in the fresh woods of the West.
> These were Gothic monsters, though perhaps of Grecian ancestry.

They seem to be figures representative on American earth of an
age of innocence before the Fall, when the notion of sin did not
exist. Describing the Maypole, Hawthorne says:

> On the lowest green bough hung an abundant wreath of roses,
> some that had been gathered in the sunniest spots of the forest,
> and others, of still richer blush, which the colonists had reared from
> English soil. *O people of the Golden Age, the chief of your husbandry*
> *was to raise flowers!*

The italics are mine. What we are witnessing, Hawthorne
seems to imply, is an attempt to re-create in the New World the
Golden Age, an age of innocence.

> There was the likeness of a bear erect, brute in all but his hind
> legs, which were adorned with pink silk stockings. And here
> again, almost as wondrous, stood a real bear of the dark forest,
> lending each of his forepaws to the grasp of a human hand, and as
> ready for the dance as any of that circle. His inferior nature rose
> halfway, to meet his companions as they stooped.

The sensual implications of the scene are not shirked, but the
sensuality is, as it were, an innocent sensuality. And for all its
merriment, the dance round the Maypole is a solemn occasion,
for a youth and a girl are to be married, by "an English priest,
canonically dressed, yet decked with flowers, in heathen fashion,
and wearing a chaplet of the native vine leaves . . . the very
Comus of the crew". It is a true marriage; "The Lord and Lady

of the May, though their titles must be laid down at sunset, were really and truly two partners for the dance of life, beginning the measure that same bright eve". But both boy and girl are struck with sudden sadness while waiting for the marriage rites to be performed:

> No sooner had their hearts glowed with real passion than they were sensible of something vague and insubstantial in their former pleasures, and felt a dreary presentiment of inevitable change. From the moment that they truly loved, they had subjected themselves to earth's doom of care and sorrow, and troubled joy, and had no more a home at Merry Mount.

Hawthorne seems to suggest that the consequence of love, which whatever else it may be means in some sense the acceptance of responsibility for another and certainly the sharing of what is most meaningful with another, is that the lover moves into the world of time and change. But at this point Hawthorne digresses to explain who the revellers at Merry Mount are. "The men of whom we speak, after losing the heart's fresh gaiety, imagined a wild philosophy of pleasure, and came hither to act out their latest day dream." They are, as we should say, escapists, their Golden Age a counterfeit. They brought with them to America "all the hereditary pastimes of Old England. . . . The King of Christmas was duly crowned, and the Lord of Misrule bore potent sway."

> Unfortunately, there were men in the new world of a sterner faith than these Maypole worshippers. Not far from Merry Mount was a settlement of Puritans, most dismal wretches, who said their prayers before daylight, and then wrought in the forest or the cornfield till evening made it prayer time again. Their weapons were always at ready to shoot down the straggling savage. When they met in conclave it was never to keep up the old English mirth, but to hear sermons three hours long, or to proclaim bounties on the heads of wolves and the scalps of Indians. Their festivals were fast days, and their chief pastime the singing of psalms. Woe to the youth or maiden who did dream of a dance! The selectman nodded to the constable, and there sat the light-heeled reprobate in the stocks; or if he danced, it was round the whipping post, which might be termed the Puritan Maypole.

Unseen themselves, a band of such Puritans, as Hawthorne has already told us, are watching the revels; they compare "the

masques to those devils and ruined souls with whom their
superstition peopled the black wilderness". At sunset they
attack: their leader, "the Puritan of Puritans", Endicott himself,
cuts down the Maypole with his sword; its worshippers are bound,
preparatory to being whipped, set in the stocks and perhaps
branded and having their ears cropped; the dancing bear is
shot through the head. "I suspect witchcraft in the beast," says
Endicott.

He turns to the young couple. "Do with me as thou wilt,"
the young man says, "but let Edith go untouched"; to which
Endicott answers: "Not so. We are not wont to show an idle
courtesy to that sex, which requireth the stricter discipline."
Nevertheless, at the sight of the young lovers "the iron man was
softened; he smiled at the fair spectacle of early love; he almost
sighed for the inevitable blight of early hopes". He orders them
to be led away, to be reclaimed for Puritanism. And the story
ends:

> And Endicott, the severest Puritan of all who laid the rock founda-
> tion of New England, lifted the wreath of roses from the ruin of the
> Maypole, and threw it, with his own gauntleted hand, over the
> heads of the Lord and Lady of the May. It was a deed of prophecy.
> As the moral gloom of the world overpowers all systemic gaiety,
> even so was their home of wild mirth made desolate amid the sad
> forest. They returned to it no more. But as their flowery garland was
> wreathed of the brightest roses that had grown there, so, in the tie
> that united them, were intertwined all the purest and best of their
> early joys. They went heavenward, supporting each other along the
> difficult path which it was their lot to tread, and never wasted one
> regretful thought on the vanities of Merry Mount.

The story is much more than a simple contrast between
Puritanism and its opposite; and to both of these Hawthorne's
attitude is ambiguous. From one point of view he is criticising
Puritanism even while accepting its necessity and its triumph.
For though the revellers round the Maypole may be decadent
escapists, nevertheless they represent a major part of the European
past as far back as pre-history. They are celebrating the instinctive life, the unity of nature, both human and animal, and
their celebration is essentially an imaginative response to nature.
Hawthorne is identifying this imaginative response not merely
with its primitive expressions in the ancient fertility rites that
lie behind the worship of the Maypole but also with art and with

love. This is plain from the way in which Hawthorne calls upon all the resources of his poetry for the expression, indeed the glorification, of his vision of Merry Mount. It is his own imaginative response to the past, to the world before the Fall, before the Puritan discovery of sin, with its consequent emphasis on repression, its moral gloom. Nor is Puritan repression, with all its rigours, quite powerful enough to withstand the force of love. Even Endicott himself is softened by the spectacle of the young lovers.

Among other things, then, "The Maypole of Merry Mount" is a story of reconciliation, of the demands of the natural life with those of Puritanism, of art with responsibility.

"Young Goodman Brown" is a much darker story, one of Hawthorne's finest investigations into the psychology of sin, the knowledge of evil. "Young Goodman Brown", the story opens, "came forth at sunset into the street at Salem village." He has a journey to make, though his young wife, Faith—the name is significant—begs him not to go: " 'Dearest heart, prithee put off your journey until sunrise and sleep in your own bed tonight. A lone woman is troubled with such dreams and such thoughts that she's afeared of herself sometimes. Pray tarry with me this night, dear husband, of all nights in the year.' " As the action shows, the night is October 31, All Saints' Eve, the "trick-or-treat" of modern American children but for the Puritans of New England the most sinister night of the year. But Goodman Brown is not to be persuaded. He sets off into the forest and is joined by a middle-aged man carrying a staff that bore the likeness of a great black snake. Walking together, they "might have been taken for father and son". Brown has his scruples and is for turning back, but his companion tells him:

> "Well said, Goodman Brown! I have been as well acquainted with your family as with ever a one among the Puritans; and that's no trifle to say. I helped your grandfather, the constable, when he lashed the Quaker woman so smartly through the streets of Salem; and it was I that brought your father a pitch-pine knot, kindled at my own hearth, to set fire to an Indian village, in King Philip's War. They were my good friends, both; and many a pleasant walk have we had along this path, and returned merrily after midnight."

Through his curiosity, Brown allows himself to be overborne. Along the path ahead he sees Goody Cloyse "a very pious and exemplary dame, who had taught him his catechism in youth, and

was still his moral and spiritual adviser, jointly with the minister
and Deacon Gookin. She greets Brown's companion—Brown
having gone into hiding, out of guilt—familiarly as the devil,
"in the very image of my old gossip Goodman Brown, the grandfather of the silly fellow that now is".

Brown is still reluctant to go on; but he seems to hear the
voices of the minister and Deacon Gookin on their way to the
rendezvous; and when he reaches it, though he cries, "With
heaven above and Faith below I will yet stand firm against the
devil!" he seems to see gathered there the whole community of
the Saints, "a grave and dark-clad company". He cries out for
his wife. There is no answer. " 'My Faith is gone!' cried he,
after one stupefied moment. 'There is no good on earth, and sin
is but a name. Come, devil, for to thee the world is given.' "
So at the devil's altar in the forest he joins the congregation to
be received into the devil's care. He hears the devil's sermon:

'. . . By the sympathy of your human hearts for sin ye shall scent
out all the places—whether in church, bedchamber, street, field, or
forest—where crime has been commited, and shall exult to behold
the whole earth one stain of guilt, one mighty blood spot. Far
more than this. It shall be yours to penetrate, in every bosom, the
deep mystery of sin, the fountain of all wicked arts, and which
inexhaustibly supplies more evil impulses than human power—
than my power at its utmost—can make manifest in deeds. . . . Lo,
there ye stand, my children. Depending upon one another's
hearts, ye had still hoped that virtue was not all a dream. Now
are ye undeceived. Evil is the nature of mankind. Evil must be
your only happiness. Welcome again, my children, to the communion of your race.'

As he waits to be confirmed into the group, Brown finds himself side by side with a young woman. It is Faith. He cries:
"Faith! Faith! look up to heaven, and resist the wicked one."

Whether Faith obeyed he knew not. Hardly had he spoken when
he found himself amid calm night and solitude, listening to a roar
of the wind which died heavily away through the forest. He
staggered against the rock, and felt it chill and damp; while a
hanging twig, that had been all on fire, besprinkled his cheek with
the coldest dew.

He returns at dawn to Salem, "staring around him like a
bewildered man". There are all the respectable whom he has

seen in the forest the night before: the minister, from whom he shrinks "as if to avoid an anathema", Old Deacon Gookin, Goody Cloyse, "catechising a little girl who had brought her a pint of morning's milk". Brown "snatched away the child as from the grasp of the fiend itself". At the end of the street Faith is waiting for him. "She skipped along the street and almost kissed her husband before the whole village. But Goodman Brown looked sternly and sadly into her face, and passed on without a greeting."

Hawthorne asks: "Had Goodman Brown fallen asleep in the forest and only dreamed a wild dream of a witch meeting?" We may decide as we choose; Hawthorne's concern is with psychological reality, and this is not affected by simple questions of waking and dreaming. In any event, Goodman Brown is initiated into consciousness of sin, sin as a universal experience, inescapable, transmitted from generation to generation; and we may note that Hawthorne bestows on Brown his own early family history. He reveals in this story the black underside of Puritanism, the overt signs of which appear in history precisely in such events as the whipping of Quaker women and the torturing and execution of witches. Yet for Brown the results of this initiation into the universal experience of sin is the opposite of what might be expected. It brings him, not closer to his fellows, but further removed from them. In a sense, it is all one whether the depravity he experienced exists objectively, as a fact in the life of the community of Salem and the Commonwealth of Massachusetts, or only within himself; the experience blights him and cuts him off from his fellows, so that he becomes "a stern, a sad, a darkly meditative, a distrustful, if not a desperate man", haunted always by the sense of sin and the suspicion of sin. "Often, awakening suddenly at midnight, he shrank from the bosom of Faith." "When the family knelt down at prayer, he scowled and muttered to himself, and gazed sternly at his wife, and turned away."

> And when he had lived long, and was borne to his grave a hoary corpse, followed by Faith, an aged woman, and children and grandchildren, a goodly procession, besides neighbours not a few, they carved no hopeful verse upon his tombstone, for his dying hour was gloom.

In "The Maypole of Merry Mount" we see, in the figure of Endicott, the moral gloom of the first generation of New England Puritans: in "Young Goodman Brown" we are shown its consequences in the third.

Hawthorne's greatest work is *The Scarlet Letter*. Partaking of the qualities both of "The Maypole of Merry Mount" and of "Young Goodman Brown", it is a masterpiece of psychological realism; and it proliferates with symbols, ambiguities, hidden meanings and conflicts of meanings. The subject of the novel is that of "Young Goodman Brown": "the moral and psychological results of sin—the isolation and morbidity, the distortion and thwarting of the emotional life," to borrow Richard Chase's words; and we are shown the results as they work themselves out in three lives, Hester Prynne's, the Reverend Arthur Dimmesdale's and Roger Chillingworth's. The novel opens with old Roger Chillingworth, an English scholar who has sent his young wife Hester Prynne on before him two years earlier to make a home for them, arriving in Boston to find Hester standing in the pillory with her illegitimate child in her arms. She refuses to name her lover and is condemned to wear a scarlet A, signifying adulteress, as the sign of her sin. Chillingworth conceals his identity and, practising as a doctor, sets out to discover the identity of her lover, Dimmesdale, the seemingly saintly young minister. He is tortured by consciousness of his guilt, preyed upon by Chillingworth, and in the end, having refused to flee with Hester, makes a public confession in the pillory, dying in Hester's arms.

When the novel was published in 1850 it was seen by some critics as a condonation of adultery. This, of course, is a tremendous over-simplification. Nevertheless, Hester is the dominating figure in the book, the heroine, as we cannot say Dimmesdale is the hero. Hawthorne pours his poetry into her rather as he does into the scenes of the revels in "The Maypole of Merry Mount". She is passionate, beautiful, spontaneous, the embodiment, at any rate in the beginning, of the life of impulse. When we first see her, in the pillory with her baby in her arms, she appears like "the image of Divine Maternity". She is that part of life which is irrepressible even by Puritans and which is vividly rendered in the image of a wild rose in the second paragraph of the first chapter, in which Hawthorne describes the town jail:

> The rust of the ponderous iron-work of its oaken door looked more antique than anything else in the New World. Like all that pertains to crime, it seemed never to have known a youthful era. Before this ugly edifice, and between it and the wheeltrack of the street, was a grass-plot, much overgrown with burdock, pig-weed, apple-pern, and such unsightly vegetation, which evidently found something

congenial in the soil that had so early borne the black flower of civilised society, a prison. But on one side of the portal, and rooted almost at the threshold, was a wild-rose bush, covered, in this month of June, with its delicate gems, which might be imagined to offer their fragrance and fragile beauty to the prisoner as he went in, and to the condemned criminal as he came forth to his doom, in token that the deep heart of nature could pity and be kind to him.

This rose-bush, by a strange chance, has been kept alive by history; but whether it had merely survived out of the stern old wilderness, so long after the fall of the gigantic pines and oaks that originally overshadowed it, or whether, as there is fair authority for believing, it had sprung up under the footsteps of the sainted Ann Hutchinson as she entered the prison-door, we shall not take upon us to determine.

That second paragraph, incidentally, is typical of Hawthorne's calculated exploitation of ambiguity, of what the critic Yvor Winters has called his "formula of alternative possibilities". The wild-rose bush may be simply the product of chance; or it may be in a sense supernatural; and here one can only admire the daring with which Hawthorne attributes to Mrs Hutchinson, who was expelled from Massachussetts in 1638 for heresy, an occurrence reminiscent of ancient Greek or medieval Catholic legend. Later in the novel, Hawthorne specifically associates Hester with Mrs Hutchinson. But for the existence of her child, Hawthorne says, "she might have come down in history, hand in hand with Ann Hutchinson, as the foundress of a religious sect. She might, in one phase, have been a prophetess." For one consequence of her sin is that she becomes a greater and nobler woman than she was before it. As a result of her sin, "the links that united her to the rest of mankind . . . had all been broken". She turns the scarlet letter itself, "glittering in its fantastic embroidery," into a symbol of defiance, symbol, as it were, of self-declared otherness from the rest of the community. Within herself, she is a free spirit as no one else in the colony could be at the time.

It was an age in which the human intellect, newly emancipated, had taken a more active and a wider range than for many centuries before. . . . Hester Prynne imbibed this spirit. She assumed a freedom of speculation, then common enough on the other side of the Atlantic, but which our forefathers, had they known it, would have held to be a deadlier crime than that stigmatised by the scarlet letter. In her lonesome cottage, by the seashore, thoughts visited her such as dared to enter no other dwelling in New England: shadowy guests, that would have been as perilous as demons to their entertainer, could they have been seen so much as knocking at her door.

Yet it would be wrong to say that Hester redeems her sin. The truth is, she hardly sees it as sin. "What we did", she tells Dimmesdale in the forest, "had a consecration of its own." Here she is expressing a romantic, one might say a nineteenth-century view, of the sanctity of love which is its own justification irrespective of the claims of conventional morality; and she dreams that at "some brighter period, when the world should have grown ripe for it, in Heaven's own time, a new truth would be revealed, in order to establish the whole relation between man and woman on a surer ground of mutual happiness."

The fact remains, by her sin Hester has destroyed the object of her love. If she, in a very real sense, is made by it, Dimmesdale is utterly undone by it, the victim of dreadful remorse which in the end has to be publicly expressed by him from the pillory: "People of New England, ye, that have loved me—ye, that have deemed me holy—behold me here, the one sinner of the world!" And as he tears away his clergyman's band from his breast, the townspeople see, or think they see, the scarlet letter imprinted in his flesh.

But there is the third person in the relationship, Chillingworth, Hester's husband and Dimmesdale's physician and persecutor. On him Dimmesdale's public confession and death have a remarkable effect:

All his strength and energy—all his vital and intellectual force— seemed at once to desert him, insomuch that he positively withered up, shrivelled away, and almost vanished from mortal sight, like an uprooted weed that lies wilting in the sun. This unhappy man had made the very principle of his life to consist in the pursuit and systematic exercise of revenge; and when, in its completest triumph and consummation, that evil principle was left with no further material to support it—when, in short, there was no more Devil's work on earth for him to do—it only remained for the unhumanised mortal to betake himself whither his Master would find him tasks enough, and pay him his wages duly.

Throughout the novel, Chillingworth is presented as the agent of the Devil; he is feared as being in league with the powers of darkness. More certainly, because this aspect of him is expressed in all Hawthorne's riddling ambiguity, he is guilty of what the author calls in his story, "Ethan Brand," the Unpardonable Sin. As Dimmesdale tells Hester: "He has violated, in cold blood, the sanctity of the human heart," and, Dimmesdale suggests, the sin is greater than either his or Hester's. Yet Hawthorne still has his comment to make, and it is one that shows the intensity of his phychological insight:

> It is a curious subject of observation and inquiry, whether hatred and love be not the same thing at bottom. Each, in its utmost development, supposes a high degree of intimacy and heart-knowledge; each renders one individual dependent for the food of his affections and spiritual life upon another; each leaves the passionate lover, or the no less passionate hater, forlorn and desolate by the withdrawal of his subject. Philosophically considered, therefore, the two passions seem essentially the same, except that one happens to be seen in a celestial radiance, and the other in a dusky and lurid glow. In the spiritual world, the old physician and the minister—mutual victims as they have been—may, unawares, have found their earthly stock of hatred and antipathy transmuted into golden love.

"Mutual victims"; Chillingworth and Dimmesdale exist in a symbolic relationship one with the other. "They are the two aspects of the will," Richard Chase has written, "which confused Puritan thought in New England—the active and inactive. From the beginning, Puritanism generated a strong belief in the efficacy of the will in overcoming all obstacles in the path of the New Israel in America, as in the path of the individual who strove towards Election. But at the same time the doctrine of Predestination denied the possibility of any will except that of God." Seen in these terms, Chillingworth represents the union of will and intellect, while Dimmesdale stands for the passive, will-less intellect with all its self-scrutiny and moral scruple.

And this brings us to the peculiarly American experience that Hawthorne is exploring in *The Scarlet Letter*. The moral and psychological drama he re-creates and investigates could have been the product of nowhere in the world except the New England seaboard of the seventeenth century, because nowhere else did Puritanism exist in such purity and isolation. The purity was the product of the isolation. No matter how much they dream of it, and even plan it, Hester and Dimmesdale

cannot escape from Puritan New England. The alternatives—
flight to the West, into the forest, flight to Europe—are alike
impossible. For though the forest is identified with love, it is
also, as Hawthorne calls it, a "moral wilderness", a place in
which restraints no longer exist and which is therefore dangerous.
We recall that it was in the forest that Merry Mount had its being
and that it was into the forest that Young Goodman Brown went
to meet the Devil. And to return to Europe would be to go
back to corruption, to a corrupt church, to feudal persecution,
to vanity. The seaboard strip of Puritan New England, for
Hawthorne and for his characters, is set as it were between the
heathen wilderness and the corrupt old world. It is the one
place where, however imperfectly realised, the moral law prevails.

[23]

From his boyhood, Hawthorne was steeped in Spenser's *The
Faerie Queene* and Bunyan's *The Pilgrim's Progress*, the first, for all
its Renaissance learning and sensuousness, one of the two great
English poems of the Puritan imagination, the second the
greatest Puritan prose narrative. The two works are the most
beautiful expressions we have of the Puritan way of interpreting
life. It is the way of allegory. In allegory anything may be
taken as standing for something else. But the meaning is fixed;
there is, as it were, only one correct translation. Living as they
did in a world in which they believed God was omnipresent,
the Puritans believed in consequence that everything that
happened, great and small alike, was the work either of God or
the Devil. Every occurrence was, so to speak, a sign that had
to be translated. Charles Feidelson, in his *Symbolism and
American Literature*, quotes an instance of this from Winthrop's
journal. During a sermon delivered before the synod at Cambridge, Massachusetts, a snake appeared behind the pulpit and
was killed by one of the elders. This is how Winthrop explains
the event:

This being so remarkable, and nothing falling out but by divine providence, it is out of doubt, the Lord discovered somewhat of his mind in it. The serpent is the devil; the synod, the representative of the churches of Christ in New England. The devil had formerly and lately attempted their disturbance and dissolution; but their faith in the seed of the woman overcame him and crushed his head.

Hawthorne also was a natural allegorist, and nothing shows more clearly than this how deeply engrained in him was his forebears' way of looking at the world in which he lived. It was his incurable habit of mind, as we see from this entry in his notebooks: "Meditations about the main gas-pipe of a great city—if the supply were to be stopped, what would happen? . . . It might be made emblematical of something." For Hawthorne anything could be emblematical of something else.

Yet, since he was a man of the nineteenth century and not in any theological sense himself a Puritan, he was an allegorist with a difference, how different may be seen in the simple instance of his treatment of the scarlet A Hester Prynne is forced to wear. At first it stands for adultery; but then we discover it is being interpreted by those whom Hester succours as meaning "able"; and we go on to realise that conceivably it may be emblematic of art. It can no longer be pinned down to a fixed meaning. Instead, it can carry many meanings, and in this Hawthorne is using the method of allegory in order to expose the inadequacy of allegorical interpretation. Something like this, though with greater complexity, he is doing all the time. He uses what looks like allegory to show how many-faceted experience is, how incapable it is of reduction to the single interpretation. As Daniel G. Hoffman, in *Form and Fable in American Fiction*, has said of him and Melville; "Allegory was designed for the elucidation of certainty; they used it in the service of search and scepticism. . . . In the process they transformed allegorism into a symbolic method."

Perhaps it was for this reason that Melville said that he did not wish *Moby-Dick* to be taken as a "hideous and intolerable allegory". In fact, both Hawthorne and Melville often spoke of "allegory" where we would speak of "symbolism", and though at their extremes one sees easily enough how different and indeed opposed the two modes are, nevertheless they are not always easily distinguishable, since they spring from a common root, a common assumption. The difference between them is one of complexity and ambiguity, and these may be shifting, for they reside not in the object or value itself or the word that stands for it but in what the beholder brings to it. Allegory presupposes in those who behold it a common view of what truth is, that all are agreed that the scarlet A stands for adultery. Symbolism enters with doubt, with multiplicity of possible meanings; and it can go much further than this, until it can be equated almost with Jung's description of the symbol in the psychological sense: "In so far as a symbol is a living thing, it is the expression of a thing not to be characterised in any other or better way. The symbol is alive in so far as it is pregnant with meaning."

Such a symbol is the white whale, Moby-Dick, in Melville's novel of that title. Herman Melville was born in New York City in 1819, of English, Scotch and Dutch ancestry and of Calvinist stock on both his father's and mother's sides. He went to sea in 1837 and from 1841 to 1844 sailed before the mast on a whaling ship in the Pacific, returning to America as a sailor in the U.S.S. *United States*. His first five novels come out of his immediate experience. *Typee*, which was a popular success, *Omoo* and *Mardi* all reflect his experiences in the islands of the Pacific, which were still much as they were when discovered by Captain Cook sixty years earlier. *Redburn* is based on Melville's first voyage as a cabin boy to Liverpool, *White Jack* on his memories of life in the United States Navy. None of them foreshadows the greatness of the later work, of *Moby-Dick* especially, and indeed, it was not until he was rediscovered thirty years after his death in 1891 by D. H. Lawrence and John Freeman in England and Raymond Weaver and Lewis Mumford in America, that his greatness was widely recognized. Now, *Moby-Dick* is generally accepted as the greatest of American novels and probably the greatest piece of American imaginative writing in form, a work seemingly inexhaustible and comparable in scope to Shakespeare and Dostoevsky.

There seem to have been two main causes for the astonishing leap forward Melville made in *Moby-Dick*. One is that since returning to dry land he had been soaking himself in Shakespeare —the influence of Shakespeare is everywhere on the novel, so much so that in creating Captain Ahab Melville must have been consciously vying with Shakespeare in the creation of Lear. The novel, in other words, is a deliberate bid for greatness at the Shakespearian level. And then, in 1850, he discovered Hawthorne. He reviewed Hawthorne's book of stories, *Mosses from an Old Manse* in tones of rhapsodical enthusiasm, and its effect on him was, it has been said, catalytic. He seems already to have

written one draft of *Moby-Dick* when he discovered Hawthorne.
Immediately after, he recast his novel, weaving into it deeper and
richer meanings, re-conceiving it, to use Richard Chase's description of it, as an epic romance. He was able to do so because he
had discovered from Hawthorne the mysterious value of the
symbol to express his view of the universe, which is implied in
his narrator Ishmael's statement: "Doubts of all things earthly,
and intuitions of some things heavenly; this combination makes
neither believer nor infidel, but makes a man who regards them
both with equal eye."

No two men could have been more different in temperament
and experience than Hawthorne and Melville, and their imtimacy
was short-lived. Hawthorne's was a landlocked talent; his inspiration was rooted in the local and his own family past, which
were much the same thing, and it was to these that it constantly
returned. Its limits were narrow and rigid; when it dared to
venture into the larger world of the present it was uncertain and
ineffective. By contrast, it was the oceans themselves, not the
small confines of seventeenth-century New England, that liberated
Melville's talent. The globe itself is its province, for it is there,
on the seas that span it, that Melville finds life. And there is a
greater difference. Melville is not concerned with sin in the
Calvinist New England sense, not concerned, as Hawthorne is,
with questions of right- and wrong-doing and their psychological
consequences. He is concerned with something more elemental,
with the eternal conflict between good and evil. If we say
Hawthorne's scope is local, which is not in the least to criticise
his art or question its achievement, we have to say that Melville's
is cosmic.

Moby-Dick is a long novel, and the amount of criticism and
exegesis already written on it is vast. But the first thing to be
said of it is that it is a story about the sea, probably the greatest
we have, certainly the greatest we have on whale-hunting. It
might indeed be described as a *vade-mecum* to the whole art and
trade of whaling and also as an encyclopaedic account of the
whale in all its aspects, the natural history of the animal, its uses
to man, its depiction in art, literature and mythology. In the
most literal way, it is one of the most sternly factual books ever
written. One feels that whole libraries must have gone to its
making, that there is nothing about hunting the whale that
Melville does not know. And this is of the utmost importance,
because it is on its very solidity, on what Henry James would

have called its "density of specification", that the power of the
symbolism ultimately rests.

More narrowly, it is the story of the pursuit of one specific
whale, the White Whale, Moby-Dick, by the whaler *Pequod*, and
of Captain Ahab's hatred, obsessive to the exclusion of any other
feeling in him, for Moby-Dick. The novel moves through
passages of excitement, peril and calm—almost becalmed—beauty
that seem almost to mirror the various moods of the ocean itself,
until it reaches its tremendous climax in the three-day chase of
the White Whale with the death of Ahab, the smashing of the
Pequod, and Ishmael, the narrator of the story and to some degree
Melville's spokesman, the sole survivor.

One clue to the novel may be found in the sermon Father
Mapple preaches in the Whaleman's Chapel in New Bedford,
before the *Pequod* sails, on the text, "And God had prepared a
great fish to swallow up Jonah." It ends:

'But oh! shipmates! on the starboard hand of every woe, there is
a sure delight; and higher the top of that delight, than the bottom
of the woe is deep. Is not the main-truck higher than the kelson
is low? Delight is to him—a far, far upward, and inward delight—
who against the proud gods and goddesses of this earth, ever
stands forth his own inexorable self. Delight is to him whose
strong arms yet support him, when the ship of this base treacherous
world has gone down beneath him. Delight is to him, who gives
no quarter in the truth, and kills, burns, and destroys all sin though
he pluck it out from under the robes of Senators and Judges.
Delight—top-gallant delight is to him, who acknowledges no law
or lord, but the Lord his God, and is only a patriot to heaven.
Delight is to him, whom all the waves of the billows of the seas
of the boisterous mob can never shake from this true Keel of the
Ages. And eternal delight and deliciousness will be his, who
coming to lay him down, can say with his final breath—O Father—
chiefly known to me by Thy Rod—mortal or immortal, here I die.
I have striven to be Thine, more than to be this world's, or mine
own. Yet this is nothing; I leave eternity to Thee; for what is
man that he should live out the lifetime of his God?'

Having preached his tremendous sermon, Father Mapple
disappears from the novel, and the book has to be read before
the full significance of what he says is plain. But the sermon is
at once a prologue to the action and to Ahab's tragic defeat and a
comment upon it. It cannot be said to be Melville's, for Melville's

attitude towards the story he narrates is ambiguous. But it is the Christian comment. It describes the Christian hero and in a negative sense helps to define Ahab. "Delight—top-gallant delight is to him, who acknowledges no law or God, but the Lord his God, and is only a patriot to heaven": Ahab acknowledges no law but himself and is a patriot to himself alone. He is called by one of the characters "a grand, ungodly, godlike man", and has taken to himself those prerogatives that are God's alone. This comes out in his relentless hatred and pursuit of *Moby-Dick*, the whale that has already, in a previous encounter between them, sheared off his leg. To his first mate, Starbuck, who is a Christian, Ahab's obsessive hatred of Moby-Dick is both blasphemous and mad. As he cries: "Vengeance on a dumb brute! that simply smote thee from blindest instinct! Madness! To be enraged with a dumb thing, Captain Ahab, seems blasphemous," Ahab replies:

> "All visible objects, man, are but as pasteboard masks. But in each event—in the living act, the undoubted deed—there, some unknown but still reasoning thing puts forth the mouldings of its features from behind the unreasoning mask. If man will strike, strike through the mask: How can the prisoner reach outside except by thrusting through the wall? To me, the white whale is that wall, shoved near to me. Sometimes I think there's naught beyond. But 'tis enough. He tasks me; he heaps me; I see in him outrageous strength, with an inscrutable malice sinewing it. That inscrutable thing is what I chiefly hate; and be the white whale agent, or be the white whale principal, I will wreak that hate upon him. Talk not to me of blasphemy, man: I'd strike the sun if it insulted me. For could the sun do that, then could I the other since there is ever a sort of fair play herein, jealously presiding over all creations. But not my master, man, is even that fair play. Who's over me? Truth has no confines."

Ahab, then, is a Promethean figure, a conception as grand as Milton's Satan and almost as Shakespeare's Lear, with both of whom he has strong affinities. But how are we to take Moby-Dick? For Starbuck, as we have seen, he is a mere dumb brute. For Ahab, he is "the gliding great demon of the seas of life", that element in the nature of things that is recalcitrant to and even hostile to man. For the Shaker sailor Gabriel, of the *Jeroboam*, Moby-Dick is no less than the incarnation of God Himself. And Melville ransacks scripture and myth in order to load Moby-Dick with all the attributes of mystery and power. The whalemen believe Moby-Dick is immortal and ubiquitous; throughout, Melville equates him with Leviathan.   Ishmael calls him "Job's whale", and perhaps the forty-first chapter of The Book of Job should be taken as a commentary on Melville's conception of Moby-Dick.   In it, God says: "None is so fierce that dare stir him up: who then is unable to stand before me?" and he is called "a king over all the children of pride", i.e., men. Ishmael, who maintains that the whale has no face, no recognisable feature, and presents to his beholder as it were a blank wall, remembers God's words to Moses: "My back parts you shall see, but not my face."   And the mystery that even an ordinary whale enshrines is summed up in Ahab's speech before the head of the decapitated sperm whale:

It was a black and hooded head; and hanging there in the midst of so intense a calm, it seemed the Sphinx's in the desert. "Speak, thou vast and venerable head," muttered Ahab, "which, though ungarnished with a beard, yet here and there lookest hoary with mosses; speak, mighty head, and tell us the secret thing that is in thee. Of all divers, thou hast dived the deepest. That head upon which the upper sun now gleams, has moved amid this world's foundations. Where unrecorded names and navies rust, and untold hopes and anchors rot; where in her murderous hold this frigate earth is ballasted with bones of millions of the drowned; there, in that awful water-land, was thy most familiar home. Thou hast been where bell or diver never went; hast slept by many sailors' side, where sleepless mothers would give their lives to lay them down. Thou saw'st the locked lovers when leaping from their flaming ship; heart to heart they sank beneath the exulting wave; true to each other, when heaven seemed false to them. Thou saw'st the murdered mate when tossed by pirates from the midnight deck; for hours he fell into the midnight of the insentiate maw; and his murderers still sailed on unharmed—while swift lightenings shivered the neighbouring ship that would have borne a righteous husband to outstretched, longing arms. O head: thou hast seen enough to split the planets and make an infidel of Abraham, and not one syllable is thine!"

The white whale, then, sums up the inexplicable mystery, beauty and terror of the universe.   He is both good and evil, essentially ambiguous.   Indeed, the ambiguity of everything in the world is insisted upon throughout the novel. A conspicuous instance of this is Chapter 42, "The Whiteness of the Whale", in which Ishmael, having said that "it was the whiteness of the whale that above all things appalled me", goes on to tease out, with all the multifarious learning at his command in natural history, geography, mythology, the meaning of whiteness, "the paradoxical colour", as Richard Chase puts it, "that involves all the contradictions Melville attributes to nature".

Ahab is the most striking embodiment in modern literature of man's overweening pride, his refusal to recognise limits; but once the manifold nature of the symbol that is Moby-Dick is realised it is easier to grasp Ahab's tragedy. It lies in his picking out one aspect only of the white whale and seeing it as the whole. In other words, he interprets it allegorically. For him it represents evil, and his hatred for it twists his being into a hatred of life itself, a hatred for which he is ready to sacrifice not only himself but the shipmates and his ship.

This great monomaniac hero, the most towering of all the solitary heroes of American fiction, has been taken as representative of the American individualist, indeed of American man. And certainly it is possible to apply to him D. H. Lawrence's words on Natty Bumppo, whom he saw as the archetypal American: "the essential American soul is hard, isolate, stoic, and a killer." For *Moby-Dick* is very much an American novel, not only in the almost Ahab-like ambition behind it; Melville is refusing to compete with any writer smaller than Shakespeare. In the *Pequod* and its company Melville finds a microcosm of America. Its crew is recruited from native New Englanders, Danes, Dutchmen, a Manxman, Maltese, Icelanders, Spaniards, Chinese, Sicilians, Englishmen, American Negroes and African Negroes, Red Indians, Pacific Islanders. As Lawrence says in his essay on Melville in *Studies in Classic American Literature*:

> What do you think of the *Pequod*, the ship of the soul of an American? Many races, many peoples, many nations, under the Stars and Stripes. Beaten with many stripes. Seeing stars sometimes. And in a mad ship, under a mad captain, in a mad fanatic's hunt. But splendidly handled. Three splendid mates. The whole thing practical, eminently practical in its working. American industry!
> And all this practicability in the service of a mad, mad chase.

And here, of course, the *Pequod* that symbolises the United States symbolises the whole world. The point is, the crew of a whaling ship of no other nationality could do so.

But there are other ways in which, by comparison with the novels in other contemporary literatures, *Moby-Dick* is essentially American. There is the vast range of reference the work commands. One feels that, in order to present his symbols in their full authority of mysterious power, Melville has ransacked all relevant knowledge wherever he has found it. He has taken as his province the whole world and all history. Without ever formulating it, he seems to be working according to the conception of tradition as we find it stated in T. S. Eliot's essay, "Tradition and the Individual Talent". Tradition, Eliot says:

> cannot be inherited, and if you want it you must obtain it by great labour. It involves, in the first place, the historical sense . . .; and the historical sense involves a perception not only of the pastness of the past, but of its presence; the historical sense compels a man to write not merely with his own generation in his bones, but with a feeling that the whole of the literature of Europe from Homer and within it the whole of the literature of his own country has a simultaneous existence and composes a simultaneous order. This historical sense which is a sense of the timeless as well as the temporal and of the temporal and timeless together, is what makes a writer most acutely conscious of his place in time, of his own contemporaneity.

Now this, it seems to me, is a statement on tradition very unlike anything an English poet would have made. It is the statement of a man who sees himself in some sense the heir of all literatures, all countries, all histories, who feels, as Walt Whitman said, that "the American poets are to enclose old and new, for America is the race of races". And in fact, when all differences in form and intentions are taken into account, we can see Melville anticipating in *Moby-Dick* the practice of American poets like Eliot in *The Waste Land* and Ezra Pound generally, anticipating them in their learning and their eclecticism; like them, he takes what is suitable for his purposes from wherever he finds it, and he does not confine himself to Anglo-Saxon literature alone. This comes out, too, in terms of style. By mid-nineteenth-century English standards, Hawthorne's prose was somewhat archaic, in part no doubt deliberately so; it was dictated by the nature of his subject-matter. But Melville's, which is unlike that of any prose-writer of his time, is something quite different; it is based very largely on the prose of the early seventeenth-century and on Shakespeare. Yet for all the antiquity of its models, it is a new kind of prose, the prose one might almost say, of a man who is forging his own manner of expression by a conscious and deliberate choice of what the past offers him.

Above all, there is a kind of daring, an imaginative freedom, in the novel that seems to set Melville apart from his European contemporaries. Lewis Mumford expresses it when he describes *Moby-Dick* as "one of the first great mythologies to be created in the modern world, created, that is, out of the stuff of that world, its science, its exploration, its terrestrial daring, its concentration upon power and domination over nature, and not out of ancient symbols, Prometheus, Endymion, Orestes, or medieval folk-legends, like Dr Faustus". This is not to say that *Moby-Dick* is the greatest novel of the nineteenth century or the only great mythology of the modern world the age created. There are many others, Tolstoy's, Dostoevsky's, Dickens's, Hardy's; nevertheless, Melville's is the most surprising of them all and the most original in the sense that it was the least predictable. It could, one feels, have been produced only by an American and at that point in American history.

[24]

Simultaneously with Hawthorne's and Melville's practice of it, symbolism as a means of apprehending the nature of things and of man's place in it was being preached by a man who now seems very different from either of them but in fact influenced them both. The heritage of Calvinism was heavy on Hawthorne and Melville; the problem of evil is at the heart of their work. In this they seem now at the furthest possible remove from Ralph Waldo Emerson, the leading figure in the New England philosophic and literary movement known as Transcendentalism.

Emerson, who was born in Boston in 1803, came of a long line of New England ministers; but the family had broken with Calvinism before he was born, and his father was a Unitarian

minister. By 1800 Unitarianism had largely displaced Calvinism
as the dominant faith in Boston, though not in New England
generally. It represented an extreme reaction against Calvinism.
Unitarians did not accept the Trinity or believe that Christ was
the Son of God: he was merely a man, though the best that had
ever lived. Nor did Unitarians believe in original sin, and they
were resolutely opposed to the doctrine of unconditional election.
They stressed God's goodness, not His arbitrariness. For them
man was naturally good.

After graduating from Harvard, Emerson himself became a
Unitarian minister and for three years was pastor of the Second
Church, Boston. Then in 1832 he resigned his pastorate: the
tenets of the Unitarian Church, few though they were, were too
rigid for him. He found himself unwilling to administer Holy
Communion, and, as he said to his congregation, "It is my desire,
in the office of a Christian minister, to do nothing which I cannot
do with my whole heart. Having said this, I have said all. I
have no hostility to this intuition; I am only stating my want of
sympathy with it." He was not, in any real sense, a Christian
at all. But having resigned his pastorate, he made a pilgrimage
to England to meet his heroes Wordsworth, Coleridge and Carlyle.
Back in the United States, he bought his grandfather's house, the
Old Manse, in Concord, Massachusetts, where Hawthorne was
later to live, and began his career as a lecturer propagating his
interpretation of Transcendentalism. It has to be put like that,
since Transcendentalism was essentially a vague and loose doctrine
drawing upon the German idealist philosophers as interpreted by
Coleridge and Carlyle, upon Plato and Neo-Platonism, Sweden-
borg and Indian philosophy and mysticism.

Emerson appears in T. S. Eliot's early satirical poem, "Cousin
Nancy", as, along with Matthew Arnold, the "guardian of the
faith", the representative of "the army of unalterable law"; and
he was during his lifetime and for a generation after so much an
American institution that it is difficult now to see him in his full
significance. He was, in fact, in his attitude towards Europe and
the universe alike, the intellectual manifestation of the American
as Crèvecoeur's New Man. It is also not easy to see exactly what
kind of writer he was. He was not in any formal sense a philosopher. He is best seen, perhaps, as an American variant of the
Victorian figure that has been called the sage, of whom conspicuous examples are Carlyle, Ruskin and Matthew Arnold, ethical
teachers whose teachings are based on their own powerful

intuitions into the meaning of things and are effective through the brilliantly idiosyncratic expression of them, so that they persuade, when they do persuade, not so much by logical discourse as by a characteristic literary style. Their meaning is conveyed as much by the way they write as by what they write.

Emerson found his own form of expression, and it was a new one. We read him now as an essayist—inevitably. But he was primarily a lecturer, or a preacher of lay sermons. He travelled the length and breadth of the United States, by rail, stagecoach, steamboat, canal boat, sledge—once he even had to cross the Mississippi on foot—to deliver his lectures; and what we read are the lectures refined as it were after many renderings. But the spoken voice is still strong in them. The impression the essays sometimes create has been described as "a patchwork of aphorisms more dazzling than coherent". We know from his journals that he built up his lectures from aphorisms, and the lectures, one can see, must have been stunning oratorical displays, enormously effective to the ear, aphorism piled upon aphorism, illustration upon illustration. It is only when they are read that the lack of logical structure, of coherence, becomes troublesome.

In any event, he proceeded not by logic and formal structure but by his intuitions, and he flung down his challenge to the world in the first sentences of his first essay, *Nature*, published anonymously in 1836:

> Our age is retrospective. It builds the sepulchres of the fathers. It writes biographies, histories, and criticism. The foregoing generations beheld God and nature face to face; we through their eyes. Why should we not also enjoy an original relation to the universe? Why should not we have a poetry and philosophy of insight and not of tradition, and a religion by revelation to us, and not the history of theirs? . . . The sun shines today also. There is more wool and flax in the fields. There are new lands, new men, new thoughts. Let us demand our own works and laws and worship.

In the light of the rest of the essay and of Emerson's works generally one could fairly expand that last sentence slightly to read: "Let us have our own American works and laws and worship." Emerson is demanding a new and continuing revelation for a new people in a new land, a revelation for Americans.

Almost everything Emerson was later to write is contained by implication in *Nature*. He asserts "the unity of Nature,—the unity in variety,—which meets us everywhere", and claims that Nature is, "to us, the present expositor of the divine mind". It is through Nature that God speaks. He asserts also the oneness of God and man when man sees Nature truly. And here he puts forward a view of man in relation to God and Nature very close to Wordsworth's in the Immortality Ode:

> To speak truly, few adult persons can see nature. Most persons do not see the sun. At least they have a very superficial seeing. The sun illuminates only the eye of man, but shines into the eye and the heart of the child. The lover of nature is he whose inward and outward senses are still truly adjusted to each other; who has retained the spirit of infancy even into the era of manhood. His intercourse with heaven and earth becomes part of his daily food. In the presence of nature a wild delight runs through the man in spite of real sorrows. Nature says—he is my creature, and maugre all his impertinent griefs, he shall be glad with me.

How important in the development of American writing is the premium Emerson puts on the child and the child's eye will be clear later. As in Wordsworth, "the child is father to the man", and childhood the higher state. Emerson goes on:

> In the woods, too, a man casts off his years, as the snake his slough, and at what period soever of life, is always a child. In the woods is perpetual youth. . . . In the woods, we return to reason and faith. There I feel that nothing can befall me in life, no disgrace, no calamity (leaving me my eyes), which nature cannot repair. Standing on the bare ground—my head bathed by the blithe air, and uplifted into infinite space—all mean egotism vanishes. I become a transparent eye-ball; I am nothing; I see all; the currents of Universal Being circulate through me; I am part and parcel of God.

Important here, apart from the vision of man as being part of God once he has cast off the outer skin of custom and habit, is Emerson's emphasis on the eye as the organ of truth. This is fundamental to his thought and to much in American literature.

Perhaps the key passage of the essay occurs in the section on language, in which Emerson states:

1. Words are signs of natural facts.
2. Particular natural facts are symbols of particular spiritual facts.
3. Nature is the symbol of spirit.

He continues:

> It is not words only that are emblematic; it is things which are
> emblematic. Every nature fact is a symbol of some spiritual fact.
> Every appearance in nature corresponds to some state of the mind,
> and that state of the mind can only be described by presenting that
> natural appearance as its picture. . . . Man is an analogist, and studies
> relations in all objects. He is placed in the centre of beings, and a
> ray of relation passes from every other being to him. And neither
> can man be understood without these objects, nor these objects
> without man.

The affinity with Hawthorne's and Melville's ways of symbolically interpreting man and nature is obvious; while the
insistence on the importance of the fact, the thing seen, looks
forward to later American writers such as the Imagist poets and
William Carlos Williams—"No ideas but in things," said Williams.
Facts themselves, things seen, seem to have a mystical value in
themselves.

Emerson's view of life is nothing if not optimistic. Indeed,
it is this more than anything else, perhaps, that comes between
him and many of us today. Evil scarcely exists for Emerson and
seems to be nothing more than the illusion bred by wrong
thinking:

> Build therefore your own world. As fast as you conform your
> life to the pure idea in your mind, that will unfold its great pro-
> portions. A correspondent revolution in things will attend the
> influx of the spirit. So fast will disagreeable appearances, swine,
> spiders, snakes, pests, madhouses, prisons, enemies, vanish; they
> are temporary and shall be no more seen.

The attitude towards evil expressed here is not far from that of
Christian Science, which is one of the two native American
religions and was founded in Boston in 1879.

But there is something else, which is brought out in the
sentences immediately preceding the quotation above:

> Know then that the world exists for you. For you is the pheno-
> menon perfect. What we are, that only can we see. All that Adam
> had, all that Caesar could, you have and can do. Adam called his
> house, heaven and earth; Caesar called his house, Rome; you
> perhaps call yours, a cobbler's trade; a hundred acres of ploughed
> land; or a scholar's garret. Yet line for line and point for point
> your dominion is as great as theirs, though without fine names. . . .

For Emerson, man's relation with the universe is entirely individualistic. It depends on a man's being himself, as we say, to his uttermost. So Emerson's view of man is essentially democratic, egalitarian, anti-authoritarian. Indeed, in the essay, "Self-Reliance", Emerson appears as the apostle of extreme individualism, even to the extent of his saying: "The gospel of hatred must be preached, as the counteraction of the doctrine of love, when that pules and whines. I shun father and mother and wife and brother when my genius calls me." In consequence, he is the apostle, too, of extreme nonconformity even when it takes the form of what might be called democratic truculence: "The nonchalance of boys who are sure of a good dinner, and would disdain as much as a lord to do or say aught to conciliate one, is the healthy attitude of human nature." Again the measure he is applying to human behaviour is that of childhood; the boy is "Nature's priest" is Wordsworth's phrase. But the man, Emerson says, "is as it were clapped into jail by his consciousness," his consciousness of others, of public opinion:

Society everywhere is in conspiracy against the manhood of every one of its members. Society is a joint-stock company, in which the members agree, for the better securing of his bread to each shareholder, to surrender the liberty and the culture of the eater. The virtue in most request is conformity. Self-reliance is its aversion. It loves not realities and creators, but names and customs.

Whoso would be a man, must be a nonconformist. . . . Nothing is at last sacred but the integrity of your own mind.

In his essay "The American Scholar", Emerson translates the theme of self-reliance to the national plane and produces what Oliver Wendell Holmes called "our intellectual Declaration of Independence". An attack on pedantry and traditionalism in literature and scholarship, it stresses the need for a modern democratic literature ("I embrace the common, I explore and sit at the feet of the unfamiliar, the low. Give me insight into today, and you may have the antique and future worlds."), announces, "We have listened too long to the courtly muses of Europe," and declares:

We will walk on our feet; we will work with our own hands; we will speak our own minds. The study of letters shall no longer be a name for pity, for doubt, and for sensual indulgence. The dread of man and the love of man shall be a wall of defence and a wreath of joy around all. A nation of men will for the first time exist, because each believes himself inspired by the Divine Soul which also inspires all men.

[25]

In many respects, Emersonian man, as depicted in "Self-Reliance" and "The American Scholar", appeared in the flesh in the person of his younger friend, Henry Thoreau. It even seems significant that, whereas Emerson bought a house in Concord, Thoreau was actually born there and stayed there as long as he lived; as he said in an entirely characteristic phrase, "I have travelled a good deal in Concord". Emerson was the philosopher, the preacher, telling men what they should do, from the height of his pulpit or podium, in a language that, though concrete enough, still exists in the realm of generalities: Thoreau was the man who went out and did, who turned precept into practice. One of the greatest of phrase-makers, he wrote: "If a man does not keep pace with his companions, perhaps it is because he hears a different drummer." Throughout his life Thoreau marched to a different drummer. He remains, and it is here that the great part of his value still lies, the arch-individualist, the complete noncomformist.

Born in 1817, he came of stock which included Yankee, Channel-Island French and Scots, Puritan and Quaker. After graduating from Harvard, he took up no profession. For a time he taught school; he made a trip by rowing boat up the Concord and Merrimack Rivers, which gave him the material of his first book; from 1841 to 1843 he worked as Emerson's gardener, tutored his children and helped in the editing of the Transcendentalist monthly magazine, *The Dial*. But mostly he supported himself by following his father's trade of making lead-pencils. His aim was to keep himself free. Then, in July, 1845, he built himself a hut at Walden, on the outskirts of Concord, and lived there alone until the September of the following year. It was while there that he was arrested for refusing to pay his poll-tax.

He did so as a gesture against the Mexican War, the institution of slavery and the American Government's treatment of the Indians. To co-operate with government when government is behaving unjustly, he argued, is to condone its crimes, and an "honest man," he said, "must withdraw from his partnership." In fact, he spent only one night in jail, for a friend paid his tax for him; but the essay it inspired, *Civil Disobedience*, which develops the idea of passive resistance, was to influence both Tolstoy and Gandhi and remains one of the great statements on man's duty to his conscience.

But Thoreau's reputation rests mainly on *Walden, Or Life in the Woods*, his account of his twenty-six months at Walden Pond. In the sojourn itself there was nothing very remarkable, and it is easy to make Thoreau appear absurd or even a phony. After all, he was less than two miles away from a village that contained more than the usual proportion of distinguished minds, Emerson and Hawthorne among them. He had not cut himself off from their society; he had not retreated into the wilderness but remained, as has been said, "almost within smell of his mother's cooking." As an experiment in living, the sojourn at Walden, hostile critics have suggested, was largely an exercise in make-believe. The Concord woods were far from being the frontier; the test Thoreau set himself by living there was hardly a challenging one.

But this is to misconceive Thoreau's purpose. There was nothing dramatic about it; if he was attempting to prove anything at all it was to himself, not to the outside world, and for the purpose a hut in Emerson's back-garden was as good as a log cabin on the Iowa River. As he says himself:

> I went to the woods because I wished to live deliberately, to front only the essential facts of life, and see if I could not learn what it had to teach, and not, when I came to die, discover that I had not lived. I did not wish to live what was not life, living is so dear; nor did I wish to practise resignation, unless it was quite necessary. I wanted to live deep and suck out all the marrow of life, to live so sturdily and Spartan-like as to put to rout all that was no life, to cut a broad swath and shave close, to drive life into a corner, and reduce it to its lowest terms, and, if it proved to be mean, why then to get the whole and genuine meanness of it, and publish its meanness to the world; or if it were sublime, to know it by experience, and to be able to give a true account of it in my next excursion.

"I did not wish to live what was not life." It seemed to Thoreau that the overwhelming mass of men lived lives that were not life; they lived "meanly, like ants". "Our life," he says, "is frittered away by detail," by shams and delusions; by work—and "as for *work*, we haven't any of any consequence"; by an obsession with the passing of time as evidenced in waiting for letters—"To speak critically, I never received more than one or two letters in my life that were worth the postage"—and reading the news-papers: "To a philosopher all *news*, as it is called, is gossip, and they who edit and read it are old women over their tea." But what is worth a man's attention? The answer is one that strikingly parallels Emerson's thinking:

> God himself culminates in the present moment, and will never be more divine in the lapse of all the ages. And we are enabled to apprehend at all what is sublime and noble only by the perpetual instilling and drenching of the reality that surrounds us. The universe constantly and obediently answers to our conceptions; whether we travel fast or slow, track is laid for us. Let us spend our lives in conceiving then. The poet or the artist never yet had so fair and noble a design but some of his posterity at least could accomplish it.

The reality that surrounds us is, of course, nature, though, as Tony Tanner has pointed out in *The Reign of Wonder*, Thoreau's nature is not quite Emerson's. It is not a "revelatory symbol of some ubiquitous divinity" but as it were an end in itself, sufficient to itself, which "offered him symbols of his own internal life . . . conveyed to him intimations of things spiritual and powers in-finite". As Tanner says: "He did not wish to be merged with the Over-Soul but rather to become as fine as the hawk." But, as much as in Emerson, there is the emphasis on the wisdom of the eye:

> As I sit at my window this summer afternoon, hawks are circling about my clearing; the tantivy of wild pigeons, flying by twos and threes athwart my view, or perching restless on the white pine boughs behind my house, gives a voice on the air; a fish-hawk dimples the glassy surface of the pond and brings up a fish; a mink steals out of the marsh before my door and seizes a frog by the shore; the sedge is bending under the weight of the reed-birds flitting hither and thither; and for the last half hour I have heard the rattle of railroad cars, now dying away and then reviving like the beat of a partridge, conveying travellers from Boston to the country.

Indeed, the emphasis Thoreau sets on the eye seems greater even than in Emerson, simply because the visual detail is so much more concrete, rendered so much more vividly and exactly. Thoreau is a man seeing: in comparison with him, Emerson a man talking about seeing.

Yet *Walden* is very much applied Emerson. Along with the emphasis on the eye goes the emphasis, which is really part and parcel of it, on the necessity of direct experience, for which, as Emerson claims in "The American Scholar", book-learning is no substitute at all; it may indeed be a barrier between man and reality. Thoreau gives us his description of the Canadian who visits him, "a wood-chopper and post-maker, who can hole fifty posts in a day, who made his last supper on a woodchuck which his dog caught". The Canadian is not illiterate, "but when Nature made him, she gave him a strong body and contentment for his portion, and propped him on every side with reverence and reliance, that he might live out his threescore years and ten a child. He was so genuine and unsophisticated that no introduction would serve to introduce him, more than if you introduced a woodchuck to your neighbour." Yet he reminded a townsman of "a prince in disguise", and Thoreau found his thinking, "so primitive and immersed in his animal life", "more promising than a merely learned man's". The Canadian is one with nature because he has remained a child; which again takes us back to Emerson.

In the last section of *Walden* Thoreau writes:

I learned this, at least, by my experiment: that if one advances confidently in the direction of his dreams, and endeavours to live the life which he has imagined, he will meet with a success unexpected in common hours. He will put something behind, will pass an invisible boundary; new, universal, and more liberal laws will begin to establish themselves around and within him; or the old laws be expanded, and interpreted in his favour in a more literal sense, and he will live with the license of a higher order of beings. In proportion as he simplifies his life, the laws of the universe will appear less complex, and solitude will not be solitude, nor poverty poverty, nor weakness weakness. If you have built castles in the air, your work need not be lost; that is where they should be. Now put the foundations under them.

[26]

Both Emerson and Thoreau on occasion wrote poetry, and though it is fair to say that it was a by-product of their prose, it is much more considerable than it is sometimes said to be. It is idiosyncratic in a way that most American poetry of the time was not and can be seen now as genuinely American utterance. The verse of both is laconic and compressed, direct and conversational, the voice behind it a New England voice. In the tone of its speech, in individual lines particularly, it looks forward to a later New England poet, Robert Frost, as in these lines of Thoreau's:

> Far in yon hazy field there stands a barn,
> Unanxious hens improve the sultry hour
> And with contented voice now brag their dead—
> A new laid egg—Now let the sun decline—
> They'll lay another by tomorrow's sun.

The first three lines are conventional enough, but in its casually conversational tone the last would not surprise us if we met it in Frost.

But neither was anything approaching the American poet that Emerson had demanded of the times. The poet appeared in 1855, significantly on July 4, with the first edition of *Leaves of Grass*. There was no author's name on the title-page but opposite it was a daguerreotype of a bearded workman in his shirt-sleeves. One hand is in his pocket, the other on his hip. His hat is tilted at a rakish angle; he is nothing if not nonchalant. The absence of the poet's name together with the poet's photograph constitutes a sort of manifesto. This is a different kind of poet, the spokesman of ordinary people with whom, as the photograph shows, he identifies himself. Those who bothered to read the book discovered its author was

Walt Whitman, a Kosmos, of Manhattan the son,
Turbulent, fleshy, sensual, eating drinking and breeding,
No sentimentalist, no stander above men and women or apart
    from them,
No more modest than immodest.

There had been no poetry like it before in the English language. Emerson recognised its quality immediately but for a quarter of a century it was largely a scandal in the United States, even to the point of its being banned in 1881, though it was greeted with enthusiasm in England by Tennyson, Swinburne and William Rossetti.

Whitman was consciously the American as New Man and the poet of the New Man. What he was up to was made quite plain in his introduction to the first edition of *Leaves of Grass*, and it was reiterated in the essay "A Backward Glance O'er Travel'd Roads" written four years before his death in 1892. Though the matter of the introduction may derive from Emerson, it is expressed with a confidence, boldness and exuberance far beyond Emerson. It sets out Whitman's specifications for the "great", at times "greatest" poet—who is Whitman himself. He begins by asserting that "America does not repel the past or what it has produced under its forms or amid other politics or the idea of castes or the old religion", but then in the second paragraph announces:

> The Americans of all nations at any time upon the earth have probably the fullest poetical nature. The United States are themselves essentially the greatest poem. In the history of the earth hitherto the largest and most stirring appear tame and orderly to their ampler largeness and stir. Here at last is something in the doings of man that corresponds with the broadcast doings of the day and night. Here is not merely a nation but a teeming nation of nations.

And in his third paragraph he describes the nature of Americans:

> Other states indicate themselves in their deputies . . . but the genius of the United States is not best or most in its executives or legislatures, nor in its ambassadors or authors or colleges or churches or parlours, nor even in its common people. Their manners speech dress friendships—the freshness and candour of their physiognomy —the picturesque looseness of their carriage . . . their deathless attachment to freedom—their aversion to anything indecorous or

soft or mean—the practical acknowledgement of the citizens of one state by the citizens of all other states—the fierceness of their roused resentment—their curiosity and welcome of novelty—their self-esteem and wonderful sympathy—their susceptibility to a slight —the air they have of persons who have never known how it felt to stand in the presence of superiors—the fluency of their speech— their delight in music, the sure symptom of manly tenderness and native elegance of soul . . . their good temper and openhandedness— the terrible significance of their elections—the President's taking off his hat to them not they to him—these too are unrhymed poetry. It awaits the gigantic and generous treatment worthy of it.

So he goes on, in full spate, for a score of pages, not in argument but in rhapsodic assertion of a nationalism that is so lofty, because the evocation of an ideal America, that it cannot be called chauvinism:

The American poets are to enclose old and new for America is the race of races. Of them a bard is to be commensurate with the people. To him the other continents arrive as contributions.

Or, taking up an emphasis familiar in Emerson and Thoreau:

The greatest poet hardly knows pettiness or triviality. If he breathes into any thing that was before thought small it dilates with the grandeur and life of the universe. He is a seer . . . he is complete in himself . . . the others are as good as he, only he sees it and they do not. He is not one of the chorus . . . he does not stop for any regulations . . . he is the president of regulation. What the eyesight does to the rest he does to the rest. Who knows the curious mystery of the eyesight? The other senses corroborate themselves, but this is removed from any proof but its own and foreruns the identities of the spiritual world. A single glance of it mocks all the investigations of man and all the instruments and books of the earth and all reasoning. What is marvellous? what is unlikely? what is impossible or baseless or vague? after you have once just opened the space of a peachpit and given audience to far and near and to the sunset and had all things enter with electric swiftness softly and duly without confusion or jostling or jam.

Again, and here too the note of all-embracing acceptance takes us back to Emerson and Thoreau:

The known universe has one complete lover and that is the greatest poet. He consumes an eternal passion and is indifferent which chance happens and which possible contingency of fortune or misfortune and persuades daily and hourly his delicious pay. What baulks or breaks others is fuel to his burning progress to contact and amorous joy. Other proportions of the reception of pleasure dwindle to nothing in his proportions. All expected from heaven or from the highest he is rapport with in the sight of the daybreak or a scene of the winter woods or the presence of children playing or with his arm round the neck of a man or woman.

In "A Backward Glance" Whitman surveys the intentions of his youth rather more soberly:

> I found myself possessed, at the age of thirty-one to thirty-three, with a special desire and conviction. . . . This was a feeling or ambition to articulate and faithfully express in literary or poetic form, and uncompromisingly, my own physical, emotional, moral, intellectual, and aesthetic Personality, in the midst of, and tallying, the momentous spirit and facts of its immediate days, and of current America—and to exploit that Personality, identified with place and date, in a far more candid and comprehensive sense than any hitherto poem or book.

He is, in other words, putting himself forward as the representative American; his poetic personality tallies, i.e., corresponds exactly, with the spirit of America. To express this, "new poetic messages, new forms and expressions", were inevitable, for, "of the great poems receiv'd from abroad and from the ages, and today enveloping and penetrating America", there was none consistent with the United States or "essentially applicable to them as they are and are to be". Even Shakespeare "belongs essentially to the buried past".

> Defiant of ostensible literary and other conventions, I avowedly chant 'the great pride of man in himself', and permit it to be more or less a *motif* of nearly all my verse. I think this pride indispensable to an American.

It is indispensable, he goes on to say, permitting himself a note of criticism of democracy unheard in the introduction to *Leaves of Grass*, because democracy's "first instincts are fain to clip, conform, bring in stragglers, and reduce everything to a dead level".

The longest poem in *Leaves of Grass*, which remained the overall title of his poems, though more and more were added to editions following the original in 1855, is "Song of Myself".

It is not Whitman's supreme achievement in poetry; that is probably the magnificent elegy on President Lincoln, "When Lilacs Last in the Dooryard Bloom'd"; but it is the fundamental Whitman, the poem above all those he wrote that he envisaged the "greatest poet" of the introduction as making.

But here a word about Whitman the man seems necessary. In the first section, or movement, of "Song of Myself", he presents himself as essentially American:

> My tongue, every atom of my blood, form'd from this
> soil, this air,
> Born here of parents born here from parents the same,
> and their parents the same.

Born on Long Island in 1819, he was of mixed English and Dutch descent, the second son of the nine children of a carpenter who never found it easy to support his family. The Whitmans moved to Brooklyn, then the rival city of New York, upon which it looked from the other side of the Hudson. Whitman left school when he was twelve and was apprenticed to the printing trade. For the next twenty years, apart from two years in which he taught school on Long Island, he earned his living as a printer and journalist, occupations almost interchangeable at that time in the United States. For a time he was editor of the Brooklyn *Eagle*, and when he lost his job because of a political difference with the proprietors, he went by train, stagecoach and steamboat to New Orleans, where he worked as a journalist on the *Crescent*. He returned to Brooklyn by way of Chicago, the Great Lakes and the Hudson River to become editor of another Brooklyn paper, *The Freeman*. Again, his political convictions—he was a Free-soiler, opposed, that is, to the extension of slavery to territories acquired as a result of the Mexican War—forced him to give up his editorship and he joined his father as a carpenter and builder. During the Civil War he worked as a nurse both in the field and in military hospitals in Washington, experiences which gave him the material for his prose work, *Specimen Days*, one of the most memorable books inspired by the War. He stayed on in Washington as a government clerk employed first in the Indian Bureau, until he was fired by the Secretary of the Interior, who happened to read some of his poetry and was morally outraged by it, and then in a sinecure post in the Office of the Attorney-General. In 1873, after a stroke, he retired to Camden, New Jersey.

Lack of formal education did not prevent him from being widely read both in literature and in the sciences. His imagination responded eagerly to the ideas of evolution which were everywhere at the time; and his works in this respect comprise another of the great mythologies of the modern world created, as Mumford says of *Moby-Dick*, "out of the stuff of that world, its science, its exploration, its terrestial daring". How eagerly he responded, and with what results, are easily seen if his poetry is set side by side with Tennyson's *In Memoriam*, which appeared five years earlier than *Leaves of Grass* and is altogether more cautious and apprehensive in the face of evolution.

Whitman's identification of himself with the common man was not literary affectation. He was a great wanderer of the streets of Brooklyn and Manhattan, a great rider of the Brooklyn Ferry and of Broadway omnibuses. He was a man who needed to rub shoulders with his fellows, and one of his greatest qualities was his power of empathy, his ability not only to feel with but also to feel into the characters of the human scene, so that he seems to become them at will. His great line in "Song of Myself", "I am the man, I suffer'd, I was there", is the simple truth about him.

"I was simmering, simmering, simmering," he said; "Emerson brought me to the boil." But whatever he got from Emerson he made his own and treated in his own way. There is an obvious contrast here with Emerson's other disciple, Thoreau. Thoreau reduced the world to the narrow confines of Walden and yet made it a microcosm of the world. Whitman, on the other hand, takes the whole of the United States and indeed the whole of time as his province; he recognises no limits. The one contracts; the other expands.

"Song of Myself" is a poem of 1,855 lines built up of fifty-two stanzas or sections ranging in length from a dozen lines or so to as many as one hundred and fifty. It is, as the title indicates, a celebration of himself; but the Walt Whitman who stalks or rather, to use a favourite word, "loafes" through the poem is not quite the Whitman of actuality. He is the "greatest poet", in other words an ideal being, and sometimes the function he fulfils seems uncannily like that of Tiresias in T. S. Eliot's *The Waste Land*, who, as Eliot writes, "although a mere spectator and not indeed a 'character', is yet the most important personage in the poem, uniting all the rest. . . . The two sexes meet in Tiresias. What Tiresias *sees*, in fact, is the substance of the poem." Certainly what Walt Whitman, the "I" of "Song of Myself", sees is the substance of Whitman's poems.

"Song of Myself" is a poem of acceptance; indeed there are no limits to Whitman's acceptance. As much as Blake, he might have cried, "Everything that lives is holy." The key image to the poem is that of grass—hence the overall title of Whitman's poems. It receives its fullest treatment in the sixth stanza:

A child said *What is the grass?* fetching it to me with full hands,
How could I answer the child? I do not know what it is any more than he.

I guess it must be the flag of my disposition, out of hopeful green stuff woven.

Or I guess it is the handkerchief of the Lord,
A scented gift and remembrancer designedly dropt,
Bearing the owner's name someway in the corners, that we may see and remark and say *Whose?*

Or I guess the grass is itself a child, the produced babe of the vegetation.

Or I guess it is a uniform hieroglyphic,
And it means, Sprouting alike in broad zones and narrow zones,
Growing among black folks as among white,
Kanuck, Tuckahoe, Congressman, Cuff, I give them the same, I receive them the same.

And now it seems to me the beautiful uncut hair of graves.

Tenderly will I use you curling grass,
It may be you transpire from the breasts of young men,
It may be if I have known them, I would have loved them,
It may be you are from old people, or from offspring taken soon out of their mother's laps,
And here you are the mothers' laps.

This grass is very dark to be from the white heads of old mothers,
Darker than the colourless beards of old men,
Dark to come from under the faint red roofs of mouths.
O I perceive after all so many uttering tongues,
And I perceive they do not come from the roofs of mouths for nothing.

I wish I could translate the hints about the dead young men and
women,
And the hints about the old men and mothers, and the offspring
taken soon out of their laps.

What do you think has become of the young and old men?
And what do you think has become of the women and children?

They are alive and well somewhere,
The smallest sprout shows there is really no death,
And if ever there was it led forward life and does not wait at the end
to arrest it,
And ceas'd the moment life appear'd.

All goes onward and outward, nothing collapses.
And to die is different from what any one supposed, and luckier.

Grass is the symbol of life, of the promise of life and the
continuity of life. It sums up in itself birth, death and resurrec-
tion. It is the great uniting element, growing among all men of
all races and colour, and it is God's, "the handkerchief of the
Lord", his name written on it. To accept grass is to accept the
cycle of life and death in its totality, with the proviso that it
is life, not death, that is the reality; death is merely a stage on
the way to further life.

And once this is accepted, everything can be accepted, and in
the poem Whitman traverses the United States accepting everything. He not only accepts, he rejoices in what he accepts: "I am
satisfied—I see, dance, laugh, sing." And first he accepts himself,
his body and his soul equally:

I believe in you my soul, the other I am must not abase itself to you,
And you must not be abased to the other.

He is at once an individual and every man, and so, the implication
is clear, is everyone else. He "tramps a perpetual journey",
through space—the United States, through the course of the day
from dawn to dark, through the course of life to death, which is
the end of life but a new beginning:

The past and present wilt—I have fill'd them, emptied them,
And proceed to fill my next fold of the future. . . .

I bequeath myself to the dirt to grow from the grass I love,
If you want me again look for me under your boot-soles.

You will hardly know who I am or what I mean,
But I shall be good health to you nevertheless,
and filter and fibre your blood.

Failing to fetch me at first keep encouraged,
Missing me one place search another,
I stop somewhere waiting for you.

So the poem ends, and in the course of the eighteen hundred
and more lines that have gone before Whitman has celebrated,
in a sort of cosmic lyricism, life in many of its aspects; those that
are not there are those that his view of life prevented his seeing.
The celebration is always ecstatic; at times it reaches the heights
of lyrical affirmation:

I believe a leaf of grass is no less than the journey-work of the stars,
And the pismire is equally perfect, and a grain of sand, and the egg
    of the wren,
And the tree-toad is a chef d'oeuvre for the highest,
And the running blackberry would adorn the parlours of heaven,
And the narrowest hinge in my hand puts to scorn all machinery,
And the cow crunching with depressed head surpasses any statue,
And a mouse is miracle enough to stagger sextillions of infidels.

In that passage the specifically American theme is quite trans-
cended; we are in the presence of a mystical affirmation of the
holiness of life that is very close to William Blake's. But it is
because Whitman is capable of reaching such heights that he can
give us his panoramic picture of the teeming life, it seems, of
the whole United States; as in the remarkable fifteenth stanza
which begins "The pure contralto sings in the organ loft", and
goes on to pick out in sharp simple sentences images of men and
women at work, vignettes of domestic interiors, street scenes,
scenes of life in all parts of America. The stanza runs to sixty-
five lines and is a single sentence, the only punctuation, except
in parenthetical clauses, being the comma, until, three lines from
the end, we have a semi-colon to introduce the generalisation
from all the scenes that have gone before. The scenes, each of
which is enclosed in the single line, proceed like images in a film;
the whole stanza is an example, before the cinema existed, of

what might be called montage-writing, montage being the film-maker's technique of cutting from image to contrasted image, the separate images gaining in significance because of the mere fact of their juxtaposition with other images, as here:

> The prostitute draggles her shawl, her bonnet bobs on her tipsy and pimpled neck,
> The crowd laugh at her blackguard oaths, the men jeer and wink at her,
> (Miserable! I do not laugh at your oaths nor jeer you;)
> The President holding a cabinet council is surrounded by the great Secretaries,
> On the piazza walk three matrons stately and friendly with twined arms,
> The crew of the fish-smack pack repeated layers of halibut in the hold,
> The Missourian crosses the plains toting his wares and his cattle,
> As the fare-collector goes through the train he gives notice by the jingling of loose change,
> The floor-men are laying the floor, the tinners are tinning the roof, the masons are for mortar. . . .

Whitman builds up an impression of life going on simultaneously at many levels, but from the very way in which the picture is built up no single image of life is of greater value than any other; the matrons stately and friendly are as important as the President.   The total picture is of egalitarian democracy going about its business.

In other stanzas he picks up specific, as it were representative, episodes in American life and history, placing himself at their centre.   Saying "I was the man, I suffer'd, I was there", he is also able to say, "I am the hounded slave, I wince at the bite of the dogs".   In the thirty-fourth stanza that follows, he tells the story of the "murder in cold blood of four hundred and twelve young men" by the Mexicans. "Now I tell what I knew in Texas in my early youth"; and he ends:

> At eleven o'clock began the burning of the bodies;
> That is the tale of the murder of the four hundred and twelve young men.

In the two stanzas that follow he tells of a sea-battle between an American and an English ship presumably during the Revolutionary War.   In the next stanza he becomes a convict.   I "see myself in prison shaped like another man . . . Not a youngster is taken for larceny but I go up too, and am tried and sentenced."

For all it is a poem, "Song of Myself" remains in its all-inclusiveness in many ways the nearest any American writer has got to writing "the Great American Novel", a well-worn phrase first used, it seems, in 1868, and in a very real sense the pattern for the attempts made in this century to write it, by Thomas Wolfe in *Look Homeward, Angel* and John Dos Passos in *U.S.A.*

It is, of course, impossible to separate what a poet says from the way in which he says it. Whitman's form was as revolutionary as his content and met with as much resistance from the established taste of his times. It doesn't seem accidental that the very few poems he wrote in conventional metre and rhyme are very poor indeed, scarcely competent, including the famous poem on Lincoln, "O Captain, My Captain". He had to forge for himself a new form. Resemblances to it can be found; there is some affinity with the verse of Blake's prophetic books; but what seems the real kinship with Whitman's free verse, and probably its main source, is ancient Hebrew poetry as we know it through the Old Testament, in the Psalms especially. Like the translators of the King James's Bible, Whitman rejects metre and rhyme, which is not to say he rejects rhythm. He is a master of rhythm, which, as it must be in all poetry, is the unifying element of his verse, for all its apparent irregularity. The unit of his verse is the line, which is as a general rule complete in itself; it normally ends with a comma. His mastery is shown by the way in which he can vary and extend the length of the line at will. It has been pointed out that Whitman evolved his technique at a time when Americans were particularly "space-conscious". Within the decade immediately before the first publication of *Leaves of Grass* both the Oregon and Californian territories had been brought into the Union, and Whitman's long line is his expression, it has been suggested, of his space-consciousness. Certainly his line and the movement—one can scarcely use the word "stanza", which calls up a regularity, a formal pattern, alien to it—of which the line is the unit render incomparably the feeling of space, distance and movement, a fact which makes him among other things so superb a poet of the sea. His art is a cumulative one. It owes something, it has often been surmised, to operatic aria; and in "Song of Myself" especially it is oratorical, since the poet is seeing himself as a bard addressing democracy, a whole people.

It is also, as we have seen, an intensely visual poetry, "made up

of hundreds of brief descriptions", "snapshots of experience—
real or fictitious", each one fixed generally in the single line. But,
as we have seen, the way in which Whitman uses his snapshots,
his individual images, looks forward to the movie-director's use
of the camera. They exist in continuous flow, like beats in music.

And the use of language is as new as the verse-forms. Besides
the intensely physical quality of the words used, which is common
to all poetry—

> The blab of the pave, the tires of the carts and sluff of bootsoles
>   and talk of the promenaders,
> The heavy omnibus, the driver with his interrogating thumb, the
>   clank of the shod horses on the granite floor—

there is an attitude to language that cannot be paralleled in any
other American or English poetry of his time. He is not writing
as a scholar, like Emerson. He intends to use the whole available
language of his time, the demotic speech of the streets, the
language of editorials and political speeches, the jargon of the
sciences. No word is alien to him; he delights in technical terms,
the lore of trades and skills. It is an aspect of his appreciation
of democracy. And he goes beyond this. He draws upon non-
English words, French, Italian, Spanish. Admittedly the words
he uses are not such as to suggest a wide knowledge of the
languages in question, and one scarcely ever feels that they come
naturally to his lips; but it is easy to see what he is after: it is a
way of indicating America as "the race of races", the melting-pot.

Like any other poet, Whitman is assailable. Some famous
early criticisms now seem not quite to the point. Emerson's
comment, "I expected him to make the songs of the nation but
he seems content to make the inventories," suggests an incom-
plete understanding. The inventories, dazzling achievements as
they are, are an integral part of the songs. The criticism of the
Southern poet, Sidney Lanier, who said that Whitman's argument
seemed to be that "because a prairie is wide, therefore debauchery
is admirable, and because the Mississippi is long, therefore every
American is God", is more damaging. Whitman did not always
distinguish the bard in himself from the booster, and perhaps
indeed the booster was part of his conception of the bard.

There are more fundamental criticisms that can be made.
But these are criticisms of underlying attitudes and assumptions.
At the poetic level, the main criticisms must be of Whitman's
lapses in taste, which particularly disfigure "Song of Myself".

At times, for instance, he seems to come altogether too close to identifying himself with Christ. And for all the frankness of his treatment of the body—and here he is one of the great emancipators—when he deals with sex there is often an ambiguity which has bothered readers from the earliest days, an ambiguity rising, it is difficult not to think, from a refusal or an inability to be entirely honest about himself. He ought, one feels, to have said less if he could not say more. All the same, the greatness of what he achieved as an American Spokesman remains, and so does the greatness of the poetry.

[27]

Among other things, Whitman brought American poetry into world poetry. So too, in a wholly different way, did Edgar Allan Poe, his elder by ten years. Ironically, since Whitman is the great yea-sayer to life while Poe often seems the pornographer of death, Whitman was the one eminent American writer to attend, in 1877, the dedication of the monument to Poe at Baltimore, where the older poet had died mysteriously twenty-eight years earlier. Poe has always been a source of embarrassment to Anglo-Saxon critics; they have rarely found it possible to reconcile his actual achievement with the enthusiasm it aroused in such great French poets as Baudelaire and Mallarmé. The Poe the non-Anglo-Saxon knows often seems their invention. Of course it is not so. However meretricious it may seem to us, it was from Poe's poetry, together with his literary criticism, that they derived their own principles of poetry, their theory of symbolism, which is rather different from American symbolism. Poe was a man of genius if ever there was one. He was among other things the virtual inventor of the detective story and of what we now call science fiction. He was also the first American, indeed almost the first poet of any nationality, to see himself consciously as the artist as man apart, *le poète maudit, maudit* precisely because *poète*.

No doubt this is partly explained by the facts of his early life. If not literally, at any rate psychologically, he suffered the loss of two mothers, both of whom were betrayed by their husbands. He was born in Boston of parents who were both actors. He was two when his father deserted wife and family. The boy's mother died at Richmond, Virginia, and though never legally adopted, Poe was taken into the family of a Richmond tobacco merchant, John Allan, seemingly at Mrs Allan's behest. When he was six he was taken to England and for five years was at school at Stoke Newington, in London, where he was known by his foster-father's name. On the Allans' return to Richmond, he was sent to school there. He was deeply attached to Mrs Allan, to whom Mr Allan was unfaithful; and man and boy found each other unsympathetic. At the age of seventeen Poe entered the University of Virginia but was there only for a year. His academic record was excellent, but Allan refused to pay his gambling and drinking debts. After a violent quarrel Poe went to Boston, where he published his first book of poems, *Tamerlane and Other Poems*, at his own expense. A year later, he enlisted in the United States Army under a false name. He served in it for two years, rising to the rank of regimental sergeant-major. Mrs Allan's pleas to her husband on her deathbed brought about some sort of reconciliation between Allan and Poe and led to Allan's helping him to secure an appointment as a cadet at West Point, the United States Military Academy. Within a year, however, he managed to get himself dismissed. Allan had by now married again, and the break between him and Poe was complete. Knowing Poe's character, it seems scarcely possible that there could ever have been much sympathy between them. Poe saw himself slighted and humiliated; as he wrote to Allan: "You suffer me to be subjected to the whims and caprice, not only of your white family, but the complete authority of the blacks."

He was, then, psychologically, twice a foundling, twice as it were a displaced person. Having left West Point, he went to live in Baltimore with an aunt, Mrs Clemm, whose fourteen-year-old daughter, Virginia, he married five years later. He was to watch her die of tuberculosis at twenty-five. In terms of volume of output, Poe was as industrious a writer as there has ever been, but his life was one of poverty, culminating in his mysterious death in Baltimore at the age of forty. He had returned to Richmond and was about to marry for the second time. Going

to New York to bring Mrs Clemm to the wedding, he broke his
journey at Baltimore. What happened to him there is impossible
to say, but five days later he was found in delirium near a saloon
that had been used as a polling booth. He died four days later
without having regained consciousness.

To pronounce any moral judgement on Poe's tragic life would
be more than usually futile. At one point he wrote of himself:

> I am constitutionally sensitive—nervous in a very unusual degree.
> I become insane, with long intervals of horrible sanity. During
> these fits of absolute insanity I drank, God only knows how often
> or how much. As a matter of course, my enemies referred the
> insanity to the drink rather than the drink to the insanity.

His life and his works alike make him a gift to the psychoanalysts.

But there is another factor in his make-up that cannot be
ignored. Poe was a Southerner and identified himself totally
with the South and its values. Brought up in the conservative,
aristocratic atmosphere of Richmond, he was totally out of
sympathy with the democratic aspirations of the North and with
the faith in progress through science that went with it. He
despised the "Mob", he was fiercely anti-Abolitionist, and there
is evidence in his stories that he had the contempt for and fear
of the Negro that was so often found in those who supported
slavery. All this was bound up with the conception of *le poète maudit*
as we find it expressed in its greatest representative, Baudelaire,
for in part it was a reaction against the triumph of the commercial
values and of the middle class and what Flaubert called its
muflisme, its swinishness. As a Virginian, Poe was also free of the
tyranny of the Puritan conscience. In this respect, as we see
when we compare their stories, the difference between him and
Hawthorne, whose genius he acclaimed, is striking. Both are
remarkable psychologists; but Hawthorne is concerned with the
psychological effects of sin, Poe with the disintegration of the
mind through something very much like the lust for knowing,
for experiencing. And—it was part of his aristocratic, anti-
bourgeois attitude—he was the avowed enemy of the moralising,
didactic element in art, the first great exponent of art for art's
sake, which again the French Symbolists were to take up a
generation later.

His poetry comes straight out of the English romantic movement; behind it, especially, are Coleridge and Shelley. But there
is still a vital difference: Poe's is an American romanticism, a

romanticism that is the consequence of American experience. In
his creation of an ideal landscape, for instance, he goes far beyond
Shelley. He is, as W. H. Auden has noted, the first poet to create
"an entirely imaginative landscape". One goes back to Hawthorne on the difficulties of writing a romance about a country
"where there is no shadow, no antiquity, no mystery, no picturesque and gloomy wrong, nor anything but a commonplace
prosperity". Poe loathed a commonplace prosperity, and shadow,
mystery, picturesque and gloomy wrong, if not necessarily antiquity, were essential to his art. Hawthorne solved the difficulty
by setting his stories in the colonial past: Poe did so, to all intents
and purposes, by eschewing the American scene altogether. The
landscape he projects in his poems is an ideal one, self-created;
while that of his stories is anything but American. It comes
closest to the actuality of the commonplace in scene in his
detective stories, such as "The Murders in the Rue Morgue" and
"The Purloined Letter", which are set in Paris, where he had
never been except vicariously in the novels of Balzac and Eugène
Sue. His horror stories—though the word "horror" is altogether
too crude for the impression of psychological, even psychical
disintegration they render—are located vaguely in Italy and Spain
or, in the case of "The Fall of the House of Usher", possibly
Scotland. The settings in fact are as conventionalised, as literary
in their origins, as the names of the characters, Roderick, Madeline,
Ligeia, Montresor, Fortunato and so on.

As has often been said, Poe drew what might be called the
furnishings of his stories from the Gothic romance, which has
been defined as the novel of horror based upon the supernatural.
To this extent he is a follower of such late eighteenth- and early
nineteenth-century writers as Horace Walpole in *The Castle of
Otranto*, Mrs Radcliffe in *The Mysteries of Udolpho*, Lewis in *The
Monk* and Maturin in *Melmoth the Wanderer*. From them he inherits
his haunted castles, charnel houses, clanking chains, disembodied
spirits, the whole theatrical assemblage of the irrational. He was
not the first American writer to do so; the properties he took
over were the common stock of the time; but more than any
other writer, he naturalised the Gothic to America and made it
part of a continuing American tradition.

He did so because of the infinitely greater seriousness with
which he used them. We get an illustration of this in a statement
in his introduction to *Tales of the Grotesque and Arabesque*: "If in
any of my productions terror has been the thesis, I maintain that

terror is not of Germany (i.e., the Gothic) but of the soul." He
is not, in other words, primarily interested in doing anything so
simple and mechanical as making his readers' flesh creep. He is
using the properties of the Gothic in order to furnish, as it were,
an interior landscape, a landscape of the soul; and the terror
rises from the unflinchingness with which he pushes back the
frontiers of consciousness to the point of disintegration and in
the end annihilation.

How Poe dramatises the terror may be seen in "The Fall of
the House of Usher", which, unusually for him, is told by an
outside observer, a representative of what might be called the
normal world. It is through his eyes that we first see the House
of Usher, which, we are later told—and the significance needs no
underlining—was "an appellation which seemed to include, in
the minds of the peasantry who use it, both the family and the
family mansion":

> I looked upon the scene before me—upon the mere house, and the
> simple landscape features of the domain—upon the bleak walls—
> upon the vacant eye-like windows—upon a few rank sedges—
> and upon a few white trunks of trees—with an utter depression of
> soul which I can compare to no earthly sensation more properly
> than to the after-dream of the reveller upon opium—the bitter
> lapse into everyday life—the hideous dropping off of the veil.
> There was an iciness, a sinking, a sickening of the heart—an un-
> redeemed dreariness of thought which no goading of the imagina-
> tion could torture into aught of the sublime. What was it—I paused
> to think—what was it that so unnerved me in the contemplation
> of the House of Usher? . . . It was possible, I reflected, that a mere
> different arrangement of the particulars of the scene, of the details
> of the picture, would be sufficient to modify, or perhaps to annihilate
> its capacity for sorrowful impression; and, acting upon this idea, I
> reined my horse to the precipitous brink of a black and lurid tarn
> that lay in unruffled lustre by the dwelling, and gazed down—but
> with a shudder even more thrilling than before—upon the re-
> modelled and inverted images of the gray sedge, and the ghastly
> tree-stems, and the vacant and eye-like windows.

He looks at the house more closely:

> Its principal feature seemed to be that of an excessive antiquity.
> The discolouration of ages had been great. Minute fungi overspread
> the whole exterior, hanging in a fine tangled web-work from the
> eaves. Yet all this was apart from any extraordinary dilapidation.

No portion of the masonry had fallen; and there appeared to be a wild inconsistency between its still perfect adaptation of parts, and the crumbling condition of individual stones. . . . Beyond this indication of extensive decay, however, the fabric gave little token of instability. Perhaps the eye of a scrutinising observer might have discovered a barely perceptible fissure, which, extending from the roof of the building in front, made its way down the wall in a zigzag direction, until it became lost in the sullen waters of the tarn.

So much for the house. Within:

The room in which I found myself was very large and lofty. The windows were long, narrow, and pointed, and at so vast a distance from the black oaken floor as to be altogether inaccessible from within. Feeble gleams of encrimsoned light made their way through the trelissed panes, and served to render sufficiently distinct the more prominent objects around; the eye, however, struggled in vain to reach the remoter angles of the chamber, or the recesses of the vaulted and fretted ceiling. Dark draperies hung upon the walls. The general furniture was profuse, comfortless, antique, and tattered. Many books and musical instruments lay scattered about, but failed to give any vitality to the scene. An air of stern, deep, and irredeemable gloom hung over and pervaded all.

We meet Usher himself, with his sister Madeline the last survivor of the ancient line:

His action was alternately vivacious and sullen. His voice varied rapidly from a tremulous indecision (when the animal spirits seemed utterly in abeyance) to that species of energetic concision—that abrupt, weighty, unhurried, and hollow-sounding enunciation— that leaden, self-balanced, and perfectly modulated gutteral utterance, which may be observed in the lost drunkard, or the irreclaimable eater of opium, during the periods of his most intense excitement. . . . He suffered much from a morbid acuteness of the senses; the most insipid food was alone endurable; he could wear only garments of certain texture; the odour of all flowers was oppressive; his eyes were tortured even by a faint light; and there were but peculiar sounds, and these from stringed instruments, which did not inspire him with horror.
    To an anomalous species of terror I found him a bounden slave. "I shall perish," said he, "I *must* perish in this deplorable folly. Thus, thus, and not otherwise, shall I be lost. I dread the events of the future, not in themselves, but in their results. I shudder at

the thought of any, even the most trivial, incident, which may operate upon this intolerable agitation of soul. I have, indeed, no abhorrence of danger, except in its absolute effect—in terror. In this unnerved, in this pitiable, condition I feel that the period will sooner or later arrive when I must abandon life and reason together, in some struggle with the grim phantasm, FEAR."

In addition to what may be ancestral, even hereditary fears, Usher is particularly oppressed by the prospect of the imminent death of Madeline, his "tenderly beloved sister, his sole companion for long years, his last and only relative on earth". Her disease—"a settled apathy, a gradual wasting away of the person, and frequent though transient affections of a partially cataleptic character were the unusual diagnosis"—had long baffled the physicians; and narrator and Usher settle down to await her end. Usher plays "wild improvisations" on his "speaking guitar". He paints "pure abstractions".

One of the phantasmagoric conceptions of my friend, partaking not so rigidly of the spirit of abstraction, may be shadowed forth, although feebly, in words. A small picture presented the interior of an immensely long and rectangular vault or tunnel, with low walls, smooth, white, and without interruption or device. Certain accessory points of the design served well to convey the idea that this excavation lay at an exceeding depth below the surface of the earth. No outlet was observed in any portion of its vast extent, and no torch or other artificial source of light was discernable; yet a flood of intense rays rolled throughout, and bathed the whole in a ghastly and inappropriate splendour.

They read together, books of esoteric lore. Then one evening "having informed me abruptly that the lady Madeline was no more", Usher announces "his intention of preserving her corpse (previously to its final interment), in one of the numerous vaults within the main walls of the building". Together they carry the "encoffined body" to the chosen place:

Having deposited our mournful burden upon trestles within this region of horror, we partially turned aside the yet unscrewed lid of the coffin, and looked upon the face of the tenant. A striking similitude between the brother and sister now first arrested my attention; and Usher, divining, perhaps, my thoughts, murmured out some few words from which I learned that the deceased and himself had been twins, and that sympathies of a scarcely intelligible nature had always existed between them.

The suggestion of incest is unmistakable. If possible, it becomes even more so in the *dénouement*, which for all its crude theatricality is still enormously effective. Usher cries out that he has put his sister living in the tomb. "Madman!" he shrieks, "I tell you that she now stands without the door!"

> As if in the superhuman energy of his utterance there had been found the potency of a spell, the huge antique panels to which the speaker pointed threw slowly back, upon the instant, their ponderous and ebony jaws. It was the work of the rushing gust—but then without those doors there *did* stand the lofty and enshrouded figure of the lady Madeline of Usher. There was blood upon her white robes, and the evidence of some bitter struggle upon every portion of her emaciated frame. For a moment she remained trembling and reeling to and fro upon the threshold—then, with a low moaning cry, fell heavily inward upon the person of her brother, and in her violent and now final death-agonies, bore him to the floor a corpse, and a victim of the terrors he had anticipated.

The narrator flees:

> Suddenly there shot along the path a wild light, and I turned to see whence a gleam so unusual could have issued: for the vast house and its shadows were alone behind me. The radiance was that of the full, setting, and blood-red moon, which now shone vividly through that once barely discernible fissure, of which I have spoken as extending from the roof of the building, in a zigzag direction, to the base. While I gazed, this fissure rapidly widened—there came a fierce breath of the whirlwind—the entire orb of the satellite burst at once upon my sight—my brain reeled as I saw the mighty walls rushing asunder—there was a long tumultuous shouting sound like the voice of a thousand waters—and the deep and dank tarn at my feet closed sullenly and silently on the fragments of the 'House of Usher'.

One speaks of the symbolism of "The Fall of the House of Usher", but in fact the story itself is one extended symbol: the story is the meaning.

Poe's most remarkable story is his longest, *The Narrative of Alfred Gordon Pym,* which is almost of novel length. Here there is no narrator; the story is presented as a journal of Antarctic exploration. It charts the hero's flight from civilisation and ordinary human intercourse into ultimate isolation. It has been taken as a joke or a hoax, and there may well be elements of the hoax in it, though they are sinister enough. The total impression, however, is anything but that of a hoax. The story recounts Pym's experiences in four voyages. The story proper, in so far as one can speak of a story at all, begins with the second voyage, when Alfred Gordon Pym—the general resemblance of the name to Poe's cannot be accidental—stows away with the help of a friend, the captain's son, on board the whaler *Grampus* sailing from Nantucket for the South Seas. He is in effect cut off for days in the hold, buried alive; we have here, in terms of a ship, a variant on Poe's obsession with coffins, vaults and premature internment. And at this point something like Melville's ambiguities and Hawthorne's "formula of alternative possibilities" come into the story. Pym, buried in darkness, without food and drink, is in what can only be called a hallucinated state. In his dreams he is attacked by a wild animal: it turns out to be his faithful Newfoundland dog, Tiger.

When at last Pym is released it is to find that the ship has been seized by the crew and the captain murdered. With his friend the captain's son and a dwarf of fantastic strength, a half-breed Indian called Dirk Peters, he manages to seize the ship from the mutineers. Battered by storms until it is no more than a hulk, the *Grampus* drifts south. A ship they sight and that crosses their bows proves to be a death ship manned by corpses—one of Poe's sources is obviously Coleridge's "The Rime of the Ancient Mariner". Pym and his fellows are driven by hunger to kill and eat one of their number, an unnecessary act of cannibalism since they later discover the ship's stores are available to them all the time.

Pym and Peters, the sole survivors of the *Grampus*, are picked up by an English ship, the *Jane Guy*, whose captain Pym persuades to sail further south in the hope of discovering an Antarctic continent or even the South Pole itself. They pierce the ice barrier and discover land, an island that has been called "an inverted Eden" in which snakes are harmless but where everything is black, plants, animals, inhabitants, black even to their teeth. And the inhabitants are not only black but viciously stupid, for whom everything white is taboo.

It seems impossible not to think that this presentation of the black inhabitants of Antarctica is Poe's comment, satirical or otherwise, on southern Negroes and the relations between slaves and masters in the South. These black Antarcticans engineer a landslide that overwhelms the *Jane Guy*'s crew and kills them all except Pym and Peters, who leads him through gorges and caverns to the surface. The only white survivors, they escape in a stolen boat with an islander they force to accompany them.

Now, as they are driven south and further south on a mysterious current, everything changes. They move into a milder climate in which everything is white, in contrast to the blackness of the island. The sea is hot and the water "no longer transparent, but of a milky consistency and hue". When Pym takes a white handkerchief from his pocket and it flutters in the islander's face, the islander "became violently affected by convulsions". In the end his fear of the all-pervading whiteness is such that he throws himself face downwards in the bottom of the boat. They seem to be impelled irresistably towards a cataract, the summit of which "was utterly lost in the dimness and the distance. Yet we were evidently approaching it with a hideous velocity." It hangs before them like a white curtain. "Many gigantic and pallidly white birds flew continually now from beyond the veil." The islander dies; and the fragment ends—for *The Narrative of Alfred Gordon Pym* is presented as a fragment:

And now we rushed into the embraces of the cataract, where a chasm threw itself open to receive us. But there arose in our pathway a shrouded human figure, very far larger in its proportions than any dweller among men. And the hue of the skin of the figure was of the perfect whiteness of snow.

The Narrative of Alfred Gordon Pym remains a most mysterious work. The voyages it describes are interior voyages, voyages through the polar seas of its author's mind to the pole itself, the ultimate, which is death. The gigantic, perfectly white figure that waits to receive him can be nothing else. There are affinities with *Moby-Dick*, especially in the way in which Poe seems to anticipate Melville's use of the concept of whiteness and its ambiguities. And Pym like Ahab is a man who dares everything, who pits himself against the final mysteries. But the differences are much greater than the similarities. Ahab, when all is said and done, is only one character in *Moby-Dick*; and certainly it is not in him that the values of the novel are enshrined. He is in a sense called to judgement, both by Ishmael and by Starbuck. In Poe's story there is really no other character but Pym; there is no one to judge him and he is not judged.   To put it in another way, he contains the whole world; nothing exists outside him; whereas what exists outside Ahab is the white whale, which kills him. Certainly the white figure of the cataract in Poe is nothing like the white whale; it is much more like a Statue of Liberty welcoming him into the promised land.   Ethan Brand, in Hawthorne's story, describes the Unpardonable Sin as "the sin of an intellect that triumphed over the sense of brotherhood within man and reverence for God, and sacrificed everything to its mighty claims".   It is Ahab's, and he is struck down for it.   It is also Pym's—and Poe's; but with this essential difference.   Sin becomes sin only when the sinner knows it is sin: Poe had no such knowledge. D. H. Lawrence expressed the truth about him when he said: "Poe is rather a scientist than an artist.   He is reducing his own self as a scientist reduces a salt in a crucible.   It is an almost chemical analysis of the soul and consciousness. . . . His best pieces are ghastly stories of the human soul in its disruptive throes."   And here he anticipated one whole strand of American writing.

[28]

Samuel Langhorne Clemens (Mark Twain) was also a Southerner; but in every conceivable way he stands in the sharpest possible contrast to Poe and indeed to all the eminent American writers who had preceded him.   True, his father, a lawyer, was a Virginian; but he was the victim of the dream of the frontier, the dream especially of wealth acquired through speculation in land at the frontier.   He had drifted westward first to Kentucky, where he married, and then to Missouri.   Twain, who was born in 1835, was brought up in the small Mississippi River town of Hannibal, the St Petersburg of *Tom Sawyer* and *Huckleberry Finn*.   At the age of twelve, on his father's death, he was apprenticed to a printer, and for the next ten years led a roving life as journeyman printer and newspaper reporter in the Middle West and even as far afield as New York City.   In 1857, about to set out for South

America, he changed his mind and became a Mississippi steamboat pilot. When the outbreak of the Civil War brought navigation on the Mississippi to an end, he joined the Confederate forces but served only for a very short time and then went to Nevada with his elder brother, who was secretary to the Governor of the Territory. He became a frontier journalist in Virginia City, taking Mark Twain, a river term meaning "two fathoms deep", as his pen-name. He drifted to San Francisco and in 1865 achieved fame with his story, "The Celebrated Jumping Frog of Calaveras County". This was consolidated by the publication of *Innocents Abroad* in 1869, written after a tour he had made of the Mediterranean countries and the Holy Land, in which he pokes fun both at the classical and the antique and at the solemnity of American tourists in their presence.

In 1870 he married and settled down at Hartford, Connecticut, to become the most internationally celebrated American writer of his time. The seal was set on his literary reputation when he was awarded honorary degrees by Yale and Oxford. He died in 1910.

It has often been observed that the modern view that Twain created, in Huck Finn, "one of the permanent symbolic figures of fiction, not unworthy to take a place with Ulysses, Faust, Don Quixote, Don Juan, Hamlet,"—the words are T. S. Eliot's—would have seemed incomprehensible to Twain's contemporaries. To the nineteenth century he was a humorist; and that he certainly was, a humorist, moreover, in a vein idiosyncratic to America and especially to the frontier. It was the kind of humour called the tall story. Boorstin has noted that in America "tall" means not only "high" or "lofty" but also "unusual", "remarkable", "extravagant". The essential feature of the tall story is the extraordinary, the unparalleled. Tall stories accreted round folk-heroes, some of whom were historical personages, like Davy Crockett, others, like Mike Fink and Paul Bunyan, probably figures of myth. The Bunyan stories may be taken as typical.

Paul Bunyan was a giant lumberjack, the inventor of the logging industry of the Pacific North-West. His blue ox, Babe, measured forty-two axe-handles and a plug of chewing tobacco between the horns. Paul was responsible for the creation of Puget Sound and the Grand Canyon. He was surrounded by a company of loggers comparable to himself and living in conditions as remarkable. One Christmas Day the thermometer in the camp office dropped to four hundred degrees below zero, at which the tube burst and no one could tell what the temperature was, though it got appreciably colder. The next morning the boiling coffee froze on the stove and the loggers had to drink hot brown ice for breakfast. They had to work so hard to keep warm that they didn't talk or swear much. Which was a good thing, for on New Year's Day it was so cold that every word spoken froze solidly in the air as soon as it was uttered, and loggers bruised their mouths walking into hallos and damns; the words did not thaw out until the next Fourth of July and then did so with a great din. That was the Year of the Hard Winter.

The Bunyan legend seems to have its origin in 1837 in the Papineau Rebellion in Canada against the British. It was taken over by loggers south of the border, and by 1860 Paul Bunyan had become an authentic American folk-hero.

Twain, it will be remembered, was born in 1835, and "The Celebrated Jumping Frog of Calaveras County" brought him fame when published in the *New York Saturday Press* in 1865. The story is about the gambler, Jim Smiley, who is always eager to back his horse or dog or, in the end, frog against any rival. Stories like it had been long current; one had been in print in California as early as 1853. In a notebook he kept at Angel's Camp, California, Twain had recorded the following incident: "Coleman with his jumping frog—bet a stranger $50. Stranger had no frog and C. got him one:— In the meantime stranger filled C.'s frog full of shot and he couldn't jump. The stranger's frog won." And that is the climax of the story. Put down thus baldly, it does not seem to amount to much, but the point lies in the telling.

The tall story was an oral and popular form, preceding the written word. It was a product of tall talk, which was a product of American experience. As Boorstin has said: "No language could be American unless it was elastic enough to describe the unusual as if it were commonplace, the extravagant as if it were normal. The extravagance of the American experience and the inadequacy of the traditional language made tall talk as necessary a vehicle of the expansive age of American life as the keel boat or the covered wagon." As the Paul Bunyan myth, which was the communal creation of a generation of anonymous lumberjacks, shows, both the tall story and tall talk were the expression of the imaginative response to conditions hitherto unparalleled of ordinary men and women who happened to be frontiersmen.

How genuinely and spontaneously of the people tall talk was

Boorstin, in *The Americans: The National Experience*, illustrates by a quotation from Thomas Low Nichols, a doctor and journalist who travelled widely in the Mississippi Valley and whose *Forty Years of American Life* was published in 1864:

> The language, like the country, has a certain breadth and magnitude about it. A Western man "sleeps so sound, it would take an earthquake to wake him". He is in danger "pretty considerable much", because "somebody was down on him, like the whole Missouri in a sand-bar". He is a "gone coon". He is "down on all cussed varmints", gets into an "everlasting fix", and holds that "the longest pole knocks down the persimmons". A story "smells rather tall". "Stranger," he says, "in bar hunts I am numerous."
>
> American humour consists largely of exaggeration, and of strange and quaint expressions. Much that seems droll to English readers is very seriously intended. The man who described himself as "squandering about promiscuous" had no idea that his expression was funny. When he boasted of his sister—"She slings the nastiest ankle in old Kentuck", he only intended to say that she was a good dancer. To escape rapidly, west of the Mississippi, might be "to vamose quicker'n greased lightnin' down a peeled hickory".

Tall talk, then, for the people whose lips uttered it, was not consciously humorous in intention. It was a form of poetry, the imaginative response, as has been said, to what by Western European standards were the exaggerations of the living conditions of Americans, exaggerations of geography and climate. It mirrored those exaggerations as, one is tempted to say, the tall buildings of New York and Chicago, the skyscrapers, were later also to mirror it. No doubt it early became a source of joy to those who used it naturally, for it was enhancing; one remembers the innocuous and tragic Arkansas drunk, Boggs, shot down by Colonel Sherburn in *The Adventures of Huckleberry Finn*, who roared into town once a month shouting "Cler the track, thar. I'm on the wawpath, and the price uv coffins is a-gwyne to raise." Tall talk became humorous only when it became conscious, when it was addressed to an audience sophisticated enough to make the comparison with traditional and educated forms of speech. It was consciously exploited, for instance, by Artemus Ward, whose burlesques of an itinerant showman were highly successful both when delivered in lecture-form in London and when published in *Punch*.

Twain, who wrote "The Celebrated Jumping Frog" originally

for Ward to deliver in lecture-halls and who went on to become
a highly successful humorous lecturer himself, was only one of
a host of writers and lecturers who exploited tall talk and the
tall story for comic ends, though he was no doubt the best of
them.   That is now the least important aspect of him.   His great
achievement was to bring into American writing native American
speech, the vernacular poetry of the people, and establish it as a
valid medium of literary expression through the seriousness of
his subject-matter.   It is here that the real contrast with his
forbears in American prose rests.   It would be absurd to say that
Twain was more "American" than Cooper, Hawthorne, Emerson,
Thoreau and Melville; but their prose was based on English
norms.

Twain's reputation rests ultimately on a single book, *The
Adventures of Huckleberry Finn*.   It has been called the most
universal book to have come out of the United States of America,
and it is easy to see why this should be so.   Only a man from the
West could have written it; it is as American as the Mississippi
itself.   At the same time, it is the classic of boyhood everywhere.
It dramatises every man's dream of freedom, or rather, every
man's dream of the freedom that he was robbed of as a boy.   It
was Twain's own dream of freedom.   Written as a sequel to *The
Adventures of Tom Sawyer*, published in 1876, it is a very different
book from that, splendid boys' book though *Tom Sawyer* is.   It
exists on an altogether higher plane of intention and achievement.
It was Mark Twain's return to his childhood in Hannibal,
Missouri, but obviously not a realistic return.   The boy Sam
Clemens may have been Tom Sawyer; he had never been Huck
Finn, for Huck is the representative of a freedom he had only
dreamed of.

It is difficult not to see Twain as a martyr to respectability.
He was brought up as a Calvinist for whom it was almost
axiomatic that success in this world was the counterpart, almost
the guarantee, of salvation in the next; and success, both on the
frontier of his boyhood and in the America of his middle age,
was reckoned almost entirely in terms of the money a man
acquired.   He had all the feelings of personal guilt that goes with
Calvinism.   His father had been anything but a success: he had
squandered his life seeking to invent a perpetual-motion machine.
The burden of the family had fallen upon his wife, Tom Sawyer's
Aunt Polly; she had, it seems, never loved her husband, and it
was to her son that she turned for support and affection.   When

his father died, "The boy Sam", says his official biographer, "was
fairly broken down. Remorse, which always dealt with him
unsparingly, laid a heavy hand on him now. Wildness, disobedience, indifference to his father's wishes, all were remembered; a hundred things, in themselves trifling, became
ghastly and heart-wringing in the knowledge that they would
never be undone." While he was in this state his mother led
him into the room where his father lay. "Only promise me,"
she said, "to be a better boy. Promise not to break my heart."
It was a crucial moment in his life. From then on, success, the
good life, was represented by his mother's values, which were
wholly conventional. It was almost inevitable that when he
married his wife she would be a similarly narrow, conventional
woman who saw it as her task to groom him for conventional
middle-class society. She groomed not only his person but his
writing; she was his censor. And without open resistance, he
suffered his genius to be trammelled in the narrowest, most
Philistine code of what was probably the vulgarest epoch in
the Western world.

But there was resistance. It manifested itself in his private
pessimism, in his blank materialism philosophically, in the uncompromising atheism which lay beneath his Presbyterian mask.
It manifests itself, too, in seemingly innocent form, in *Huckleberry
Finn*, which got by as a book about boys for boys; and Mrs
Clemens's part in its making was limited to cutting out the
swear-words.

Tom Sawyer is a delightful creation: Huck is much more. It
is part of Mark Twain's skill that Huck presents himself always
as a sort of juvenile Sancho Panza to Tom's Quixote. Nothing
could be further from the truth. Tom is already caught by
respectability; his activities, his flights of fancy, exist simply as
play; when he organises the elaborate rescue of Jim from Uncle
Silas's hut, with all the necessary rituals—"Here, homeless and
friendless, after thirty-seven years of bitter captivity, perished a
noble stranger, natural son of Louis XIV"—he can do so because
he knows, as Huck does not, that Jim is no longer a slave but
has already been given his freedom by Miss Watson. Tom's
imagination exists and functions in order to make dull reality,
the constricting facts of existence, tolerable. But Huck is not
living at the level of play at all; he is in earnest. Freedom from
restraints, from "sivilisation", is for him a way of life. He does
not need Tom's imagination because he does not wear Tom's

chains. Tom plays at freedom; Huck acts. Quietly and inexorably, he is obsessed by the necessity of freedom. He has no ties, and his ambition is to have none.

Huck is also the touchstone of moral truth in the novel, and moral truth is at odds at every point with the conventional morality, the accepted values, of the community in which he lives. Indeed, the book turns on a moral problem, a problem of conscience illustrated in the relationship between Huck and his friend Jim, the runaway slave, "Miss Watson's nigger":

> Conscience says to me, "What had poor Miss Watson done to you, that you should see her nigger go off under your eyes and never say one single word? What did that poor old woman do to you, that you should treat her so mean? Why, she tried to learn you your book, she tried to learn you your manners, she tried to be good to you every way she knowed how. That's what she done!" . . . Jim talked out loud all the time I was talking to myself. He was saying how the first thing he would do when he got to a free state he would go saving up money and never spend a single cent, and when he had got enough he would buy his wife, which was owned on a farm close to where Miss Watson lived and then they would both work to buy the children, and if their master wouldn't sell them, they'd get an Abolitionist to go and steal them.
>
> It most froze my blood to hear such talk. He wouldn't ever dared to talk such nonsense in his life before. Just see what a difference it made to him the minute he judged he was about free. It was according to the old saying, "Give a nigger an inch and he'll take an ell." . . . Here is this nigger which I had as good as helped to run away, coming right out flat-footed and saying he would steal his children—children that belonged to a man I didn't even know; a man that hadn't ever done me no harm.

It is a superb piece of irony. Huck resolves the problem of conscience it raises by opting for damnation. He writes his letter to Miss Watson, telling her that Mr Phelps has Jim and will give him up for the reward.

> I felt good and all washed clean of sin for the first time I had ever felt so in my life, and I knowed I could pray now. But I didn't do it straight off, but laid the paper down and set there thinking—thinking how good it was all this happened so, and how near I come to being lost and going to hell. And went on thinking. And got to thinking over our trip down the river; and I see Jim before

me, all the time, in the day, and in the night-time, sometimes moon-
light, sometimes storms, and we a-floating along, talking, and
singing, and laughing. But somehow I couldn't seem to strike
no places to harden me against him, but only the other kind. I'd
see him standing my watch on top of his'n, 'stead of calling me,
so I could go on sleeping; and I see him how glad he was when I
come back out of the fog; and when I come to him again in the
swamp, up there where the feud was; and such-like times; and would
always call me honey, and pet me, and do everything he could think
of for me, and how good he always was; and at last I struck the
time I saved him by telling the men we had smallpox aboard, and
he was so grateful, and said I was the best friend old Jim ever had
in the world, and the *only* one he'd got now; and then I happened
to look around and see that paper.

It was a close place. I took it up, and held it in my hand. I was
a-trembling, because I'd got to decide, for ever, betwixt two things,
and I knowed it. I studied a minute sort of holding my breath,
and then says to myself:

"All right, then, I'll *go* to hell"—and tore it up.

It was awful thoughts, and awful words, but they was said.
And I let them stay said; and never thought no more about reforming.
I shoved the whole thing out of my head; and said I would take up
wickedness again, which was in my line, being brung up to it,
and the other warn't. And for a starter, I would go to work and
steal Jim out of slavery again; and if I could think up anything
worse, I would do that too; because as long as I was in, and in for
good, I might as well go the whole hog.

We have seen how Emerson and Thoreau took as axiomatic
the belief in the natural and inherent superiority in virtue and
wisdom of the child to the man that is summed up in Wordsworth's
lines:

> Thou best Philosopher, who yet dost keep
> Thy heritage, thou Eye among the blind.

Huck is that best philosopher, that Eye among the blind. He is
the child of nature, innocent, unspoilt, because uncorrupted by
education. He sees truly and therefore he feels truly, even
though he knows that what he feels is wrong by the standards
of those who would educate him. He is like the child in
Andersen's story, who blurts out the truth that the emperor is
naked. He is in his wholly artless way the exposer of shams:

Next Sunday we all went to church, about three mile, everybody a-horseback. The men took their guns along, so did Buck, and kept them between their knees or stood them handy against the wall. The Shepherdsons done the same. It was pretty ornery preaching—all about brotherly love, and such-like tiresomeness; but everybody said it was a good sermon, and they all talked it over going home, and had such a powerful lot to say about faith, and good works, and free grace, and prefore-ordestination, and I don't know what all, that it did seem to me to be one of the roughest Sundays I had run across yet.

His naïve eye unfailingly registers truth, distinguishes between appearance and reality. Again at the Grangerford's:

On the table in the middle of the room was a kind of lovely crockery basket that had apples and oranges and peaches and grapes piled up in which was much redder and yellower and prettier than real ones is, but they warn't real because you could see where pieces had got chipped off and showed the white chalk or whatever it was, underneath.

And as he sees, he feels. His responses, not only in the great moral decisions such as whether or not to hand Jim back to slavery, are always the humanly right ones. Sometimes the sense we have of their rightness is expressed in the limpidity and accuracy of the prose he speaks, as in this passage on the murder of the drunkard Boggs by Colonel Sherburn:

They took Boggs to a little drug-store, the crowd pressing round, just the same, and the whole town following, and I rushed and got a good place at the window, where I was close to him and could see in. They laid him on the floor and put one large Bible under his head, and opened another one and spread it on his breast—but they tore open his shirt first, and I seen where one of the bullets went in. He made about a dozen long gasps, his breast lifting the Bible up when he drawed in his breath, and letting it down again when he breathed it out—and after that he laid still; he was dead. Then they pulled his daughter away from him, screaming and crying, and took her off. She was about sixteen, and very sweet and gentle-looking, but awful pale and scared.

It would be impossible to overpraise writing such as that: it is flawless, without the least suspicion of false simplicity.

More often the rightness comes out as direct response, as in

the scene in which Huck, hidden in a tree, sees the two young
Grangerfords murdered by the Shepherdsons:

> All of a sudden, bang! bang! bang! goes three or four guns—
> the men had slipped around through the woods and come in from
> behind without their horses! The boys jumped for the river—
> both of them hurt—and as they swum down the current the men
> run along the bank shooting at them and singing out, 'Kill them,
> kill them!' It made me so sick I most fell out of the tree. I ain't
> agoing to tell *all* that happened—it would make me sick again if
> I was to do that. I wished I hadn't ever come ashore that night,
> to see such things. I ain't ever going to get shut of them—lots of
> times I dream about them.

It comes out, too, in much less serious scenes, as that at the
circus when the drunk man jumps on the circus horse:

> And at last, sure enough, all the circus men could do, the horse
> broke loose, and away he went like the very nation, round and
> round the ring, with that sot laying down on him and hanging on
> his neck, with first one leg hanging most to the ground on one side,
> and then t'other one on t'other side, and the people just crazy. It
> wasn't funny to me, though; I was all of a tremble to see his danger.

In this instance Huck is fooled, as it were, by his own sensibility:
the drunk rider is in no danger, he is not even drunk; it is a hoax.

No other character in the novel has anything like Huck's
purity of feeling except, significantly, Jim, who, as an illiterate
Negro slave, is almost by definition forced into the role of child
and can therefore possess the virtues of the child, virtues denied
to adults simply by being adults.

Huck's sweetness of mind and common sense, which is the
product of seeing truly, irradiate the book. He is, in fact, that
rarest of characters in fiction, the human being who convinces
us as being positively good. There is nothing more difficult for
a novelist to do, as Dostoevsky noted when writing *The Idiot*;
and Twain is successful with Huck partly because he makes Huck
a child and therefore cut off from whole areas of experience, and
partly by making him a comic figure. But while it is right to
emphasise the sweetness of Huck's character—it makes him one
of the most attractive figures in world literature, and is a triumph
of the highest order for his creator—to concentrate on this aspect
of him to exclusion of all others will be to see him, and the book,
wrong. *Huckleberry Finn* is a very violent book; if it were not

that the violence is mediated for us through Huck, one would say it was a very brutal book. Huck is continually beaten by his father; in his progress down the river he is often in danger of sudden death; and all the time he is exposed to scenes of gross brutality, the delirium tremens of his father, the robbers on the wreck, the feud between the Grangerfords and Shepherdsons, the shooting down of Boggs in cold blood, to mention only the most notable. It has been observed that there are thirteen corpses in the book. "Every major episode in the novel ends with violence, in physical brutality, and usually in death": the words are Philip Young's in his very fine chapter on *Huckleberry Finn* in his *Ernest Hemingway*. And the point of this gauntlet of violence that Huck has to run is, as Young demonstrates, that it *wounds* him. "Violence had made him sick."

This means that Huck cannot be wholly equated with the Wordsworthian child; and he is certainly a long way from the "nonchalance" of Emerson's "boys who are sure of a good dinner." He has retained his innocent eye but he has been bruised and hurt, so much so that his one ambition is to escape. Significantly, when, having seen the two Dangerford boys murdered, he finally comes down from the tree after dark, he made up his mind, "I wouldn't ever go a-near that house again"; and he releases Jim as they make for the raft. "I never felt easy till the raft was two mile below there and out in the middle of the Mississippi."

But the violence Huck is fleeing is part and parcel of society, inseparable from it. The feud between the Grangerfords and Shepherdsons is a case in point. Huck tells us that Colonel Grangerford was a gentleman and he convinces us:

> There warn't no frivolishness about him, not a bit, and he warn't ever loud. He was as kind as he could be—you could feel that, you know, and so you had confidence. Sometimes he smiled, and it was good to see; but when he straightened himself up like a liberty-pole, and the lightning begun to flicker out from under his eyebrows, you wanted to climb a tree first, and find out what the matter was afterwards. He didn't ever have to tell anybody to mind their manners—everybody was always good-mannered where he was. Everybody loved to have him around, too; he was sunshine most always—I mean he made it seem like good weather.

There is no irony here; the Colonel is a Southern gentleman, and his household lives by ritual and ceremony. So far admirable;

nevertheless, it is the feud with the Shepherdsons round which this civilised way of life revolves; just as the genuine kindliness of Aunt Sally and Uncle Silas seems fatally implicated in the institution of slavery. They are presented as being, within the terms of the values of the society in which they live, as good as human beings can be. Yet they are quite unable to see Negro slaves as human beings:

> ". . . We blowed out a cylinder-head."
> "Good gracious! anybody hurt?"
> "No'm. Killed a nigger."
> "Well, it's lucky, because sometimes people do get hurt."

It is civilisation, then, perhaps community itself, that is the enemy, the inevitably corrupting element in which violence and inhumanity are bred; so that when Huck makes his famous announcement in the last sentences of the novel—

> But I reckon I got to light out for the Territory ahead of the rest, because Aunt Sally she's going to adopt me and sivilise me, and I can't stand it. I been there before—

Twain is not just providing his novel with a flip ending or Huck merely betraying his reluctance to becoming house-trained, as it were. The sentences sum up the whole burden of the book: that to be civilised, to allow oneself to become civilised, is to acquiesce in violence, inhumanity and hypocrisy.

The symbol of escape and freedom, and therefore of safety, is the River. And the River scenes, especially those in which we see Huck and Jim alone together on the raft at night, have a quality that is at once idyllic and compelling, that moves us as though by a myth the significance of which we feel deeply but scarcely understand. The River is more powerful as a symbol because of this, and, as symbols are, it is Janus-faced; in it, Huck is reborn, but it has, too, the hypnotic attraction of "easeful death". But however it is interpreted, it stands, in its magnificence and might, the magnificence and might of its storm and its calms, as the eternal opposite of the world that men have made, the world whose value Huck repudiates.

One other American writer of the nineteenth century remains: the poet Emily Dickinson. She was born in 1830, a member of a family that had lived for eight genèrations in the Connecticut Valley, and died in 1886. Just as Thoreau said, "I have travelled a good deal in Concord," so with no less truth Emily Dickinson might have said, "I have travelled a good deal in Amherst." She left the small Massachusetts college-town only four times in her life; for rather less than a year when, aged sixteen, she was a student at Mount Holyoke Female Seminary at the nearby town of South Hadley; again in 1855 when she visited Washington, D.C., where her father was serving as a congressman; and in the summers of 1864 and 1865 when trouble with her eyes forced her to go to Cambridge and Boston for treatment. She was unmarried, a spinster who for the latter part of her life dressed only in white. She was not quite a hermit; she had contacts with the world outside Amherst; but she remains the most striking instance of what seems a tendency ingrained in American writers, the tendency to be a recluse, to shun the company of their fellows, as Hawthorne and Melville both did and as Faulkner, for long periods of his life, was to do; as though the towns in which they lived, even the houses in which they lived, were large enough to contain the whole world.

Only seven of Emily Dickinson's poems were published during her life, though she wrote many hundreds. When a selection of one hundred and fourteen of them were published in 1890 they were greeted by critics with almost total bewilderment, not surprisingly, for though Emily Dickinson's idiosyncrasies of punctuation had been edited out and her metres and rhymes tailored to conform with conventional practice, they were still completely original. They are almost invariably very brief, many of them no more than a single four-line stanza. She found their metrical basis in the hymns she had learned as a child, but out of those familiar rhythms made something disconcertingly new, so that it was not until the nineteen-twenties, the period of modernist poetry, that they were appreciated at their own true value. And then, with her innovations, her use of half rhymes and quarter rhymes, her delight in incongruous juxtapositions and what seemed her daring use of language, she herself appeared very much a modernist poet.

It is easy for us to be wise after the event. In her colloquial directness, the Yankee homeliness of her speech, she falls into a tradition of American poetry that begins with Emerson and Thoreau and continues after in Robert Frost; and in her brevity, with its concentration on a single vivid image, she anticipates the Imagist poets and the many present-day poets who are related to them. She was a remarkable innovator, as in her poem on a railway train:

> I like to see it lap the miles,
> And lick the valleys up,
> And stop to feed itself at tanks;
> And then, prodigious, step
>
> Around a pile of mountains,
> And, supercilious, peer
> In shanties by the side of roads;
> And then a quarry pare
>
> To fit its side, and crawl between,
> Complaining all the while
> In horrid, hooting stanza;
> Then chase itself down hill
>
> And neigh like Boanerges;
> Then, punctual as a star,
> Stop—docile and omnipotent—
> At its own stable door.

Reading that poem for the first time, without knowledge of its author, one would almost certainly assume it was written in the twenties of this century.

And though every poem she wrote is indubitably stamped with her mark, so that we know that only she, Emily Dickinson, could have written it, nevertheless her range is large. One might set against the poem on the train the following:

Pain has an element of blank;
It cannot recollect
When it began, or if there were
A day when it was not.

It has no future but itself,
Its infinite realms contain
Its past, enlightened to perceive
New periods of pain.

Her great subjects are infinity and immortality.   Like Blake, she
saw infinity in a grain of sand, eternity in an hour.   But somehow
she domesticated them, or rather, she expressed them in her
own terms as a woman busy about the house in a country district.
"God", it has been said of her, "was a next-door neighbour to
talk pleasantly with; the burdens of human existence were to be
expressed in terms of the trivialities of a household."   God is
there in her poetry, and the immensities; but so is the life of a
small New England country town in the nineteenth century, and
God and the immensities are seen and rendered through it.
And throughout her poetry there is the ring of absolute assurance:

I never saw a moor;
I never saw the sea,
Yet know I how the heather looks
And what a billow be.

I never spoke with God,
Nor visited in heaven.
Yet certain am I of the spot
As if the checks were given.

[30]

These, then, were the founding fathers of American writing: Cooper, Hawthorne, Melville, Emerson, Thoreau, Poe, Whitman, Twain, Emily Dickinson. You cannot make anything like a school or a group or a movement out of them; all were very different from one another. But there are no parallels to them in nineteenth-century English writing, with the possible exception of Emily Brontë, who is an isolated figure in the English literature of her time. In some ways the case of Emily Brontë throws light on them. She too seems as it were a self-created writer; she has no antecedents and she seems to write in complete disregard for anything done in fiction before her. Moreover, at any rate on the face of it, her great novel has nothing to say about the lives of men in society, because that she is not concerned with.

There, except conceivably with Emily Dickinson, the parallel breaks down. Cooper and the rest were great innovators because they had to be. Each in his own way was creating a consciously American literature; they were as much pioneers as though they were cutting down forests and fighting Indians on the frontier, and they beat out trails that American writing was to follow in the twentieth. Between them they state the themes that dominate American writing that comes after them and assert what, in the light of that later writing, we recognise as characteristic American modes of apprehending experience. Fundamental to these is symbolism, whether it appears as the natural phenomenon, the fact, which becomes the symbol of a spiritual reality or as the larger-than-life character who in his solitariness takes on the quality of a figure of myth. By contrast with what we commonly find in English writing, the emphasis is on man alone, naked man, opposed to or unaware of the claims of society, obsessed with his relation to the universe or to the forces that shape men's lives. These, for some of the writers, are dark, incomprehensible, destructive, evil. They are never simple, and their mystery can be expressed only by paradox. When they are seen as benign they demand of the writer, if they are to be received as such, an innocence as of childhood, a sense of wonder which recreates the world daily, a trust which is to be obtained only when the writer has broken free of the constraints of society and the conventional habits of seeing that society imposes upon its members. When it is not merely irrelevant, society is generally seen as the enemy, the enemy of free communion with nature or with other men; and when it is accepted, as in Whitman, the acceptance seems possible only because the poet himself, through his gifts of empathy, has become all men, contains society within himself.

In many respects it is a very strange literature, one is tempted to say a naturally existential literature. It is certainly a literature of extremes, in which white as it were is set against black and there is no room for grey, though white is by no means invariably to be associated with good. It can be deeply pessimistic. It can also be as challengingly optimistic, resonant with the sense of infinite possibility for man. Yet in every instance, whichever extreme is in command, one has the strongest feeling that it is essentially American. Neither the pessimism of Hawthorne nor that of Poe is a European pessimism, just as the optimism of Emerson and Whitman is not a European optimism. Both are equally the products of American experience, which primarily and racially, is the experience of alienation, indeed of a double alienation, since, after the alienation from Europe, signalised by the initial emigration from Europe, came the experience of alienation in a new world in which climate and inhabitants were alike hostile.

The writers we have been discussing so far, it is important to remember, were all from relatively old American families. Their ancestors had helped to build up the country and their immediate forbears, their grandfathers and fathers, had made the republic, which had been made in an act of rebellion against Britain. They had, as we say, a stake in the country, and the country itself, as a nation, was still new and, even to them, only in its beginnings. The interior had yet to be subdued and populated. So they were consciously, even self-consciously, American; and they could not fail to feel themselves deeply implicated in the American experience, which was a continuing, unfolding thing. For some of them, Cooper for instance, its unfolding seemed to mean a falling off of the American ideal: for others, Emerson and Whitman, it offered infinite possibilities for man's future. But all were committed Americans who, as writers, shared the self-confidence of a young nation that, against all hazards, had survived and was undergoing an expansion unprecedented in history. That this is so is shown by their confidence as writers and as innovators in writing. And here their political opinions were largely irrelevant. Whitman's opinions, for example, would have been anathema to Poe, but in the absolute confidence with which Poe lays down his critical dogmas and offers us his stories he is as much the American, the "new man" of Crèvecoeur, as Whitman. He is, as it were, the New Man in the realm of art.

In a sense, they were very privileged Americans, privileged because of the very time at which they were born. They belong to an America that was, so far as its settled areas were concerned, comparatively small and still rural and pastoral, yet with all the rich promises of the hinterland that was waiting to be developed. They belong to the pre-industrial America and, Twain excepted, to pre-Civil War America.

Yet they belong even more to present-day America, as may be seen from the fact that Emily Dickinson was not in any real sense discovered until the twenties, at much the same time as the true greatness of Melville was first recognised by pioneer critics in American studies like Lewis Mumford. Before this, apart from Whitman and Twain, who were significantly different in language and expression from the others, they seemed to belong to a past that was only imperfectly American. In the later years of the nineteenth century many writers reacted against what seemed to them the established tradition of American writing, what was often called "the genteel tradition" of New England and of Boston in particular. It was then easy, though wrong, to lump Hawthorne, Emerson and Thoreau with much lesser writers like Longfellow, Bryant, Whittier, Holmes and James Russell Lowell, because they were of New England. This reaction was the literary counterpart of the political reaction against the old dominance of New England that began as soon as the West, the states beyond the Appalachians, realised their power. The writers who wrote in reaction against the literary tradition of New England did so because they regarded it as a sub-species, as it were, of English writing. Inevitably Boston, as the cultural centre of the United States, gave way to the much more cosmopolitan city of New York. Later, it seemed that New York might have to yield its pre-eminence to other cities. The "real" United

States was identified with what seemed the growing-points of the country. So, round about 1912, it seemed that the literary centre of America might be shifting to Chicago, the metropolis of the Middle West, to which Mid-Western poets like Carl Sandburg, Edgar Lee Masters and Vachel Lindsay naturally gravitated.

This tendency to see the more raw America as the more real America is linked with something else, with the question of language. During the thirties a novel was published called *Talk United States*. The implication of the title was obvious: American writers had not been using what Wordsworth called the real language of man and it was time they did. It is of course in colloquial speech that the differences between British and American English are most glaring, and it is possible that the gap between the written language and the spoken is generally greater in the United States than it is in England. But in fact, ever since Mark Twain, who was the great liberator here, American writers have been exploring the resources of vernacular speech. One thinks of Faulkner's novels, of the baseball stories of Ring Lardner, of Hemingway and Farrell and of Henry Roth in *Call It Sleep*, of E. E. Cummings in some of his poems; and the instances could be multiplied. But these names alone indicate how many different vernaculars there are in the United States; and when a novelist urges his fellow-writers to "talk United States" by "United States" he probably means his own vernacular, which may be of region, of class, of immigrant origins, or even of age-group. One thinks of *Catcher in the Rye*.

This problem of speech is one that has been more pressing for some writers than for others. It does not seem ever to have worried Robert Frost, in whose poems we seem always to hear the natural speaking voice of a rural, though educated, New Englander. His verse was the distillation of a region's way of speech. William Carlos Williams, on the other hand, who, by the time of his death in 1963, had become one of the most influential of recent American poets, grappled with the problem all his life, and it is not difficult to see why. Williams, who was a physician as well as a poet and a man equally dedicated in both vocations, was born in the industrial city of Rutherford, New Jersey, and spent his life there practising medicine. He strove to use the speech-rhythms of his patients, who came of many national stocks but not often of English, as the basis of his writing. In this he was more successful, it seems to me, in his fiction than in his poetry.

What is very much to the point is that Williams was writing in direct opposition to T. S. Eliot, whom he saw as the great enemy of American poetry. "Critically," Williams wrote, "Eliot returns us to the classroom just at the moment when I felt we were on the point of an escape to matters much closer to the essence of a new art form itself—rooted in the locality which should give it fruit." The significant word here is "locality". Eliot had abandoned the local in favour of the international, as Ezra Pound had also done. Eliot's great international poem, both in its sources and in its influences, was *The Waste Land*: Williams describes its appearance as "the great catastrophe to our letters". Of Ezra Pound, a lifelong friend with whom he had been at college, he spoke more kindly, as "the best enemy United States verse has"; but the use of the word "United States" instead of America is noteworthy. Williams is advocating a national poetry; he is writing in full reaction against European and especially English modes of poetry.

Eliot became an Englishman and thereby renounced the United States. But it does not in the least follow that because a writer talks or writes United States that he is therefore any more automatically American than one who writes something like standard English. Hemingway used English as it had not been used before and as certainly no contemporary Englishman could have done. It made him, no question, a distinctively American writer. All the same, it would be impossible to say that it made him more American than a novelist like Thornton Wilder, whose use of English is often scarcely distinguishable from an Englishman's.

Wilder has always been an extremely literary writer, the kind of writer, whether as novelist or dramatist, who approaches life through art; which has not prevented him from writing, in *Heaven's My Destination*, one of the best comic novels about a Bible-Belt American that we have. His first novel *The Cabala* was published in 1926; it is very plainly not autobiographical, but it must all the same stem from his experiences as a young man at the American Academy in Rome, where he went after graduating from Yale. It relates the experience of a young graduate student in Rome. Early on, one discovers, despite the plausible realistic surface, that it is not a realistic novel. This becomes evident when the hero meets a young English poet, great but unknown, who is dying from tuberculosis: Keats—it cannot be anyone else. The theme, it is apparent, is the young American hero's response to Rome as the rich, many-faceted symbol of

European civilisation. He falls in with and becomes the pet of Roman aristocracy, of distinguished priests and grand ladies. And here is another surprise. These distinguished priests and grand ladies, who are the initiates of the secret society of the novel's title, are the dwindled remains of the gods and goddesses of classical antiquity.

The Cabala ends with the hero sailing back home to the United States. On his first night out of Naples he cannot sleep for wondering why he is not more reluctant to leave Rome, the enchanted and enchanting city. He invokes Virgil, who appears to him and says: "Romes existed before Rome, and when Rome will be a waste there will be Romes after. Seek some city that is young. The secret is to make the city, not to rest in it." And then Virgil tells the young American hero about New York, the city whose towers "have cast a shadow across the sandals of the angels". *The Cabala* ends with this paragraph:

> The shimmering ghost faded before the stars, and the engines beneath me pounded eagerly towards the new world and the last and greatest of all cities.

Thomas Wolfe, who was a novelist of a very different kind from Wilder, had a phrase he used for what he particularly disapproved of in writing. It was "the European and fancy". It is pretty safe to say that he would have dismissed *The Cabala* as "European and fancy". Yet nowhere in American literature is Europe, the old world, more thoroughly repudiated than in Wilder's novel—or more elegantly. The repudiation is as complete as William Carlos Williams's. There is, however, a fundamental difference between Wilder's repudiation and Williams's, which is worth looking at in the light of the distinction Philip Rahv had made between those American writers he calls redskins and those he sees as palefaces. It is not a distinction that can be pressed too far, and there are cases when it is more apparent than real. Yet it is a suggestive one.

The redskin—and here I am borrowing Rahv's terms rather than following his theory—is the writer who has turned his back on Europe, the "stripped European", in Mumford's phrase, whose mind is "not buoyed up by all those memorials of a great past that floated over the surface of Europe" and who is determined to make an American literature out of American materials solely. Historically, Twain was such a writer, as was Hemingway. Williams was another, and here his prose work

In the American Grain is relevant. In this book, which is a series of impressionistic renderings of figures in North American history from Eric the Red to Lincoln, Williams sees the Puritans as the villains, the greatest perverters, and in a sense identifies himself with the Indians. This is, obviously, anything but paleface behaviour. For the paleface writer Wilder, America, the United States, includes Europe and transcends it. It is the stage beyond Europe in historical and cultural development. Europe, or what is significant in its past, has merged into America. New York, as it were, is the Third Rome. The American is the inheritor of Europe.

It is here that the distinction between redskin and paleface breaks down. On the face of it, Whitman is the primordial redskin who repudiates European modes of poetry, so much so that at times his work seems an expression of American nationalism or literary chauvinism. But in fact Whitman sees himself—and the American poet—precisely as the inheritor of Europe and even of beyond. "The American poets are to enclose old and new for America is the race of races. Of them a bard is to be commensurate with a people. To him other continents arrive as contributions." We are not, I am sure, to interpret the phrase "the race of races" as meaning *la crème de la crème*. Whitman is not promulgating any doctrine of Americans as *herrenvolk*. He means simply that Americans are the people made up of all other peoples. So that when he puts himself forward, in his poetic capacity of "Walt Whitman, a Kosmos", as the representative American he is also claiming to be the representative modern man who is the heir of all the past of man throughout the world.

This notion of the American as the inheritor of the whole cultural past of the world, a notion largely the product of the American's relationship to Europe, has influenced the poetic practice and the poetic theory of later American poets at first glance very dissimilar from Whitman. The two obvious names here are those of Ezra Pound and T. S. Eliot. Both spent the greater part of their lives in Europe, and Eliot became an Englishman at a comparatively early age. But his poetry is best seen as American rather than as English; while Pound, despite his eccentricities and his tragic differences with his country, has remained obstinately American. Indeed, the fact that they were expatriates is largely irrelevant to their poetry. In the chapter, "Harvard: 1904–1907", in his autobiography *Scenes and Portraits*

Van Wyck Brooks sees Eliot as the "quintessence of Harvard" in his day. Brooks shows how the characteristics that we think of as especially Eliot's, what we might almost call his properties —his royalism, classicism, Anglo-Catholicism, "the cults of Donne and Dante, the Sanskrit, the Elizabethan dramatists and the French Symbolist poets"—were all acquired by Eliot as a student at Harvard. They were part of the intellectual atmosphere of the Harvard of his time, though perhaps he made them his own as no other Harvard man of his generation did, just as he made his own, as we see from the imagery of his early poetry, the Italian Renaissance paintings in Mrs Jack Gardner's collection at Cambridge.

Eliot did not have to go to Europe to discover the literary and artistic masterpieces of the European past that were necessary to his poetic purpose: they were all there for him at Harvard. It seems that his decision to stay in England and take up British citizenship was much more likely the consequence of his religious and political beliefs than any sense that England was necessary to him as a poet. He cannot have believed that the English in the mass were more cultured or more interested in culture than Americans. "A certain kind of European overrates the comparative importance, in the present age of the world, of a good deal of his cultural tradition, and often of his own interest in it. For myself, as an American, I have not the least doubt that I have derived a good deal more benefit of the civilising as well as of the inspirational kind from the admirable American bathroom than I have from the cathedrals of Europe." This apparently Philistine statement comes from Edmund Wilson and was, I suspect, meant to be deliberately provocative. In fact, Wilson rather weakens his case by going on to describe the pleasures of soaking in the bath, whereas the normal American practice is surely to take a quick shower. But what would be Philistine or plain foolish in another man is not necessarily so in Edmund Wilson, as his record as writer and critic shows. He is an American who has made himself in the most impressive way a master of European literature in several languages as well as a superb critic of American literature and American institutions. He does in fact know Europe at first hand but, so far as his writing is concerned, he does not need to.

Perhaps the most extreme example of this sense that the whole world may be contained in the United States is to be found in the career of the poet Wallace Stevens. He was a modern poet in the sense that Eliot is, one who was much influenced by the French Symbolists and who ransacked the whole civilised world for his material. He was emphatically not, in Rahv's terms, a redskin. By profession he was a business man, an executive in a Hartford, Connecticut, insurance company. He was a fine, at times a great poet, but poetry for him was a sparetime activity. This is how the English critic V. S. Pritchett, reviewing his *Letters,* has described his career:

> There is the peculiar sight of a man who looks like a double. He is a fabricator of chinoiserie, lacquer work and ingenious metaphysic, yet he travels on his exacting legal work of one-night stands from conference to conference. His poems are filled with the bric-à-brac of mediaeval France and the France of the decadents; of Spanish Florida, Mexico, China, Ceylon, Japan and even Ireland, but he was never out of America in his life and he got home from the office to suburban Hartford to doze in esoteric weekends. Eliot found his Royalism in Europe: Stevens constructed it out of an exotic and imaginary court in Connecticut.
>
> How did he obtain these antiquities and these sensual nostalgias? By reading, by dreaming, and by writing to all those places for them; teas from China, figurines from Ceylon, pictures and special editions from France. The enterprises with which Stevens created his inner world of aristocratic bits and pieces, the efficiency with which he attempted to furnish a bare room in the American imagination, is commanding; one thinks of Henry James's earnestly and successfully pursued campaign to acquire London and European society as if it were up for sale at Sotheby's. . . .

It is possible to detect a certain undercurrent of British irony in Pritchett's account of Stevens's cultural activities. Even so, it is difficult not to recall again Thoreau's "I have travelled a good deal in Concord". Stevens had travelled a good deal in Hartford, Connecticut. He had made it the centre of the world and made the rest of the world contribute to it. He behaved, in other words, as though the United States were not only an extension of Europe but also the culmination of all that had gone on before it, as though it were the heir of all ages and all the civilisations. And in this he was behaving very much as Emerson, Thoreau and Whitman had done.

[31]

Though it was writers born mainly on the eastern seaboard in the first half of the nineteenth century who discovered and expressed what were to be the major themes of American writing, the themes themselves received very different treatment as they were taken up by writers from other parts of the country at later stages in the country's development. In terms both of origin and of environment many of these writers had almost nothing in common with those of New England and its long history of settlement. Consider the Chicago poet Carl Sandburg, who was born in Galesburg, Illinois, the son of a Swedish immigrant. He left school at the age of eleven and earned his living working in a barber's shop and later as the driver of a milkwagon, as a porter and dishwasher, a newspaper reporter, an itinerant harvester in the wheatfields of Kansas and then as a soldier in the Spanish-American War. He became a poet by profession with the publication of *Chicago Poems* in 1916. In this and later volumes he attempted to express Chicago—

> Hog Butcher for the World,
> Tool Maker, Stacker of Wheat,
> Player with Railroads and the Nation's Freight Handler;
> Stormy, husky, brawling,
> City of the Big Shoulders—

and the life of its heterogeneous people. A leading figure in what is called "the Chicago Renaissance", the vehicle of which was Harriet Monroe's magazine *Poetry*, Sandburg announced:

> I am the people—the mob—the crowd—the mass.
> Do you know that all the great work of the world is done through me?
> I am the workingman, the inventor, the maker of the world's food and clothes.

I am the audience that witnesses history. The Napoleons come from me and the Lincolns. They die. And then I send forth more Napoleons and Lincolns. . . .

The debt to Whitman is unmistakable; indeed, Sandburg's "barbaric yawp" is more obviously barbaric than Whitman's. He is a much smaller poet than Whitman, lacking Whitman's lyrical eloquence and his intensity of vision, his epic quality. What he does do is re-state Whitman's democratic fervour and his acceptance of common humanity. One of his later volumes, *The People, Yes*, he has described as "a footnote to the Gettysburg Address", and the description could be justly applied to his poems generally. It is not a coincidence that he now perhaps is best known as the biographer of Lincoln.

Chicago also excited the imagination of another first-generation American, Theodore Dreiser, who was born in Terre Haute, Indiana, in 1871. His father was a German immigrant who, after initial success in his new country, failed in business, so that Dreiser was brought up in poverty of the miserable kind. One of his sisters became a prostitute; a brother went to jail. Dreiser himself came to reading and to writing largely as a newspaper reporter. All Dreiser's writings were conditioned by the bitterness of his childhood experiences; and perhaps it was his father's lack of success that was responsible for the fascination that American success in its most spectacular and ruthless forms always exercised upon him. So in his novels *The Financier* and *The Titan*, Dreiser depicts the rise from humble origins of a multi-millionaire who is generally believed to have been modelled on Charles T. Yerkes, the street-car magnate. Dreiser's character, Frank Cowperwood, as a boy sees a lobster devour a squid and then realises, "Things live on each other—that was it." Cowperwood is a predator. We leave him at the end of *The Financier* released from jail after having served a sentence for larceny and about to seek a new fortune in Chicago. Dreiser compares him to the black grouper fish, which survives "because of its very ability to adapt itself to conditions". He goes to make his immense fortune, using to do so all the ruthlessness of which he is capable. What is impressive in these novels is the way in which Dreiser interprets the workings of finance capitalism in terms of a theory of human behaviour that he derives from his readings of the evolutionary theories of the day, as the workings of natural law. Nature is red in tooth and claw, and so is man, because he is part of nature.

Cowperwood appears almost as a magnificent animal, who triumphs and deserves to do so because of his superior vitality and ruthlessness.

Dreiser's attitude to the spectacle of Cowperwood, who is at times equated with a merchant prince of the Italian Renaissance, is one of moral neutrality. This, he seems to be saying, is the nature of life. But what he also has, and it is here that his greatness lies, is a deep and comprehensive pity for all created things. This comes out especially in his novel *An American Tragedy*, which tells the life-story of Clyde Griffiths, the son of street evangelists in Kansas City, who dreams of a life of luxury and becomes a bellboy in an hotel. He leaves Kansas City because he is involved in a motor accident and goes to New York. There, working in a club, he meets his uncle Samuel Griffiths, a factory owner in New York state. Griffiths gives the boy a job in his factory. Clyde seduces a workgirl, Roberta Alden, gets her pregnant, and then realises he has the chance of marrying a rich girl. He decides to murder Roberta and to do so takes her rowing on a lonely lake, only to discover he lacks the courage to kill her. But the boat overturns and Roberta is drowned. After a long trial, in which the question of his innocence or guilt becomes a political issue, Clyde is sentenced to the electric chair.

In every way Dreiser is an exceedingly clumsy writer. It is doubtful whether he ever in his life wrote a sentence capable of giving pleasure in itself. And it is not easy at first to see in what sense Clyde Griffiths can be considered a tragic figure. He is the passive victim of circumstances; he is, as Dreiser says, a "soul that was not destined to grow up". Dreiser insists upon his selfishness; he is weak and incapable of decisive action, characterised by "the most feeble and blundering incapacity". He is, and this Dreiser intends, anything but a tragic hero. Yet Dreiser's pity for him is so vast and so deep that that is not how we see him while reading the novel. He is not sentimentalised, and Dreiser's pity for him is wholly impersonal. Because of this, we accept Clyde as something of a universal figure, for Dreiser plainly sees man as the victim of circumstances. The tragedy lies in the implicit contrast between what a man expects of life and what he gets. But why an American tragedy? Here, it seems to me, we have to go back to Dreiser's own childhood as the son of poverty-stricken, defeated immigrants. The tragedy is specifically American because of the contrast between the promise of the United States, its materialism and wealth, and the poverty in

which so many millions of its people lived. And, as Dreiser
shows, the poverty is not only an economic poverty but one also
of values, of the spirit; we see this in Clyde's identification of
himself with the hotel in Kansas City, the symbol of American
success, and in the terror he feels when he sees the poverty in
which Roberta lives.

Dreiser shows us the American dream unrealised and turned
sour. He was one of the first American novelists to do so, and
certainly none before him had done so with anything like his
power. In the nineteenth century, the novelist W. D. Howells,
who had made a highly successful migration from rural Ohio to
Boston and thence to New York, had equated "the more smiling
aspects of life" with "the more American". After Dreiser's
worm's eye view of the American dream and the American
struggle, it was impossible for writers to fall in with Howells's
optimism; and Dreiser becomes the central figure of a miscel-
laneous group of poets and novelists who from many points of
view question the assumptions beneath Howells's optimism.

One of the characters of Dreiser's last novel, *The Stoic*, says,
"I am crying out for life": it was a cry increasingly heard in the
writings of the decade that began about 1914. It sounds through
Edgar Lee Masters's *Spoon River Anthology*, which was the first
of many books expressing what was called "the revolt from the
village". Masters was born in Kansas in 1869 and brought up
in that state and in rural Illinois, where his father was a lawyer.
Masters, too, became a lawyer and for many years practised in
Chicago. Based on the *Greek Anthology, Spoon River Anthology*,
which was published in 1915, consists of a series of free-verse
poems that are monologues or self-epitaphs spoken from the
grave by inhabitants of the fictitious Illinois village of Spoon
River. There are some two hundred and fifty of them, representing most of the ordinary occupations of men and women,
and through them nineteen stories develop. Masters seems to
have conceived of the work, which should be read as a whole and
not as a collection of poems, as a sort of Divine Comedy; but
what most powerfully impresses now is its naturalism, its emphasis on individual isolation and frustration, on the constrictions
of American small-town village life.

A writer it influenced was Sherwood Anderson, the novelist
and short-story writer whose most important work is probably
the collection *Winesburg, Ohio*, published in 1919. Anderson,
who was born in Camden, Ohio, in 1876, was by turn, after a

sketchy schooling, newsboy, house painter, farm-hand, race-course hand and soldier in the Spanish-American War until, after a year at college, he became first an advertising copywriter in Chicago and then a paint manufacturer in Ohio. In 1913, a fairly prosperous business man, he walked out of his factory for good to return to Chicago and learn how to write.

Though there had been great American short-story writers— Hawthorne, Poe, James—before Anderson, he stands out, in *Winesburg, Ohio*, as the founding father of the modern short story in America. The very date of the book's publication is significant: 1919, the year after the first world war ended. The United States had participated in that war; the war had drawn it, whether Americans liked it or not, into the great world,' and the country emerged from the war a great power. It marked, perhaps, the end of American innocence, for it led thousands of young Americans, soldiers and sailors, to discover they were, in Frank O'Connor's words, "isolated, unique, and complacent". Anderson's stories are not about war, but the characters that are central to the stories in *Winesburg, Ohio* are men and women who have dis-covered they are isolated and unique. The book is a collection of stories that almost becomes a novel, for, apart from the unity imposed upon it by the setting, most of the stories impinge upon young George Willard, the son of the town's hotel-proprietor and a reporter on the *Winesburg Eagle*. It is difficult not to think of Willard as the young Anderson: he too wishes to be a writer, and one feels all the time that *Winesburg, Ohio*, is the book he is destined to write.

Anderson prefaces to the collection a story that, on the face of it, has nothing to do with Winesburg. It is called "The Book of the Grotesque" and describes an unpublished book. When we turn to the Winesburg stories we find that Anderson is dealing with men and women who are in some sense grotesques. They are frozen, as it were, in postures of estrangement and alienation from which they attempt in vain to break away, generally through some effort to communicate with George Willard, who appears to them as a sort of priest, at any rate a free spirit as they are not. They are represented as people intolerably isolated, trapped in their grotesqueness, cut off by it from any communion with their fellows in Winesburg. They appear as drunks, homosexuals, women-haters, voyeurs, frigid women, religious maniacs. They are the defeated, people distorted by alienation and the con-sciousness that they are different from other people, and condemned thereby to inexorable loneliness. Yet at the same time they are shown as being better than their fellow-citizens who acquiesce and accept, who are "normal". Though the stories in *Winesburg, Ohio*, plainly spring from a criticism of the quality of American small-time life at the time Anderson was writing, its narrowness, its conformity, its preoccupation with vulgar commercial values, it is equally plain that they go beyond this and become a criticism of life itself as Anderson saw it. They are not primarily realistic stories; and if as criticisms of the quality of American life they had much in common with the novels of Dreiser and Sinclair Lewis they have even more in common with the work of a later writer, the Southern writer Carson McCullers, who explores Anderson's themes of alienation and incommunicableness not through grotesques but through freaks.

It was from *Spoon River Anthology* that Anderson seems to have got the clue to his subject-matter, but his mode of expression was entirely his own. Turgenev's *A Sportman's Sketches* gave him his ideal of writing, and he was enabled to reach it by his study of the prose of Mark Twain and Gertrude Stein. The one showed him how to render vernacular speech; the other, how to break up the texture of conventional literary prose in order to express direct intuition. The result was a prose freer, more idiomatic, lyrical, less "literary", than anything written since Twain.

A much more immediately successful and popular criticism of American life of the time, though also much coarser and more superficial, is to be found in the novels of Sinclair Lewis, especially in *Main Street* and *Babbitt*, which, when they were published in 1920 and 1922 respectively, were international bestsellers. Indeed, their success abroad may be seen as the literary manifestation to the world at large of the United States as a great power, and much of their success was due to the rest of the world's curiosity about America the new phenomenon. How novel the phenomenon was is indicated by the fact that when the English edition of *Babbitt* was published it appeared with a glossary of American words. In 1930 Lewis became the first American to win the Nobel Prize for Literature. The award was much criticised, and not unreasonably, yet in a way it was fitting, since for millions of readers in Europe at this time Lewis, far more than many better American writers, *was* America.

He was born in the small Minnesota town of Sauk Center in 1885, and both date and place are important. Until seven years before he was born the town's sole link with the outside world was the stagecoach; while by the time he came to boyhood Minnesota had been settled by successive waves of immigrants, Germans, Bohemians, Swedes, Norwegians. From Sauk Center Lewis, who was the son of a country doctor, went East to Yale and then on to New York, where he worked in publishing. He published six novels before *Main Street*, which, according to himself, he had planned as a sophomore at college, appeared. A satirical description of life in the fictitious small town of Gopher Prairie, Minnesota, it hit Sauk Center and all the Sauk Centers of the United States like a tornado. Lewis's point of view is made plain in the epigraph to the novel:

> This is America—a town of a few thousand, in a region of wheat and corn and dairies and little groves.
>
> The town is, in our tale, called 'Gopher Prairie, Minnesota'. But its Main Street is the continuation of Main Streets everywhere . . .
>
> Main Street is the climax of civilisation. That this Ford car might stand in front of the Bon Ton Store, Hannibal invaded Rome and Erasmus wrote in Oxford cloisters. What Ole Jensen the grocer says to Ezra Stowbody the banker is the new law for London, Prague, and the unprofitable isles of the sea; whatever Ezra does not know and sanction, that thing is heresy, worthless for knowing and wicked to consider . . .

Lewis, in other words, is set on destroying by ridicule the smugness and provincialism of small-town life. As a novelist, he was fighting the same war as that soon to be waged by H. L. Mencken in the pages of his magazine the *American Mercury* against what he called the "booboisie", whose opinions and behaviour were pilloried every month in the famous column of *bêtises* taken from the American press called "Americana". Most of them could be summed up in a statement made in 1922 by the President of the day, Warren Gamaliel Harding: "If I could plant a Rotary Club in every city and hamlet in this country I could then rest assured that our ideals of freedom would be safe and civilisation would progress."

The protagonist of Lewis's values, such as they are, is his heroine, Carol Kennicott, who is first presented as a girl on a hilltop "drinking the air as she longed to drink life". Becoming a librarian in St Paul, she dreams of bringing beauty to the small towns of the Middle West. She marries Will Kennicott, doctor in Gopher Prairie, whose inhabitants are for him "the best people on earth. And keen." He invites her to make the town "—well—make it artistic". But how? The citizens of Gopher Prairie—Sam Clark from the hardware store, Harry Haydock and his wife Juanita, of the Bon Ton, Dave Dyer the druggist, Ezra Stowbody, president of the Ionic Bank, Professor George Edwin Mott, superintendent of schools, Nat Hicks the tailor, Luke Dawson, the richest man in town, Jack Elder of the Minniemasha House—are all perfectly satisfied with themselves as they are; and when she tries to brighten their lives by re-decorating her house according to the modes of Chicago and St Paul and inviting them to romp-and-fancy dress parties, they suspect she is patronising them and give her the cold shoulder.

As satire *Main Street* seems pretty feeble now, just as Carol seems pretty silly as a heroine; and it is clear that Lewis no more knows what to do about Gopher Prairie and its inhabitants than Carol does. In the end she leaves her husband and Gopher Prairie.

Lewis's best novel remains *Babbitt*. The action takes place in in the city of Zenith, in the imaginary state of Winnemac, and the place-name, with its suggestion that there can be nothing better or higher than Babbitt's city, is the counterpart to the ironical epigraph to Main Street. Babbitt became the universal name for the stereotype of the small American business man; and perhaps that is Lewis's great achievement. The name itself is a triumph, with its hints of "rabbit" and of "baby", of a being easily frightened and only half formed. What Lewis records in the novel are the timid rebellions of Babbitt against the pressures of conformity. They seem now to amount to very little. Babbitt is an "Elk, a Booster, and a member of the Chamber of Commerce"; the "standard advertised wares, socks, tyres, cameras, instantaneous hotwater heaters—were his symbols and proofs of excellence; at first sight the signs, then the sub-stitutes, for joy and passion and wisdom". He has his moments: a camping trip to Maine with a friend who has dreamt of being a violinist but has become a salesman; a clandestine affair with a vaguely bohemian lady; a flirtation with Radical politics, which leads to his temporary ostracism by his friends. They are symbolised, perhaps, by the "fairy child" whom he sees in his dreams, "so slim, so white, so eager!"

Lewis was no Dickens, except intermittently; he was not blasting commercial culture as Dickens did in *Our Mutual Friend* in the figures of Podsnap and the Veneerings. He was no H. G. Wells, with whom he was often compared and by whom he was undoubtedly influenced. Babbitt is a thin and vague conception compared with Wells's Mr Polly; and there is no question at all of where Wells stands in relation to Mr Polly. Polly for all his pathos and his endearing qualities, is exposed as the product of false educational and social values. But where Lewis stands in relation to Babbitt is not by any means clear. Lewis presents Babbitt's pale fantasies deadly seriously, so that one feels that they are not only, in spite of their poverty, the best Babbitt can achieve but also the best Lewis himself can. The thinness of the fantasy, the poverty of the inner life, seem as much Lewis's as Babbitt's. Certainly they expose the threadbare texture of existence in Zenith, but they suggest that Lewis's own rebellion against American life did not go much further than his character's. "I wrote *Babbitt*," Lewis said years after the book was published, "not out of hatred for him but out of love," and it is not difficult to believe him. Nevertheless, it was the best thing he did; for if Babbitt himself is little more than a symbol of only half-reluctant conformity, there are still the other characters, Chum Frink and Virgil Gooch and Willis Ijams, the Rev. Dr Drew and Sheldon Smeeth of the Y.M.C.A. These, the whole procession of boosters for Zenith and the American Way of Life, Lewis mimics and caricatures with a relish and zest that can truly be called Dickensian. And parts of the novel, as when Babbitt attends the annual convention of the State Association of Real Estate Boards, remain horribly funny. But the satire is intermittent. Lewis was too close to Babbitt himself for it to be anything but inhibited.

[32]

But Dreiser, Anderson and Lewis were not the only writers from the Middle West at this time; indeed, it would not be exaggeration to say that during the years of the first world war and for the decade that followed it Middle West writers dominated American literature, certainly in fiction. There was F. Scott Fitzgerald,

who was born in St Paul, Minnesota.   While it is true that the
settings of his novels and stories are rarely in the Middle West
itself but more often in the East, in New York and the French
Riviera, it is not irrelevant that Jay Gatsby, whom Fitzgerald
presents almost as the platonic idea of the American, is from
South Dakota, and that the narrator of *The Great Gatsby*, Nick
Carroway, from Minnesota.   The other main characters of the
novel, Daisy and Tom Buchanan and Jordon Starr, are also from
the Middle West.   The novel is, as Nick Carroway says, "a story
of the West, after all—Tom and Gatsby, Daisy and Jordon and
I, were all Westerners, and perhaps we possessed some deficiency
in common which made us subtly unadaptable to Eastern Life".
They stand, in fact, in much the same relation of suspicion and
self-mistrust to New York and the East as Henry James's New
Englanders did to Europe.

Another writer from the Middle West, older than Fitzgerald,
was Willa Cather.   We have already seen how in *My Antonia*,
her novel of Czech immigrant life in Nebraska, she noted the
cultural loss that some immigrants suffered on their arrival in
America.   Through her work she developed a subtle criticism of
contemporary life that was not the less damaging because it was
oblique.   *My Antonia* can perhaps best be seen as a pastoral.
For Jim Burden, the successful, unhappily married New York
lawyer, whose memories of his life as a boy and a young man
in Nebraska form the content of the novel, the prairie of his
childhood is a symbol almost of paradise, of Eden before the fall.
For him this Eden is summed up in the figure of Antonia, the
Czech immigrant girl who was his playmate as a child.   But
Eden had been lost to him long before he arrived in New York.
At the age of thirteen he moves with his parents to town, to
Black Hawk, where Antonia goes into service as a "hired girl",
after the way of the daughters of Central European immigrants.
And already the town is seen as corrupting: vitality belongs to
the country, the frontier, and the hired immigrant girls come to
represent life as opposed to death.

Willa Cather's notion of the frontier as a paradise which is
inevitably to be destroyed by those who follow after and exploit
it is not so very different from Fenimore Cooper's.   It comes out
plainly in her novel *A Lost Lady*, which appeared in 1923.   The
action is set in the small Nebraska town of Sweet Water in the
late eighteen-eighties.   Again, as the centre of the novel there is
a young man, Niel Herbert, twelve when the action begins,

through whose consciousness we follow and interpret the action, which is concerned with the life of Mrs Forrester, the lost lady of the title. Her husband Captain Forrester, much older than she, is a veteran of the Civil War and pioneer railway-builder across the great plains. Through Niel's eyes we watch her gradual degeneration and moral corruption during the boredom of her husband's long years as an invalid, a declension only partly masked by her façade of gaiety and finally revealed to Niel when, as a young man, a student of architecture, he returns from the East to find her in the hands of a vulgar, loutish lawyer, Ivy Peters. To him has passed part of the Captain's estate, for the Captain has ruined himself by accepting moral responsibility for the affairs of a bank with which he is associated.

The symbolism could scarcely be more plain. Captain Forrester sums up in himself the men who made the Old West, men of action who were also dreamers. Peters is the man who comes after, the calculating exploiter, the embodiment of commercial values. Mrs Forrester, the lost lady, one is forced to see as the West itself, lost in the sense of being no more and lost, too, in the sense of having been corrupted, of having fallen. Willa Cather was writing myth, not history. It is difficult to believe that all the men who made the West were as gallant and chivalrous as Captain Forrester; and Miss Cather has nothing to say about the evils that attended the opening up of the West and of the building of the railways, the wholesale destruction of the buffalo-herds and the decimation and expulsion of the Indians. In this respect, *A Lost Lady* should be read alongside Michael Straight's novel *Carrington*, which is a more historically accurate picture of the opening of the West after the Civil War.

Willa Cather was possessed by an ideal dream of the American past and by a revulsion from the American present. Both receive their finest expression in a late novel, *Death Comes to the Archbishop*, published in 1927. The novel describes the missionary activities of two Roman Catholic priests, Bishop Jean Marie Latour and Father Joseph Vaillant, in New Mexico in the eighteen-fifties. They are missionaries in a feudal, pastoral world, preaching to Pueblo Indians and to the descendants of the Spanish settlers. The revulsion from the American present appears as a hatred of the industrial North with its urban, commercial values. It becomes scarcely less than a hatred of Anglo-Saxon America, which is seen as the destroyer of natural beauty and of pastoral innocence.

Another variant of the modern writer's relationship to his frontier ancestors is to be found in the fiction of Glenway Wescott, who was born in Wisconsin in 1901. During the thirties Wescott was an expatriate in Paris but was unable, on the evidence of his stories and novels, to escape from his native state, which appears as much a state of mind as a place. The title of his first book of stories, *Goodbye, Wisconsin*, is ironic; the characters of the stories, men and women who have made their physical escape from Wisconsin, are seen by Wescott as "a sort of vagrant chosen people like the Jews". He had by then, in his first novel, *The Apple of the Eye*, defined Wisconsin in terms of a repressive Puritanism, a grim conformity. But though he believed that Puritanism "makes people sick", Wescott did not underrate its appeal to the imagination, and it is this divided view of Puritanism, and hence of Wisconsin, which gives his novel, *The Grandmothers*, its distinction. Very early on in the novel, we meet Alwyn Tower, a young man from Wisconsin, an intellectual, sitting on a balcony above a French Mediterranean harbour. Drunken sailors from an American warship are quarrelling below, while he reads an essay he had written at the age of nineteen on what he has discovered about his family. The essay is, "as it were, a short biography of America". Tower is pondering, in other words, what it means to be an American; and the novel, which springs out of the essay, flows between the present and the past. It is a re-creation of the past, the young man's imaginative reconstruction of the lives of his grandparents, their families and relations who were pioneers in the opening up of Wisconsin in the middle years of the nineteenth century. In this remarkably solid evocation of pioneering life, a place and period are summed up, and summing them up, the author—or his narrator—comes to terms with them, recognises his ancestors in himself and recognises especially their regret "that the time for laughter and ease, even for him, never seemed to come".

The most famous writer from the Middle West is unquestionably Ernest Hemingway, who was born in the Chicago suburb of Oak Park, Illinois, in 1898 and brought up there and among the lakes of Michigan, the scene of his first collection of stories, *In Our Time*. More than any writer since Mark Twain, he forged for himself a prose style that was distinctly American, in the American grain, it seemed, as no prose, apart from the speaking voice of Huck Finn, had been before. It became in many ways the characteristic utterance of a generation. As, after the publication of *The Waste Land*, young poets tried to write like Eliot, so, after the publication of *In Our Time, Men without Women* and *The Sun Also Rises*, young prose-writers tried to reproduce the cadences and laconicisms of Hemingway.

Yet as soon as one looks at his literary career in relation to the American life of his time one realises that Hemingway's was a very strange case indeed. He was always—the phrase is Frank O'Connor's—a displaced person. As American as any American who has ever lived, it was as though there was no place for him in the United States, as though it had nothing to offer him as a writer. This, no doubt, is to exaggerate, but, outside the stories of *In Our Time*, which was his first book to appear from a commercial publisher, even when the scene is America it seems true what O'Connor says of him, that no one has a job or home and that the characters are those "associated with recreation rather than with labour", waiters, barmen, boxers, jockeys and, one might add, gangsters, hobos and small-time crooks. There is little of the United States in the pages of Hemingway. Since Hemingway is one of its greatest writers, this is surely very extraordinary.

Light on the problem is thrown by the stories in *In Our Time*. There are thirteen of them, and in them is contained, by implication, almost all Hemingway's later work. The stories mainly relate the boyhood experiences of Nick Adams among the woods and lakes of Michigan, initiations into life in the company of his father, a doctor, and of the Indians his father works among; but there are also stories of Nick as a young man, returned from the war. They are extremely violent stories; or rather, violence, Hemingway seems to be suggesting, whether that of hunting and fishing, of sex and childbirth, is the condition in which man must live and which he must learn to accept. Philip Young, in his fine book on Hemingway, has shown how closely the boy Nick's experiences chime with Huck Finn's; but for Huck there is always the possibility of escape. Even if we know the dream is delusive, he at any rate believes that he can "light out for the Territory", the open spaces beyond the frontier, beyond the corruptions of civilisation. In Hemingway, however, escape can be temporary only. In what perhaps is the most remarkable story in the collection, "Big Two-Hearted River", Nick returns to the scene of his boyhood in Michigan. On the surface, the story is merely an account of a trout-fishing trip, but in its

context and in the light of our knowledge of Nick's war experiences it is much more, a story of re-birth through return to
the healing waters of his childhood.

That escape can only be temporary is indicated by the brief
vignettes of violence, often not more than a paragraph long,
that appear in italics between the stories proper. These vignettes
of death in battle in the world war, in which Hemingway fought
in Italy, and in the war between the Greeks and the Turks which
he observed as a war correspondent, point to the future; we are
invited to see Nick's experiences of violence as a boy as rehearsals
for the violence he must experience as a man. In one of these
vignettes we see Nick as a wounded soldier on the Italian front.
He has been shot in the spine. Beside him lies an Italian soldier,
also badly wounded. Nick says to him, "You and me we've made
a separate peace." Making a separate peace is Nick's equivalent
to lighting out for the Territory.

As his life showed, it was also Hemingway's, for his life, with
its ceaseless quest after violent action in big-game hunting, in the
bull-ring, in war, seemed often a coarse and even brutal parody
of the life style expressed in his writings. There it appears as a
code of honour, in which the element of style is of great importance. In a sense, the code of honour he asserts is an aesthetic
response to the all-pervading fact of violence. It may be summed
up like this. Man dies; since man dies, it is intolerable that a
man should die less than well, with a sense of style; and as a
man dies, so should he live.

In his bullfighting book, *Death in the Afternoon*, Hemingway
said he wrote "to tell honestly the things I have found true".
What he found true was physical sensation; and of the life of
physical sensation, the exhilaration of hunting and fishing, of
violent exercise and of certain aspects of war, he was the unrivalled interpreter. But, love and war excepted, the life of
physical sensation that he explored is of a kind that is marginal
to life in modern industrial society. It exists as sports or re-
creation, so that in order to find what may be called the real
thing Hemingway had to roam far and wide from the contemporary United States, to Spain, to Africa, to Cuba. When
Melville wrote *Moby-Dick* he could base his story firmly in what
at the time was a great American industry, one central to the
American economy of the period. Hemingway's long short
story, *The Old Man and the Sea*, which has some affinities with
Melville's novel, could be set only in a relatively primitive

society, in Cuba. It would be difficult to over-estimate the violence that seems inherent in modern industrial society, especially in the United States, but it is violence of a kind and on a scale Hemingway could make nothing of. Its complexity made his code of honour almost grotesquely irrelevant to it, so that in many ways Hemingway appears as pre-industrial man. He made his separate peace with America by opting out of it, and the peace he made was very much, one cannot help thinking, that of a twentieth-century Natty Bumppo who in his old age plunged further and further into the prairies beyond the frontier, fleeing the settled communities—and their corruption—in which the mass of his fellows lived.

[33]

Hemingway turned aside from the America of his day. Some of his contemporaries, following the model of Whitman, sought to embrace it. Thomas Wolfe was one of these. So in their different ways were the novelist John Dos Passos and the poet Hart Crane. All sought to synthesise experience, American experience, the two novelists through a central figure resembling in function the "I, Walt Whitman" of "Song of Myself".

Wolfe was born in the South, in Asheville, North Carolina, in 1900, and studied both at the University of North Carolina and at Harvard. The facts of his life are to be found in his four novels *Look Homeward, Angel* and *Of Time and the River*, the only ones to appear in his lifetime, and *The Web and the Rock* and *You Can't Go Home Again*, published after his death in 1938. Whatever he called his central character, whether Eugene Gant in the first two novels or George Webber in the second pair, Wolfe was always his own hero. The four novels are indeed really a single work, a vast work; and even so, the books as we possess them are only a part of what he actually wrote, for they were carved out or assembled from works originally much longer by his editors. Words poured out of him in full spate, millions of them. He was physically a very large man, six feet five inches tall, with energies and appetites in proportion; his novels are correspondingly enormous. Their theme is always Wolfe himself, who is in constant reaction against wherever he is at any particular moment, whether at home in North Carolina, at university, in Brooklyn, Paris or London. He is always seeking, always fleeing. The titles of his first and last novels, *Look Homeward, Angel* and *You Can't Go Home Again*, seem to sum up the story of his search and frustration. What he describes in his millions of words is a permanent and inescapable estrangement:

Around him lay the village; beyond, the ugly rolling land, sparse with cheap farmhouses; beyond all this, America—more land, more wooden houses, more towns, hard and raw and ugly. He was reading Euripides, and all around him a world of black and white was eating fried food. He was reading of ancient sorceries and old ghosts, but did an old ghost ever come to haunt this land? The ghost of Hamlet's Father, in Connecticut,

> . . . I am thy father's spirit,
> Doomed for a certain term to walk the night
> Between Bloomington and Portland, Maine.

He felt suddenly the devastating impermanence of the nation. Only the earth endured—the gigantic American earth, bearing upon its awful breast a world of flimsy rickets. Only the earth endured—this broad terrific earth that had no ghosts to haunt it. Stogged in the desert, half-broken and overthrown, among the columns of lost temples strewn, there was no ruined image of Menkaura, there was no alabaster head of Aknaton. Nothing had been done in stone. Only this earth endured, upon whose lovely breast he read Euripides. Within its hills he had been held a prisoner; upon its plain he walked alone, a stranger.

O God! O God! We have been an exile in another land and a stranger in our town. The mountains were our masters; they went home to our eyes and our heart before we came to five. Whatever we can do or say must be forever hill bound. Our senses have been fed by our terrific land; our blood had learned to run to the imperial pulse of America which, leaving, we can never lose and never forget. We walked along a road in Cumberland, and stopped, because the sky hung down so low; and when we ran away from London, we went by little rivers in a land just big enough. And nowhere that we went was far; the earth and sky were close and near. And the old hunger returned—the terrible and obscure

hunger that haunts and hurts Americans, and that makes us exiles
at home and strangers wherever we go.

Not the least interesting thing in a very interesting passage is
the way in which the "he" of the first two paragraphs suddenly
becomes "we" in the third. The individual experience becomes
what Wolfe sees as the American experience: "the terrible and
obscure hunger . . . that makes us exiles at home and strangers
wherever we go". The Wolfe figure—Gant, Webber—becomes
a figure of myth, American myth. He contains the whole novel
and contains within himself universal references. Wolfe really
does see his characters *sub specie aeternitatis*; as Pamela Hansford
Johnson has said, Dixieland—the boarding house kept by
Gant's mother—"is the sad house of King Admetus".

But the passage shows something else: the nature of Wolfe's
prose. The passage could be re-set, without much change or
editing, as blank verse. Normally, we would regard this as a
grave flaw, but this is not necessarily so with Wolfe. Words are
in full spate; we are in the presence of whole Niagaras of rhetoric,
torrents of sound. His prose is, as Malcolm Cowley has said,
"a sort of chant, like the declamation of a Homeric bard".
Which, in his way, Wolfe was. The prose, heavily rhythmical,
exploiting the devices of poetry, serves to enlarge and elevate
his subject-matter, to maintain the heroic note, to project Eugene
Gant as a figure of myth, the embodiment of what for his creator
is the essential American experience of estrangement.

Another attempt to express the whole of America in fiction, as the
title of the trilogy, *U.S.A.*, shows, was made in the thirties by
John Dos Passos, who was born in Chicago in 1896. The scope
of *U.S.A.* is vast, and the book must be considered as an attempt
to write an American epic of the twentieth century. The writer
Dos Passos is nearest to is Whitman, but he is very much a
latter-day Whitman. The nineteenth-century poet could preach
the brotherhood of man as though it were actually materialising
in nineteenth-century America. Dos Passos is a Whitman who
has fallen from that state of innocence; for him, in *U.S.A.*, the
brotherhood of man is frustrated by the facts of twentieth-
century American life. *U.S.A.*, which is one of the remarkable
technical experiments in modern fiction, consists of the three
novels *The 42nd Parallel* (1930), *1919* (1932) and *The Big Money*
(1936), and together they offer a radical criticism, radical in both
senses, of American society during the first thirty years of this

century. The criticism is not cosmic, as it tends to be in Wolfe, but social, and it is only fair to say that Dos Passos's views are different now from what they were in the thirties. The work embraces the whole of the United States and its history from the Spanish-American War at the beginning of the century to the execution of the anarchists Sacco and Vanzetti in 1927. During this span of time it follows the lives of nine principal characters and, in doing so, takes in American industry, labour, politics, the war, the peace that followed, the new profession of public relations, and the arts.

It does this in a number of ways, the total effect of which is perhaps to operate against the success of the trilogy as a work of art. But what remains is a very remarkable book, even if one sees it as fragmented, is a unique anthology of one man's work. Dos Passos's aim is to show his characters in the context of their times, to implicate them in the whole history of their times. To this end, he employs a number of technical devices which are in a sense separable from the characters but within which they have their being.

First, there is what Dos Passos calls "Newsreel", which is exactly what it says, the background of the times against which the characters move. Newsreel is built up from, is a kind of montage of, newspaper headlines, extracts from newspaper reports and snatches from popular songs. Then appearing less often but interspersed between the chapters, are a number of biographies or representative Americans of the first quarter of the century. These, which in some ways constitute the most impressive feature of the book, are written in a typographically patterned prose which is really a kind of free verse. Among the historic personages celebrated in these prose poems are Eugene Debs, the American socialist leader; Luther Burbank, the Californian botanist; Big Bill Haywood, the labour leader who led the revolutionary organisation International Workers of the World; William Jennings Bryan, the famous orator, advocate and presidential candidate; the steel millionaire Andrew Carnegie; Edison; the Progressive senator Robert La Follette; John Reed, Dos Passos's contemporary at Harvard who went to Russia at the time of the Bolshevik Revolution, became a communist and wrote *Ten Days That Shook the World*; Theodore Roosevelt; President Wilson; Thorstein Veblen, the left-wing economist whose thinking much influenced Dos Passos; the pioneer aviators the Wright brothers; the great financial house of the

Morgans; Henry Ford; the architect Frank Lloyd Wright; and
Insull, the financier. The biography that ends the book is that
of an anonymous young vagrant who is trying to bum a lift
from passing cars. These biographies alone would have been
enough to make Dos Passos's literary reputation.

Dos Passos calls his third device "The Camera Eye". In a
sense this is the interior life of the novel. Existing in counter-
point to the characters proper, it is written in a stream-of-con-
sciousness prose which again often approximates typographically
to free verse. It is essentially subjective. But whose eye is it?
Partly the author's, for certainly Dos Passos's own experiences
of the first world war, in which he served first as an ambulance
driver with the French and then a private in the medical corps of
the U.S. Army, contribute to it; but also of a more generalised
figure, something like Whitman's "I was the man, I suffer'd, I
was there".

Within these devices exists what might be called the novel
proper, the adventures of the various characters, all in their
different ways meant to be representative figures, capitalists, exploiters, rebels and so on. It is here, where the work comes
closest to being what we conventionally expect a novel to be,
that *U.S.A.* is at its weakest. Nevertheless, it is still an achievement of some magnitude, and its criticism of American life rises
to its climax in its pages, when we see the young hitch-hiker,
unemployed, nameless, epitome in himself of nameless thousands
of unemployed, standing at the roadside somewhere in the Mid-
West trying to thumb a lift, while above him the aeroplanes
fly with their cargoes of business men between New York and
Los Angeles. Here Dos Passos seems to show us the United
States in mid-continent in all its contrasts, which cancel one
another out: progress on the roads, in the air, transport moving
faster and faster—while the anonymous workless American still
walks, begging a lift and not getting one, mocked by the promise
of opportunity, mocked by the American promises. What Dos
Passos shows us is a United States that is the negation of the
brotherhood of man to man Whitman conceived it to be.

Necessarily, since he was a poet, Hart Crane's intentions were
very different from Dos Passos's. A tragic figure—he killed
himself at the age of thirty-three—he was born in Garrettsville,
Ohio, in 1899; his parents' ancestors had migrated from New
England in covered wagons to Ohio when it was still the
Western Reserve. A poet from the age of thirteen, Crane,

despite limited formal education, became a learned poet whose
influences were not so very different from those on T. S. Eliot:
the Elizabethan dramatists, Donne, Blake and the French
Symbolists, especially Baudelaire and Rimbaud, powerfully
affected him. But he used these influences for purposes other
than, indeed opposed to, those of Eliot. Crane's work *The
Bridge*, on which, though unfinished, his reputation will probably
rest, may be seen as a riposte to *The Waste Land*. In the last
analysis, Crane is in the tradition of Whitman.

Crane, in a statement of his general aims and theories, said
that he was concerned with the future of America, not because
he thought America had any "so called par value as a state"
but because he was persuaded that in America there were destined
to be discovered "certain as yet undefined spiritual, perhaps a
new hierachy of faith" going beyond anything known elsewhere.
He added that he liked to feel himself a potential factor in this
process. Elsewhere he wrote: "Unless poetry can absorb the
machine, i.e., *acclimatise* it as naturally and casually as trees,
cattle, galleons, castles and all other human associations of the
past, then poetry has failed of its full contemporary function."
In the same essay he stated that he saw Whitman, despite his
faults, as "the most typical and valid expression of the American
psychosis", by which he can only have meant *psyche*.

The Bridge, which is a sequence of fifteen poems, seeks to
create the myth of America through a restatement of crucial
American experiences. Crane's difficulty was to find the element
that would unify them. He found it in Brooklyn Bridge, which
he saw as the symbol of the "initial impulses" of the American
people, their unique identity and their hopes of the future. The
poem "To Brooklyn Bridge" stands as the prologue to the work
as a whole, and he was in fact living in Brooklyn when he wrote
it, and not only living there, but, as he discovered later, living in
the very house and working in the very room from which
Washington Roebling, the paralysed engineer of the Bridge, had
watched its construction.

The Bridge ranges across American history and in Crane's
choice of events and characters has its resemblances to William
Carlos Williams's prose work *In the American Grain*. Pocahontas
is celebrated, and so is Rip Van Winkle. The Indians are com-
memorated in the poem "The Dance", the pioneers in the poem
"Indiana". The whalers and seafarers of New England inspire
"Cutty Sark", which is followed by "Cape Hatteras", which takes

in the exploits of the Wright brothers with their "sinewy silver biplane" and ends with an apotheosis of Whitman. Perhaps the most remarkable section of all is the evocation of modern New York in "The Tunnel"—the New York subway—in which appears Edgar Allen Poe, his eyes "like agate lanterns . . . below the toothpaste and dandruff ads".

Crane is not an easy poet; he had a way of telescoping images that is often baffling. But he had great intensity, almost hallucinatory power of vision, and a soaring eloquence. He wrote in full consciousness of the fissured, atomised modern world, and perhaps in his life it defeated him; but he also had a vision of unity and of two worlds existing simultaneously, the world of time and the world of eternity. He said himself that in his poetry he was "really building a bridge between so-called classic experience and the many divergent realities of the seething, confused cosmos of today". Roebling's Brooklyn Bridge is at once a great engineering feat and a great artistic achievement: whether it is an adequate enough symbol to carry Crane's sense of American unity in diversity has been doubted, but it produced in the dedicatory poem, "To Brooklyn Bridge", one of the finest of American poems.

The bridge is invoked in winter and the poem opens with the image of a gull rising from the water and flying beyond the Statue of Liberty. The gull in its flight suggests sails, which are seen as crossing the figures in a ledger in an office in a sky-scraper near the river. The contrast is with routine, as shown in the life of a clerk whose day is spent bent over ledgers and whose evenings are spent in the cinema whose "panoramic sleights" promise but do not provide answers to the problems of every day. This restlessness and frustration is in turn contrasted with the serenity of the bridge, which is apostrophised almost as though it were God and which is plainly meant to be seen as a symbol of integrity, freedom and harmony rebuking the "subway scuttle" from which emerges the madman who flings himself to death from its parapet. So, packed with meaning, densely compressed in expression, the poem proceeds stanza by stanza to its conclusion:

> O Sleepless as the river under thee,
> Vaulting the sea, the prairie's dreaming sod,
> Unto us lowliest sometime sweep, descend
> And of the curveship lend a myth to God.

In these lines the bridge seems to take on the immortal attributes of the rainbow as symbol of promise to man and seems also to be invited to become the embodiment in myth of God.

The Bridge remains a most impressive attempt to create a myth of America. But Crane was not the only poet of his time to attempt it. At a much lower level, for he had little of Crane's poetic quality and intensity, Stephen Vincent Benét in 1928 nevertheless pulled off the almost impossible feat of writing a genuinely popular long poem in *John Brown's Body*, on the famous Abolitionist and the Civil War. Here again the Whitmanic note is plain to hear, in the "Invocation", in which Benét summons the American muse, "as various as your land". The American muse is shown to be the sum-total of American attributes and history.

At much the same time Southern writers were creating a myth of the South. We have already glanced at Allen Tate's novel *The Fathers* and at William Faulkner, whose exploration of the complex fate entailed in being a Southerner is the profoundest we have had. But what happened in the Southern novel happened also in poetry, in such poems as John Crowe Ransom's "Antique Harvesters", Tate's "Ode to the Confederate Dead" and his elegy on Jefferson Davis and Robert Penn Warren's *Brother to Dragons*. In the works of these writers and others such as Caroline Gordon and later William Styron the South seems, at first glance, presented almost as a separate nation; and certainly the kind of fate that is represented is very different from those of the majority of Americans. Yet when this literature of the South is looked at more closely it is seen as fundamentally American. Whatever the difference between the New England experience and the Southern and when all differences arising from the times in which they wrote are taken into account, Hawthorne and Faulkner have more in common with each other than either has with any of his English contemporaries. They share similar modes of assessing the past and its influence on the present and of apprehending experience.

[34]

During the thirties, however, the Southern writing of the decade, which now seems its greatest glory, appeared marginal to American writing of the times generally. This was because its preoccupations were very different from those of the North. American writing became, to an extent it has not been before or since, a socially oriented literature. In this respect, it was behaving similarly to contemporary writing in Britain and in Western Europe generally, and for the same reasons: the pheno-menon of economic depression and widespread unemployment and, arising from it, the threat of fascism and world war. The great names in American fiction at this time were John Dos Passos, James T. Farrell, with his *Studs Lonigan* trilogy and John Steinbeck, with *In Dubious Battle* and, in particular, *The Grapes of Wrath*. All three were championing the under-dog against the power of finance-capitalism. Yet the novels they and others wrote were significantly different from any produced in England. They were much more powerful and they were much more violent. The violence is easily explained: it reflected a tradition of violence in American industrial relations, of the use of firearms and terrorisation to suppress strikes, that had no counterpart in English experience. Also, though the lot of the unemployed man in Britain was wretched enough, it was never quite so miserable as the American's; unemployment insurance benefits had existed in Britain for almost twenty years, so that to a small extent at least the British working man was cushioned, as the American was not until later in the decade, against complete poverty.

As to the much greater power of American writing at this time, two contributing factors may be isolated. One was the much greater sense of shock caused by the depression in the United States. When the Wall Street crash occurred in October 1929, the event which set off the chain-reaction of economic disasters throughout the world, Britain had scarcely recovered from the effects of the first world war and the labour troubles, culminating in the General Strike of 1926, that followed it. The United States, on the other hand, had been experiencing the greatest boom in its history; Americans, it seemed, were becoming richer and richer, and there appeared no end to the riches in store for them. The riches disappeared over-night, and millions were plunged from comparative affluence into poverty. The bottom had fallen out of things, for most people with scarcely any warning at all. The shock was traumatic and the reaction as extreme. If bewilderment was the first emotion felt, anger was the next.

The other factor has something to do with the differences in class-structure between the two countries. The most successful English attempt to render the period in terms of the demoralisation caused by unemployment and the threat of fascism is to be found in Christopher Isherwood's novel *Mr Norris Changes Trains* and the stories in *Goodbye to Berlin*. These are set in Germany. Admittedly, Isherwood had gone to the scene where the demoralisation and the threat were at their most dramatic. But the point is, no English writer succeeded anything like so well with the English scene. No amount of sympathy or political identification with unemployed workers could compensate for the middle-class English novelist's lack of first-hand knowledge of life outside his own class. He was imprisoned, as Americans like Dos Passos, a Harvard man, and Steinbeck were not, in a comparatively rigid hierarchical structure in which the various social classes were differentiated one from another by the kind of education they had received and the assumptions engendered by it, the outward and visible signs of these being the modes of speech that branded most English with the stamp of their class origins. This is not to say that class did not exist in the United States; but it was much less consciously felt and much less of a barrier between man and man than in England. Equality as between man and man, at any rate so long as the men were white, was taken much more for granted in America; and there was also the American tradition of work, of young people taking vacation jobs as waiters, petrol-station attendants and so on and working their way through high school or college. The experience of work, in other words, of hard physical labour, was much more widely shared by all classes in the United States than in England.

Like social fiction throughout the western world at the time,

the American novel tended to be Marxist.   Much stronger than
the Marxist note today appears a native American radicalism or
populism, even a harking back to Jacksonian democracy.   The
emphasis was on egalitarianism, in the old sense of Jack being as
good as his master.   Indeed, many of these novels seemed to
restate the American dream in its simplest form.   This comes
out particularly in the fiction of John Steinbeck.

Steinbeck's first major novel, *In Dubious Battle*, published in
1936, describes an attempt by Communists to organise the
itinerant fruit-pickers of California into a trade union and the
industrial warfare that follows.   On the surface, it is a story of
Radical heroism, of the oppressed and illiterate restored to their
dignity as men by their fight against victimisation: and it ends
on a note of fervent rhetoric.   But it is a much more ambiguous
novel than it seemed at the time.   Steinbeck's spokesman seems
to be the doctor, Burton, who acts as medical officer in the
striking fruit-pickers' camp.   He is certainly no Marxist.   When
challenged by the Communist organisers to state what he believes,
why he is there risking his life and reputation, he says, "I don't
believe in the cause, but I believe in men."   He believes, in fact, in
men in much the same way as Whitman believed in what he called
"the en-masse", a kind of biological unanimism that seems also to
have much in common with Emerson's notion of the "over-soul".
Man in the mass, man as a species, seems for Burton—and one
guesses for Steinbeck too—to have almost religious connotations.

In his later novel *Of Mice and Men*, which deals with individuals
rather than men in a group, the dream that is expressed is
primitively and fundamentally American.   This is a story about
the relationship between two men, one a feeble-minded giant,
who exists at what seems the lowest level of articulateness.
Almost the one thing that differentiates them from the animals is
their capacity to dream; and what they dream is of something
they will never attain, a little white house standing in its own
few acres at the end of the trail.   This is essentially, though it is
told on a much vaster scale, the story of *The Grapes of Wrath*, the
most successful in popular terms of American novels of social
protest of the thirties.   It describes how the dispossessed
share-croppers of Oklahoma, uprooted by economic depression,
pour in their broken-down old cars across the mountains and the
desert into the promised land, the rich valleys of California.   They
are doomed to disillusionment: California is settled; no one
wants them there.   Again, Steinbeck sees the "Okies" as "group

men", almost as a biological species on the move, and indeed, when Steinbeck tries to render them as individuals, he fails almost completely, a fact which makes it almost impossible to see him as a major novelist. But all the time there is in his work a generous sense of man's equality with man, and a sense too of human goodness even at the lowest levels, as in this passage:

> The cars of the migrant people crawled out of the side roads on to the great cross-country highway, and they took the migrant way to the West. In the daylight they scuttled like bugs to the westward; and as the dark caught them, they clustered like bugs near to shelter and to water. And because they were lonely and perplexed, because they had all come from a place of sadness and worry and defeat, and because they were all going to a new mysterious place, they huddled together; they talked together; they shared their lives, their food, and the things they hoped for in the new country. Thus it might be that one family camped near a spring and another camped for the spring and for the company, and a third because two families had pioneered the place and found it good. And when the sun went down, perhaps twenty families and twenty cars were there.

From one point of view, Steinbeck's "Okies" appear sub-human, a horde of lemmings plunging heedlessly, as though driven by blind instinct, to destruction. But from another, they seem to assert a principle of recurrence in American experience, recreating the experience of their forbears as they huddled together in the stinking steerage in the immigrant ship bound for a dream, comforting themselves with thoughts of the dream, and as they gathered together later with their covered wagons to cross the great plains in further pursuance of the dream.

The Grapes of Wrath was published in 1938: in the same year appeared another novel which now seems in some ways a sour comment upon it, or at any rate on the almost instinctive westward drive it celebrates. This is Nathanael West's *The Day of the Locust*. West had already written, five years earlier, *Miss Lonelyhearts*, a bitterly comic story about a New York newspaperman, a "sob sister" on a daily paper, who is appalled and obsessed almost to madness by the sufferings and loneliness of the thousands of readers who write to him for advice. For West, the human lot, as presented in *Miss Lonelyhearts*, is outrageous and intolerable, intrinsically absurd, and bearable only when translated into the comic.

In *The Day of the Locust* the scene is Los Angeles; and just as in his earlier novel West had seized upon the sob-sister's column as the symbol of hopeless suffering, so in the later one he takes Hollywood as the symbol of unreality, the world of illusion in which for him Americans largely live.   The unreality and illusion are brilliantly conveyed in the first chapter in the description of a film set.   But, as immediately after we walk through Los Angeles with the hero, Tod Hackett, we realise that the film set is no more unreal than the world outside it.   Tod is a painter who has come to Hollywood to learn to paint film sets but also in order to paint a large apocalyptic painting to be called "The Burning of Los Angeles"; and the people he meets in the course of the novel's action are to be seen as figures, as it were, in his canvas. But behind these people, all of them emblems of unreality or illusion, existing on the fringe of the film industry, there is the nameless horde, the locusts that have borne down upon California from the Middle West.

It is here that the parallel with *The Grapes of Wrath* is inescapable. But there is this difference between Steinbeck's lemmings and West's locusts.   Whereas Steinbeck's "Okies" flood into California in search of the good earth, West's anonymous crowds are retired people—"senior citizens" they would be called today— who have migrated from the Middle West, driven, as the title of the novel suggests, by an instinctive urging to California, to wait for death there in a sort of indignant boredom in what has proved to be a Never-Never land, a phony paradise.   The novel ends with these bored displaced Mid-Westerners pouring in their boredom into Hollywood to watch the guests arriving at a fashionable film premiere.   The crowd turns into an angry mob, gets out of control and almost crushes Tod to death; and in the behaviour of the mob Tod realises that here is his painting "The Burning of Los Angeles" become a reality.   What he sees, and the reader through him, is something like the ultimate ironical presentation of the American Dream.

West was killed at the age of thirty-six in a car accident in 1940, almost unknown as a novelist.   His novels had been commercial failures, and he had earned his living writing scripts for B pictures.   After the war his novels were rediscovered, and he can now be seen as the first of a whole generation of American novelists whose work has been motivated by what has been called "the vision of the ludicrous catastrophe".   The works of these novelists, which include Ralph Ellison's *Invisible*

Man and Joseph Heller's *Catch-22*, are characterised by black comedy often farcical and outrageously funny even when, and in a sense because, it is being pessimistically nihilistic. Fundamental to these novels seems to be the view of individual man as helpless and impotent in the face of the great impersonal forces of modern technological society. But this view of modern man is raised to what one is tempted to call the metaphysical plane, and this links these novels to the later works of Herman Melville and even more, perhaps, to the fiction of Franz Kafka.

It is as though helplessness, chaos and absurdity are basic to the human condition; but the distinguishing quality of these novels is that the emphasis falls as much on the absurdity as on the helplessness and the chaos. If it did not, these novels would probably be tragic. Their authors are describing the universal human condition as they see it. Their view of it is one that is widely held throughout the western world, at any number of levels of seriousness; something like it is expressed, for instance, in the film *Dr. Strangelove*, with its highly significantly alternative title, *How I Learnt to Love the Bomb*. But since their vision of it is rendered in purely American terms it is bound to appear first of all as a criticism of the quality of American life. The dream of infinite possibilities has become a nightmare, nightmare that can be endured only because it is felt as funny. Life—but in the first instance American life—is seen as a hideous comedy.

The phrase, "the vision of the ludicrous catastrophe", cannot, of course, be applied to anything like the whole of contemporary American writing. But what is still almost universally apparent in it is the obsession with the nature of the American experience, a continual scrutinising of its values, of its promises and its achievements. It seems noteworthy that Norman Mailer has actually entitled one of his more recent novels *An American Dream*, even though on the face of it the matter of the book seems quite unrelated to the title. But light on this is thrown by his latest novel *Why Are We in Vietnam?* Again, the novel seems to have nothing to do with its title; the war in Vietnam is mentioned only once, right at the end of the book. On the surface, the novel describes the attempts of a Texan millionaire and his son to shoot a bear in Alaska. There are links here with a theme that runs through American literature and is treated in different ways in Hemingway's *The Old Man and the Sea*, Faulkner's long short story *The Bear* and Melville's *Moby-Dick*. But Mailer is using the archetypal theme for a purpose rather different from those earlier writers. He is using it to dramatise, as it were, his criticisms of Texas and its values, which he seems to see as representing the essence of aggressive America.

This continued obsession with America and the idea of America can be illustrated equally well from contemporary poetry, and as instances one might take two poets who exist in obvious contrast one with the other and who belong to quite separate and indeed opposed traditions of American poetry, Allen Ginsberg and Robert Lowell.

Ginsberg is the most famous of the Beat poets. The Beats, like their successors the Hippies, reject the majority values of the United States, the Puritan heritage and what is usually understood by the phrase The American Way of Life, with its implied emphasis on the commercial virtues. Their criticism of these majority values may be summed up, perhaps, in a sentence from Jack Kerouac's novel *The Dharma Bums*: ". . . my karma was to be born in America where nobody has any fun or believes in anything, especially freedom."

In fact, the Beats are not nearly as new as they seemed to be when they first appeared in the 1950s. They represent a mid-twentieth-century version of mid-nineteenth-century American Transcendentalism. They are, in other words, the descendants of Emerson, Thoreau and Whitman—particularly of Whitman. The behaviour of Dean Moriarty in Kerouac's first novel *On the Road* springs, we are told, from "a wild yea-saying overburst of American joy". The implication is plain: it is the old notion of the American as the New Man, free of bondage, any bondage, all bondage, at one with nature. The modern American is of course no more free of bondage than anyone else. As a young man, he is liable to be drafted into the armed services; and it is difficult at this point not to quote the last sentence of the preface to the second edition of *Europe without Baedeker*, by that great recalcitrant old-fashioned Yankee, Edmund Wilson: "I did not foresee the present development of our huge official bureaucracies, Pentagon, C.I.A., Internal Revenue Bureau, or that a human bureaucracy of clerks and officials, invested with special powers which are more or less mechanically exercised, would resort in the long run to a mechanical bureaucracy of computers."

Wilson's sentence suggests admirably the America to which the Beats are opposed, as Thoreau was to the America of his day. What they would put in its place is very much the America and its values that Whitman depicts in *Leaves of Grass*. One's

objection to the Beats is not to their ideas but to the fact that the
ideas have been better expressed before, precisely by Thoreau,
Emerson and Whitman.   Nevertheless, Ginsberg at his best is a
powerful poet, and he is at his most powerful when he is most
Whitmanic.   But Whitman could see himself as the poet of a new
country and an advancing democracy; he was, consciously, the
spokesman of his time.   By contrast, Ginsberg is writing against
his time, which makes the permissiveness he preaches seem often
outrageous, as also does the language in which he preaches it.
He is the poet as critic of his age and of his society.   He is not
the less American for that.   America is his subject, as we see from
the opening lines of what is still his most famous poem, "Howl":

> I saw the best minds of my generation, destroyed by madness,
>   starving, hysterical, naked,
> dragging themselves through the negro streets at dawn looking for
>   an angry fix,
> angelheaded hipsters burning for the ancient heavenly connection
>   to the starry dynamo in the machinery of night . . .

Ginsberg has the right origins for a Whitmanic poet: born in
the industrial city of Newark, New Jersey, across the Hudson
from New York, he worked as a dish-washer and a spot-welder
before going to Columbia University.   Robert Lowell comes
from one of the most illustrious of New England families, and
after two years at Harvard went to Kenyon College, Ohio, to
study writing under John Crowe Ransom, who is technically
one of the most influential of modern critics.   Lowell, then, is a
learned poet in much the same way that Ransom himself or
T. S. Eliot or W. H. Auden may be called learned poets: and
besides this, his poetry is characterised, to borrow Coleridge's
phrase, by "a more than usual state of emotion with more than
usual order".   His poetry has changed in manner since his first
collection was published in 1944; it has become much more
acutely personal, direct, "confessional".   Yet it remains in some
ways an intensely local poetry in that it is rooted in the landscape
and history of New England.   What is perhaps the most famous
of his early poems is called "The Quaker Graveyard at Nantucket",
and at times he seems almost as much obsessed with his Puritan
ancestors as Hawthorne was.   In another famous early poem,
"Mr Edwards and the Spider", he seems to identify himself
with Jonathan Edwards; in this poem he fuses, as it were,
Edwards's essay on the flying spider, written when he was a

student at Yale, with his great sermon "Sinners in the Hands of an Angry God". And although, with his collection *Life Studies*, published in 1959, Lowell seemed to have moved into a much vaster poetic world, in a later volume, *For the Union Dead*, we find him again contemplating Edwards and his spider in the poem "Jonathan Edwards in Western Massachusetts", while in the title-poem itself, from which I have already quoted, he may be seen assessing Boston's present in terms of its past—and by extension, the present of the whole United States in terms of its past.

PART 3

America and the Rest of the World

[35]

In his *History of the United States during the Administrations of Thomas Jefferson and John Madison* Henry Adams has some pages on European misconceptions of Americans and America in the early days of the Republic. His brilliant analysis is relevant to the United States today.

The mass of Americans at the end of the eighteenth century, Adams tells us, "were sanguine and self-confident, partly by temperament, but partly also by reason of ignorance; for they knew little of the difficulties which surround a complex society". It was the ignorance that struck European visitors. It was illustrated by such a proposal as that made in the House of Representatives in 1796 to insert in the Reply to the President's Speech a statement that the nation was "the freest and most enlightened in the world". Adams comments:

> ... a nation as yet in swaddling-clothes, which had neither literature, arts, sciences, nor history; nor even enough nationality to be sure that it was a nation. The moment was peculiarly ill-chosen for such a claim, because Europe was on the verge of an outburst of genius. Goethe and Schiller, Mozart and Haydn, Kant and Fichter, Cavendish and Herschel were making way for Walter Scott, Wordsworth and Shelley, Heine and Balzac, Beethoven and Hegel, Oersted and Cuvier, great physicists, biologists, geologists, chemists, mathematicians, metaphysicians, and historians by the score. Turner was painting his earliest landscapes; Napoleon was taking command of the French armies, and Nelson of the English fleets; investigators, reformers, scholars, and philosophers swarmed, and the influence of enlightenment, even amid universal war, was working with an energy such as the world had never before conceived.

And yet, Adams goes on to suggest, Americans might have argued that, all this notwithstanding, "in matters which for the moment mainly concerned themselves Europe was a full century

behind America.   If they were right in thinking that the next
necessity of human progress was to lift the average man upon
an intellectual and social level with the most favoured, they
stood at least three generations nearer than Europe to their
common goal."   This American belief in progress, which
Adams, not ironically I think, calls a "doubtful and even im-
probable principle", was stated in 1800 by Jefferson in the
following terms:

> Progress is either physical or intellectual.   If we can bring it
> about that men are on the average an inch taller in the next genera-
> tion than in this; if they are an inch larger round the chest; if their
> brain is an ounce heavier, and their life a year or two longer—
> that is progress.   If fifty years hence the average man shall in-
> variably argue from two ascertained premises where he now jumps
> to a conclusion from a single supposed revelation—that is progress!
> I expect it to be made here, under our democratic stimulants, on
> a grand scale, until every man is potentially an athlete in body and
> an Aristotle in mind.

The key to this progress was "our democratic stimulants",
which can well be expressed in a string of negatives: no mon-
archy, no aristocracy, no state church, no class system, no
education for an *élite* only, no standing army.   The consequences,
as Adams states them, are these:

> Stripped for the hardest work, every muscle trim and elastic, every
> ounce of brain ready for use, and not a trace of superfluous flesh on
> his nervous and supple body, the American stood in the world a
> new order of man.   From Maine to Florida, society was in this
> respect the same, and was so organised as to use its human forces
> with more economy than could be approached by any society
> of the world elsewhere.   Not only were artificial barriers carefully
> removed, but every influence that could appeal to ordinary ambition
> was applied.   No brain or appetite active enough to be conscious
> of stimulants could fail to answer the intense incentive.   Few
> human beings, however sluggish, could long resist the temptation
> to acquire power; and the elements of power were to be had in
> America almost for asking.   Reversing the old-world system, the
> American stimulant increased in energy as it reached the lowest
> and most ignorant class, dragging and whirling them upward as
> in the blast of a furnace.   The penniless and homeless Scotch or
> Irish immigrant was caught and consumed by it; for every stroke

of the axe and the hoe made him a capitalist, and made gentlemen of his children. Wealth was the strongest agent for moving the mass of mankind; but political power was hardly less tempting to the more intelligent and better-educated swarms of American-born citizens, and the instinct of activity, once created, seemed hereditable and permanent in the race.

Compared with this lithe young figure, Europe was actually decrepitude. . . .

But this was not at all how Americans and America appeared to contemporary Europe. Adams quotes a French visitor as writing, soon after 1800: "There is, perhaps, no civilised country in the world where there is less generosity in the souls, and in the heads fewer of those illusions which make the charm of the consolation of life. Man here weighs everything, and sacrifices everything to his interest." The instinct of activity seemed to be the instinct of rapacity. "Rapacity", Adams says, "was the accepted explanation of American peculiarities," even though it scarcely made sense since European visitors were constantly struck by what seemed to them the recklessness and extravagance with which Americans spent money. Adams quoted from *The Excursion* to show how even Wordsworth, the greatest English poet of the age, could create no conception of the United States "more poetical than that of any Cumberland beggar he might have met in his morning walk". And yet, Adams adds, "Wordsworth might have convinced himself by a moment's thought that no country could act on the imagination as America acted upon the instincts of the ignorant and poor, without some quality that deserved better treatment than poignant scorn". What Wordsworth and Europeans generally failed to see, Adams says, was that "the hard, practical, money-getting American democrat, who had neither generosity nor honour nor imagination, and who inhabited cold shades where fancy sickened and where genius died, was in truth *living in a world of dream*, and acting out a drama more instinct with poetry than all the avatars of the East, walking in gardens of emeralds and rubies, in ambition already ruling the world and guiding Nature with a kinder and wiser hand than had ever yet been felt in human history". The italics are mine: Adams was writing in 1884; I suspect this was the first time the analogy of the dream had been applied to the American experiment.

The European failure to realise that a dream was at work was probably inevitable. "The American democrat", Adams says, "possessed little art of expression, and did not watch his own emotions with a view of uttering them either in prose or verse." Besides, from its very nature the dream was all but incommunicable. Adams imagines a dialogue between an American and someone from the outside world:

> "Look at my wealth!" cried the American to his foreign visitor. "See these solid mountains of salt and iron, of lead, copper, silver, and gold! See these magnificent cities scattered broadcast to the Pacific! See my cornfields rustling and waving in the summer breeze from ocean to ocean, so far that the sun itself is not high enough to mark where the distant mountains bound my golden seas! Look at this continent of mine, fairest of created worlds, as she lies turning up to the sun's never-failing caress her broad and exuberant breasts, overflowing with milk for her hundred million children! See how she glows with youth, health, and love!" Perhaps it was not altogether unnatural that the foreigner, on being asked to see what needed centuries to produce, should have looked about him with bewilderment and indignation. "Gold! cities! cornfields! continents! Nothing of the sort! I see nothing but tremendous wastes, where sickly men and women are dying of homesickness or are scalped by savages! mountain-ranges a thousand miles long, with no means of getting to them, and nothing in them when you get there! swamps and forests choked with their own rotten ruins! nor hope of better for a thousand years! Your story is a fraud, and you are a liar and swindler!"

The passage seems to place the American habit of boasting and European reactions to it, as we see them for instance in *Martin Chuzzlewit*, in which Dickens mercilessly satirises what seemed to him the cynical exploitation of immigrant ignorance and gullibility, in a light rather different from that in which it is usually seen. If the European thought in terms of actuality, what inspired the American was the dream of possibility, of infinite possibility. And Adams ends his chapter with a passage that brings out to the full the breath-taking immensity of the American Dream:

> If the priests and barons who set their names to Magna Charta had been told that in a few centuries every swine-herd and cobbler's apprentice would write and read with an ease such as few kings could then command, and reason with better logic than any

university could then practise, the priest and baron would have
been more incredulous than any man who was told in 1800 that
within another five centuries the ploughboy would go a-field
whistling a sonata of Beethoven, and figure out in quaternions the
relation of his furrows.   The American democrat knew so little of
art that among his popular illusions he could not then nourish
artistic ambition; but leaders like Jefferson, Gallatin, and Barlow
might without extravagance count upon a coming time when
diffused ease and education should bring the masses into familiar
contact with higher forms of human achievement, and their vast
creative power, turned toward a nobler culture, might rise to the
level of that democratic genius which found expression in the
Parthenon; might revel in the delights of a new Buonarroti and a
richer Titian; might create for five hundred million people the
America of thought and art which could alone satisfy their
omnivorous ambition.

Whether the illusions, so often affirmed and so often denied to
the American people, took such forms or not, there were in effect
the problems that lay before American society: could it transmute
the social power into the higher forms of thought?   Could it
provide for the moral and intellectual needs of mankind?   Could
it take permanent political shape?   Could it give new life to religion
and art?   Could it create and maintain in the mass of mankind those
habits of mind which had hitherto belonged to men of science
alone?   Could it physically develop the convolutions of the human
brain?   Could it produce, or was it compatible with, the differentia-
tion of a higher variety of the human race?   Nothing less than this
was necessary for its complete success.

Adams is thinking in terms of a period of five hundred years,
not half of which has gone by since the time of which he was
writing.   It would be impossible to draw up a balance-sheet of
America's success and failure in the realisation of its dream, but
certain things seem clear.   It is a fact that the United States has
achieved for its citizens the highest standard of living in the
world, meaning by that the material conditions of life to which
the great majority of people everywhere now aspire.   It seems
equally certain that it offers its citizens greater possibilities of
self-realisation through education and leisure than exist anywhere
in the world.   It is also the most powerful as well as the richest
country in the world, and this has created especial problems
both for itself and the world generally.   It emerged as a world

power at the end of the first world war, and though this was probably inevitable historically, it marked the end of the isolation that was one of the pre-requisites to the success of the American Dream and the beginning of the present period of involvement with other countries, military alliances and the rest, against which Washington and the early leaders of the Republic had expressly warned their fellow-countrymen. It was the end, it might be said, of American innocence, though, paradoxically, American military adventures abroad, in Korea, Central America and Vietnam, for all they represent a radical break with the American past, can still be seen as attempts to preserve the purity of the American Dream from corruption by outside factors. To many Americans and non-Americans alike, they often seem neurotic attempts.

But there is another way of assessing the United States today and its relationship with the rest of the world, and the clue to it may be found in a statement made by A. Alvarez in his *Under Pressure: The Writer in Society: Eastern Europe and the U.S.A.*, a book that is essential reading for anyone concerned with the American experience. America, Alvarez maintains, "is, for better and for worse, squarely, uncompromisingly in the twentieth century". The twentieth century has often been called the "American century", and in Europe the stock reaction to this is one of fear, fear of what is called Americanisation, "Coca-Colonisation". In fact, much of what seems Americanisation is simply the inevitable outcome of technological development, of modern means of production and distribution, and is not specifically American at all except insofar as the Americans have pioneered them. The obvious symbol of the modern world is the airport; and airports are more or less identical throughout the world, pockets of an international no-man's land differing only in size.

There is, of course, something else to the notion of Americanisation. Outside the United States, Americanisation tends to be equated with the destruction or at any rate the corruption of specific national ways of life. For close on a century now there have always been Englishmen eager to protest against the infiltration into British English of American speech-habits and of American slang in particular; and for half a century throughout the industrialised world the really influential popular music has been American or imitations of American, jazz and its commercial manifestations and derivatives. In this field, the dominance of the United States is not now as pronounced as it was; all the same, one doesn't have to look very closely at the roots of British Pop music, for instance, to see that some of them are specifically American. British Pop is an off-shoot of rock-'n'-roll, which is itself an offshoot of the hill-billy music of the Kentucky mountaineers. Similarly, though Hollywood no longer dominates the cinema as it did, nevertheless its audience is world-wide to an extent far beyond that of other main film-producing countries; and much the same is true of American television programmes.

There is a number of aspects to this fact of Americanisation. One is that when we think of international art, art which, whatever its kind and whatever the audience aimed at, seems to rise above purely national and local considerations and to appeal to people throughout the western world irrespective of country, it is generally American art that we are thinking about. Admittedly, there is a problem of which comes first, the American art or the international. In contemporary American architecture, one thinks of Gropius, Mies van der Rohe and Saarinen, two Germans and a Finn, who became American citizens. It may be that there is nothing in their buildings that is essentially American; Gropius, after all, made his reputation in the Germany of the Weimar Republic. Yet it is in the United States that these architects have found the greatest scope for their art, and their works seem to fit naturally and inevitably into the American scene and into the context of American architecture as defined by the buildings of men like Frank Lloyd Wright. They are members of an international movement; the point is, it is in the United States that they have found the soil in which their international art can flourish.

A quite different aspect of Americanisation is to be seen in the composition of the European public that responds to it. Though one is in the realm of surmise here, it seems reasonable to assume that at any time in the past forty or fifty years the audience for jazz and for Hollywood has been mainly a young audience and probably a working-class audience, one that sees itself as under-privileged as compared with upper-class or educated *élites* and is, in simple fact, largely debarred from the full cultural tradition of the nation it belongs to by lack of education.

It is not difficult to work out the impression of America such an audience would take away from American films and popular songs from the 1920s onwards. It would be characterised by a much greater permissiveness than European, especially Latin

European society, has normally offered, by much greater equality both between man and man and between man and woman, by the comparative absence generally of restraints, parental, religious and those, psychological for the most part, imposed on behaviour and ways of thought by the existence of other social classes accepted as superior. The impression, in other words, is an image of freedom in the widest sense, of which even the violence of the American scene, which Hollywood films have never shirked representing, would seem to be a manifestation. Altogether, the United States would be seen as a paradise for the young and for the working class, a country in which even poverty was qualitatively different from European poverty, since even the poorest man had his car. This view, indeed, is supported by the observations of Americans themselves; as the American socialist Michael Harrington writes in *The Other America*, a study of poverty in the United States that had a great influence on the thinking of President Kennedy and was partly responsible for his anti-poverty campaign: "Clothes make the poor invisible too: America has the best-dressed poverty the world has ever known."

Which brings us back to Alvarez, who writes:

> . . . America is the real modern thing: a gleaming, air-conditioned, brightly packaged, technological mass society devoted, with startling single-mindedness, to making life easy. Nearly everything has or aspires to a certain surface efficiency and glimmer, an air of steel, glass, electronic device, speed and instant chic. Every single citizen assumes his right to the benefits of the mass-production society; his share, that is, of the smart, cheap clothes and the machines—of the cars, ice-boxes, TV sets.

It was, in part, this assumption that drove Negro mobs in the summer of 1967 to riot and loot in Newark, Detroit, Milwaukee and Buffalo; and it is the same assumption that is enshrined in the image of America as construed from films, television programmes and popular music by the youth and the working class of Europe. It is an image of a future the realisation of which is already taken for granted by large sections of the population of Western Europe. I have already quoted Alvarez as saying America is the only country that is "squarely, uncompromisingly in the twentieth century". He adds: "Most of the Western European countries are only reluctantly there: England and France, for example, remain emotionally around nineteen

hundred and ten, thoroughly industrialised but dreaming still of
times past—witness the cold houses, the half-hearted architecture,
the awful roads, the boring class distinctions, the gently good
manners." There is no doubt some exaggeration here; the
United States is not of a piece, and, where they exist, Oxford-
and-Cambridge snobs have nothing on Harvard-Yale-Princeton
snobs. Generally, however, Alvarez's assertion seems to me fair.
The point is, Western European reluctance to enter, squarely,
uncompromisingly, into the twentieth century is usually the
reluctance of relatively small but influential groups who see
themselves as *élites* by virtue of birth, wealth, specialised education
or political creed—and the last includes as many old-fashioned
socialists, in Britain especially, as old-fashioned conservatives.
The reluctance is understandable and not by any means unreasonable. One remembers Lewis Mumford's description of
the nineteenth-century immigrant to America as a "stripped
European". When the European fully enters the twentieth
century he may well find that part of the price of entry is that he
too has to become to some degree a stripped European.

Meanwhile, it is obvious that Europe is moving, in part
involuntarily, into something like an American condition, not all
of it, of course, equally rapidly or in the same way. Since the
war, for instance, Britain, to the considerable surprise of many of
its citizens, has become a multiracial society. Probably one in
twenty of all workers is now a coloured man. In other words,
Britain finds itself suddenly faced with problems that the United
States has been grappling with for many years. Again, the
Common Market area is becoming a multi-national society in
which workers move from one country to another and whole
cities contain large pockets of foreign immigrants. What lies
ahead of Europe, as a result of technological development and
what goes with it—the necessity to think in terms of much
larger units of trade and administration, the rise in educational
levels, the demand for ever-higher living standards—is something
that will more and more closely approximate to the American
situation as Alvarez describes it, what he calls "paradoxical
stylishness":

> This paradoxical stylishness—style in the absence of substance,
> style in the place of means—. . . is typical somehow of America's
> modernity, and is at the root of the problem we too have to face
> as we move fully into the twentieth century. It is a matter of coming

to terms with a new kind of reality, a reality in which style and being, surface and inward awareness, appearance and feeling are utterly and, apparently, irreconcilably at odds. We are beginning to have a way of life so elegantly designed that it is impermeable, it leaves no room for human muddle.

He takes as an example a flight in a jet, "at once the easiest and most forceful way of feeling what it's like to belong to the twentieth century".

You are carried miles up at a ludicrous speed in a cocoon of bottled air and bottled music, while shiny, mass-produced hostesses ply you with the food and the pilot intones his soothing creed: "Sit back, relax and enjoy your flight." When it's over, you are de-canted into airports of smooth glass and aluminium and swept whisperingly along super highways into the cities. It's marvellous, imposing—even, in a way, rather touching. But it's also unreal, a bit impossible. All that tailored glass and steel fits too closely together. There seems scarcely room, even at the interstices, to lead your own messy, inefficient life. So you get a slightly ghostly feeling, as though existence itself had become automated and you were reduced to just another hole in the computer's punch-card.

The feeling is not, of course, specifically American; it is international, experienced everywhere that the twentieth century in Alvarez's sense, which are those aspects of our age that differentiate it from all others, operates. It is the feeling we have when conscious of living in what Henry Miller has called "the air-conditioned nightmare". Miller applies the phrase to modern American life. It may be that life has always been a nightmare, but the air-conditioning makes all the difference. It makes the individual human being's environment unreal, as Alvarez says, in a way flimsy, impermanent, without a fixed meaning; it can be controlled and changed as it were by the pressing of a switch. The effect of this increasing impermanence and unreality of the outside world, in the sense that it can be altered and adjusted to suit convenience, is interesting. It is to intensify, even to exacerbate, the importance of the individual's inner world, his subjective world, and this in turn can raise problems, even doubts, about identity. Alvarez puts it like this: "In a country like Poland you can more or less ignore your own private troubles because the environment itself is so drably and inescapably in need. In the States, on the other hand, all that comfort exaggerates the personal unease, making it seem gratuitous, intolerable."

Now, if my reading of it is correct, it is exactly these elements of subjectivity, of the notion that the individual contains within himself in some sense the whole outside world, and of constant seeking and questioning of identity, that has characterised American literature and distinguished it from English from its very beginnings. These elements may be traced back to the uninhibited effects of Calvinism working on human beings isolated in an alien environment. Yet it is as though, from its beginnings, American literature has anticipated what seems to be the special nature of man in the twentieth century. I have made much of the fact that the great subject of American literature has been the search for American identity, what it means to be an American. Now that so much of the rest of the world, and Europe in particular, either aspires to the condition of America or is forced willy-nilly into it, this is tantamount to saying that the great subject of American literature is what it means to be, not American man only, but also Western man. As R. W. B. Lewis writes in the preface of his *Trials of the Word*: "For all its occasional parochialism and its periodic outbursts of cultural nativism, American literature at its most original and adventurous is also the most international, the most cosmopolitan, the most *Western* of the literatures of the Western world."

To say this is not in any way to assert that American literature is better than other literatures. Such a claim would be absurd, and in any case nothing could be more stupid than to attempt to arrange the literatures of the world in order of merit. What Lewis's statement does is to explain the special nature of American literature and its special value for us, Americans and non-Americans alike. It illuminates, as nothing else does, the complex fate that is basic to being an American, one element of which Henry James forgot to mention: the shaping force of the American Dream. For non-Americans, it has a further importance, not only for the light it throws on America but also because the American Dream, even though the phrase may not be used, has become the common property of the Western world.

BIBLIOGRAPHY

ADAMS, HENRY, *Democracy: An American Novel* (1880).
  History of the United States during the Administrations of Thomas Jefferson and James Madison (1884–89).
ALVAREZ, A., *Under Pressure; The Writer in Society: Eastern Europe and the U.S.A.* (1966).
ANDERSON, SHERWOOD, *Winesburg, Ohio* (1919).

BOORSTIN, DANIEL J., *The Americans: The Colonial Experience* (1958).
  The Americans: The National Experience (1965).
BRADFORD, WILLIAM, *History of Plymouth Plantation* (1651).
BROOKS, VAN WYCK, *Scenes and Portraits* (1954).
BURNS, JOHN HORNE, *The Gallery* (1947).

CATHER, WILLA, *Death Comes to the Archbishop* (1927).
  A Lost Lady (1923).
  My Antonia (1918).
CHASE, RICHARD, *The American Novel and Its Tradition* (1957).
CLARK, WALTER VAN TILBURG, *The Ox-Bow Incident* (1940).
CLEMENS, SAMUEL LANGHORNE (Mark Twain), *The Celebrated Jumping Frog of Calaveras County* (1867).
  The Adventures of Huckleberry Finn (1885).
  The Adventures of Tom Sawyer (1876).
COOPER, JAMES FENIMORE, *The Leather-Stocking Tales: The Pioneers* (1823), *The Last of the Mohicans* (1826), *The Prairie* (1827), *The Pathfinder* (1840), *The Deerslayer* (1841).
  Notions of the Americans (1828).
CRANE, HART, *The Bridge* (1930).
CREVECOEUR, HECTOR DE, "What Is an American?", in *Letters from an American Farmer* (1782).

DICKINSON, EMILY, *Poems,* ed. Thomas H. Johnson (3 v., 1955).

DREISER, THEODORE, *The Financier* (1912).
  The Titan (1914).
  An American Tragedy (1925).

EDWARDS, JONATHAN, *Sinners in the Hands of an Angry God* (1741).
ELIOT, T. S., *The Sacred Wood* (1920).
  The Waste Land (1922).
ELLISON, RALPH, *Invisible Man* (1952).
EMERSON, RALPH WALDO, *Essays* (1841).

FARRELL, JAMES T., *Studs Lonigan: Young Lonigan* (1932), *The Young Manhood of Studs Lonigan* (1934), *Judgment Day* (1935).
  The Face of Time (1954).
FAULKNER, WILLIAM, *Absalom! Absalom!* (1936).
FEIDELSON, CHARLES, *Symbolism and American Literature* (1953).
FITZGERALD, F. SCOTT, *The Great Gatsby* (1925).
FRANKLIN, BENJAMIN, *Autobiography* (1771).
FREDERIC, HAROLD, *The Damnation of Theron Ware* (1896).
FROST, ROBERT, *Complete Poems* (1949).

GINSBERG, ALLEN, *Howl!* (1956).
GORDON, CAROLINE, *None Shall Look Back* (1937).
GREENE, GRAHAM, *The Quiet American* (1956).

HARRINGTON, MICHAEL, *The Other Americans* (1963).
HAWTHORNE, NATHANIEL, "Young Goodman Brown" (1835), "The Maypole of Merry Mount" (1836), *The Scarlet Letter* (1850), *The House of the Seven Gables* (1851).
HELLER, JOSEPH, *Catch-22* (1962).
HEMINGWAY, ERNEST, *In Our Time* (1925), *The Sun Also Rises* (1926), *Men without Women* (1927), *Death in the Afternoon* (1932), *Old Man and the Sea* (1952).
HOFFMAN, DANIEL G., *Form and Fable in American Fiction* (1961).

JAMES, HENRY, *Hawthorne* (1879).
  The Portrait of a Lady (1881), *The Wings of the Dove* (1902).
JAMES, WILLIAM, *Pragmatism* (1907).
JONES, HOWARD MUMFORD, *O Strange New World* (1964).

KEMBLE, FANNY, *Journal of a Residence on a Georgia Plantation in 1838–39* (1863).
KEROUAC, JACK, *On the Road* (1957), *The Dharma Bums* (1958).

238   BIBLIOGRAPHY

LAWRENCE, D. H., *Studies in Classic American Literature* (1924).
LEWIS, R. W. B., *Trials of the Word* (1965).
LEWIS, SINCLAIR, *Main Street* (1920), *Babbitt* (1922).
LOWELL, ROBERT, *Poems, 1938–49* (1950), *For the Union Dead* (1964).
LURIE, ALISON, *The Nowhere City* (1966).

MAILER, NORMAN, *An American Dream* (1964), *Why Are We in Vietnam?* (1967).
MASTERS, EDGAR LEE, *Spoon River Anthology* (1915).
MELVILLE, HERMAN, *Moby-Dick* (1851).
MILLER, PERRY, *The Life of the Mind in America* (1965).
MUMFORD, LEWIS, *The Golden Day* (1926).
   Herman Melville (revised ed. 1963).

PASSOS, JOHN DOS, *U.S.A.: The 42nd Parallel* (1930), *1919* (1932), *The Big Money* (1936).
POE, EDGAR ALLAN, *The Narrative of Arthur Gordon Pym* (1838), "The Fall of the House of Usher" (1840).

RANSOM, JOHN CROWE, *Poems and Essays* (1955).
ROTH, HENRY, *Call It Sleep* (1934).
ROWLANDSON, MARY, *A Narrative of the Captivity and Restoration of Mrs. Mary Rowlandson* (1682).

SALINGER, J. D., *The Catcher in the Rye* (1951).
SANDBURG, CARL, *The Complete Poems of Carl Sandburg* (1950).
STEINBECK, JOHN, *In Dubious Battle* (1936), *Of Mice and Men* (1937), *The Grapes of Wrath* (1939).
STOWE, HARRIET BEECHER, *Uncle Tom's Cabin* (1852).
STRAIGHT, MICHAEL, *Carrington* (1960).

TANNER, TONY, *The Reign of Wonder* (1966).
TATE, ALLEN, *The Fathers* (1938).
   Poems, 1920–45 (1947).
THOREAU, HENRY DAVID, *A Week on the Concord and Merrimack Rivers* (1849).
   "On the Duty of Civil Disobedience" (1849).
   Walden: or, Life in the Woods (1854).
TOCQUEVILLE, ALEXIS DE, *Democracy in America* (1835).
TRILLING, LIONEL, *The Liberal Imagination* (1948).
TURNER, F. J., *The Frontier in American History* (1920).

WESCOTT, GLENWAY, *The Apple of the Eye* (1924), *Goodbye, Wisconsin* (1928), *The Grandmothers* (1927).

WEST, NATHANAEL, *Miss Lonelyhearts* (1933), *The Day of the Locust* (1939).

WILDER, THORNTON, *The Cabala* (1925), *Heaven's My Destination* (1935).

WILLIAMS, WILLIAM CARLOS, *In the American Grain* (1925).
  The Collected Later Poems (1950), *The Collected Earlier Poems* (1951), *Patterson* (1946–58).

WILSON, EDMUND, *A Piece of My Mind* (1956), *Europe without Baedecker* (1966).

WINTHROP, JOHN, *Journal* (1790).

YOUNG, PHILIP, *Ernest Hemingway* (1952).

OTHER BOOKS TO READ

Books on the United States, its people, history, literature and institutions, are legion. What follows is a selection of those, in addition to the books listed, I have found particularly helpful.

In history proper I would suggest: Oscar Handlin's *The Americans: A New History of the People of the United States* (2 vol., 1965); *The Growth of the American Republic*, by Samuel Eliot Morison and Henry Steele Commager (2 vol., 1930); *The History of the United States*, by R. B. Nye and J. E. Morpurgo (2 vol., 1961); Frank Thistlethwaite's *The Great Experiment* (1955).

As surveys of the intellectual background of American life from Colonial times onwards, a number of books nominate themselves: Vernon L. Parrington's *Main Currents in American Thought* (3 vol., 1927–30); Max Lerner's *American Civilization* (2 vol., 1962); and Perry Miller's and Thomas H. Johnson's invaluable anthology, *The Puritans* (1938).

The production of anthologies of American literature has for many years been almost a major academic industry in the United

States.   One of the best remains, for all it is thirty years old,
The Oxford Anthology of American Literature, edited by William
Rose Benét and Norman Holmes Pearson (2 vol., 1939).   A good
recent one is *The American Tradition in Literature*, edited by
Sculley Bradley, Richard Croom Beatty and E. Hudson Long
(2 vol., third edition, 1967).   The best British-made anthology
is Geoffrey Moore's *American Literature: A Representative Anthology
of American Writing from Colonial Times to the Present* (1964).

To my mind, the best short history of American literature is
Marcus Cunliffe's *The Literature of the United States* (1954).   A
standard work is the *Literary History of the United States,* edited
by Robert E. Spiller, Willard Thorpe and others (3 vol., 1948).
Books dealing with limited periods or special aspects of American
writing that I have found particularly valuable and stimulating
include: F. O. Matthiessen's *American Renaissance: Art and
Expression in the Age of Emerson and Whitman* (1941); Alfred
Kazin's *On Native Grounds*—on American fiction (1942); Edmund
Wilson's *Patriotic Gore*—on the literature of the Civil War (1962);
Leslie A. Fiedler's *Love and Death in the American Novel* (1960);
R. W. B. Lewis's *The American Adam* (1955).   A seminal work
in a category of its own is Constance Rourke's *American Humor:
A Study of the National Character* (1931).

INDEX